Environmentalism

The environment is one of the liveliest and most topical issues of our day. In *Environmentalism* the contributors demonstrate that anthropology has a distinctive contribution to make to current debates on 'green' issues.

Drawing on studies in sociology and law, as well as anthropology, the contributors challenge the view that environmental issues are the province of *natural* science alone and explore the interdisciplinary nature of the environmental debate. The book brings together a wide range of studies, from environmental ideology and imagery, and environmental law and policy, through local environmental activism, to ethnographic analyses of human/environment relations in indigenous societies. The contributors raise key issues such as the effects of state interests and bureaucracies on environmental activism, the cultural construction of 'hard' principles of law and policy, and the responses of indigenous peoples to industrial exploitation of their environments. They also explore important theoretical issues in anthropology, including the globalization of culture, the analytical value of dualism and the relationship between anthropology and advocacy.

An important contribution to the 'green' debate from an anthropological perspective, *Environmentalism* also sheds new light on the boundaries between anthropology and other disciplines. It will be especially valuable to social scientists with an interest in environmentalism and human ecology and to people actively involved in environmental policy and planning.

ASA Monographs 32

Environmentalism

The view from anthropology

Edited by Kay Milton

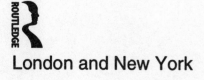

London and New York

First published 1993
by Routledge
11 New Fetter Lane, London EC4P 4EE

Simultaneously published in the USA and Canada
by Routledge
29 West 35th Street, New York, NY 10001

Typeset in Garamond by LaserScript, Mitcham, Surrey
Printed and bound in Great Britain by
Mackays of Chatham PLC, Chatham, Kent

British Library Cataloguing in Publication Data
A catalogue record for this book is available from the British Library

Library of Congress Cataloging in Publication Data
Environmentalism: the view from anthropology/edited by Kay Milton.
 p. cm. – (ASA monographs; 32)
Includes bibliographical references and index.
1. Human ecology. 2. Environmental policy. 3. Applied anthropology.
I. Milton, Kay, 1951– . II. Series: A.S.A. monographs; 32.
GF41.E55 1993   93-14815
304.2 – dc20   CIP

ISBN 0–415–09474–7 (hbk)
   0–415–09475–5 (pbk)

Contents

Illustrations

Contributors

Nurit Bird-David is Lecturer in Social Anthropology at Tel Aviv University.

Niels Einarsson is a doctoral student in the Department of Cultural Anthropology at the University of Uppsala, Sweden.

Roy Ellen is Professor of Anthropology and Human Ecology at the University of Kent at Canterbury.

Robin Grove-White is Director of the Centre for the Study of Environmental Change at the University of Lancaster.

Peter Harries-Jones is Associate Professor of Anthropology at York University, Ontario.

Tim Ingold is Professor of Social Anthropology at the University of Manchester.

Allison James is Lecturer in Social Anthropology at the University of Hull.

Tanya M. Luhrmann is Associate Professor of Anthropology at the University of California, San Diego.

Bonnie J. McCay is Professor of Anthropology and Ecology in the Department of Human Ecology, Cook College, Rutgers University, New Jersey.

Kay Milton is Lecturer in Social Anthropology at Queen's University, Belfast.

Adrian Peace is Lecturer in Social Anthropology at the University of Adelaide.

Giuliana B. Prato is a doctoral student in the Department of Anthropology at University College, London.

Paul Richards is Professor of Anthropology at University College, London.

Paul Sillitoe is Reader in Anthropology at the University of Durham and currently Nuffield Fellow at Wye College, University of London.

Lynda M. Warren is Lecturer in Law, Cardiff Law School, University of Wales, Cardiff.

Steven Yearley is Professor of Sociology at the University of Ulster.

Editor's preface

Proposing a conference theme can be like casting seeds to the wind, not knowing where they will fall, nor whether germination will be fast or slow, nor what fruits might eventually be born. So it was with the theme of the 1992 Conference of the Association of Social Anthropologists. 'Anthropological perspectives on environmentalism' represented a tentative step into unknown territory. Would colleagues come forward with enthusiasm, or maintain an uninterested silence?

The theme was motivated by a concern that an important public debate, perhaps the most important of our time, was proceeding without a significant input from anthropology. In a field dominated by the natural sciences, social scientists have, in any case, struggled for recognition, and those who have made the greatest impact have been sociologists, geographers and, most especially, economists. And yet, it seemed indisputable that anthropology, which has explored the breadth of human possibilities, should have something important to contribute to the search for a viable future.

The theme was also motivated by a sense of ignorance and personal isolation. My own research on green issues had brought contact with environmental activists and social scientists of other disciplines, but not with fellow anthropologists. Was environmentalism not recognized among anthropologists as an important object for analysis, or were others also working in relative isolation from their colleagues? The time for an exchange of views seemed long overdue.

In the event, germination was slow but sure; what started as a tentative step became an enlightening venture of which this volume is the outcome. The interdisciplinary nature of the environment as a field of study helped to shape the character of both the conference and this volume. Although it was envisaged primarily as an opportunity to explore anthropological perspectives on environmental issues, it was felt important to do this through a dialogue with other disciplines. For this reason, contributions were invited from specialists in sociology, law and geography (and some of mixed ancestry), as well as anthropologists.

The mix of disciplines and the nature of the subject matter generated a lively conference discussion in which underlying tensions were clearly evident. In particular there was a tension between the study of environmentalism as a cultural perspective, and the study of human–environment relations, in which anthropologists have more traditionally engaged. Less explicit, but perhaps more telling, was the tension between detached observation of and active involvement with environmentalism. Some attempt has been made, in the introduction to this volume, to address these tensions.

Many individual efforts have contributed to the venture. In the early stages of planning, the advice and encouragement of ASA officers and more experienced conference conveners, in particular Jonathan Webber, Jerry Eades and David Parkin, were most welcome. Bob Layton, as the local organizer, and his team of helpers at Durham, shouldered much of the responsibility and considerably lightened the convener's burden. Thanks are also due to our hosts at St Aidan's College, to Ian Simmons, who gave the opening address, and to all those who attended the conference and helped to make it a constructive and rewarding event, especially those who contributed papers and chaired sessions.

As the role of convener gave way to that of editor, I received invaluable advice from David Parkin and from Heather Gibson of Routledge, whose enthusiastic support far exceeded the call of professional duty. The Department of Social Anthropology at Queen's University provided facilities for the production of the manuscript; their support is gratefully acknowledged. The greatest debt of gratitude must be to my fellow authors, who bore my editorial demands with good-natured tolerance, and whose contributions have been a source of intellectual inspiration.

Environmentalism and anthropology

Kay Milton

> Environmentalism is as much a state of being as a mode of conduct or a set of policies. Certainly it can no longer be identified simply with the desire to protect ecosystems or conserve resources – these are merely superficial manifestations of much more deeply-rooted values. At its heart environmentalism preaches a philosophy of human conduct that many still find difficult to understand, and those who are aware seemingly find unattainable.
>
> (O'Riordan 1981: ix)

The relationship between an academic discipline and any debate pursued outside academia is rarely straightforward. Public concerns are not constrained by disciplinary boundaries and the practical business of living in the world is not governed by the canons of theory (cf. Bourdieu 1977: 109ff.). It has often been observed that the relationship is especially problematic for the social sciences, which have the tortuous task of studying that of which they are a part. Culture is both the object of anthropological analysis and the enterprise in which anthropologists, along with everyone else, subjectively engage. This uncomfortable reality has repeatedly threatened to tear the discipline apart (Schensul and Schensul 1978: 124–5), polarizing opinion between an active commitment to social reform and a detached observation of social processes. The resulting dilemmas have been reflected in many debates within the discipline, particularly in those focusing on major social commitments such as socialism and feminism.

This book is an exploration of the relationship between anthropology and environmentalism, which has emerged, since the late 1960s, as a distinctive social commitment. The relationship has to be explored rather than defined because it is still evolving. This book is a part of that process; it brings together analyses of a range of environmental issues, both conceptual and empirical, conducted from a diversity of personal and theoretical perspectives. Most of the authors are anthropologists, but contributions from specialists in sociology and law have also been included. It is a truism that nothing evolves in isolation, and the specific character of anthropology's relationship with environmentalism can only emerge through interaction with other disciplines. This is especially so given that environmentalism is a matter of public concern; such matters, in disregarding the boundaries between academic disciplines, present a challenge to them.

The purpose of this introduction is to consider what a relationship between anthropology and environmentalism might look like. It can be envisaged as consisting of two complementary processes. First, the analysis of environmentalism might contribute to the development of anthropology as a discipline, just as, in the past, particular subjects of study have yielded theoretical insights. In particular, the study of environmentalism might be expected to contribute to two important debates within anthropology. Because it entails a social commitment, environmentalism raises questions about the application of anthropological knowledge and the relationship between anthropology and advocacy (Paine 1986, Harries-Jones 1991); and the global nature of environmental problems might make the study of environmentalism an appropriate testing ground for ideas on the globalization of culture (see Hannerz 1992). In addition, an environmentalist critique of anthropology might emerge to question some of the discipline's central principles, as the feminist critique did in the 1970s (Moore 1988: 1–11); for the present, this possibility remains largely undeveloped.[1]

The second process is the contribution which anthropological knowledge might make to the public debate on environmental issues. A consideration of this potential role forms the primary focus of this introduction. The intention is not to exclude theoretical issues, however, but to use the question of anthropology's potential contribution to the environmentalist debate as a way of addressing those issues. As will become clear, the question of how anthropological knowledge can be applied to environmental issues leads to a consideration of advocacy and globalization. I shall argue that anthropology can contribute to the environmentalist cause without violating its own theoretical principles. Clearly, this argument will be open to contention. The ways in which the contributions to this volume fit into the scheme suggested here will be indicated in the discussion, but it should on no account be assumed that any of the views expressed here are shared by the other contributors.

ENVIRONMENTALISM AS A SOCIAL COMMITMENT

For those who espouse its principles, environmentalism is essentially, though not uniquely, a quest for a viable future, pursued through the implementation of culturally defined responsibilities. The general nature of these responsibilities distinguishes environmentalism from other such quests; they stem from the recognition that 'the environment' – loosely identified as the complex of natural phenomena with which we share the universe and on which we depend – is affected by human activity, and that securing a viable future depends on such activity being controlled in some way.

This general description already fails to grasp the complexity of the phenomenon, however, for there are many visions of a viable future, and diverse answers to the question of for whom, or what, it should be viable. In some versions, the survival of indigenous cultures, the rights of people to pursue their traditional patterns of resource-use, are paramount. In others, the survival of humanity in general, regardless of cultural variation, is the central issue. Still other versions of the environmentalist quest place the highest priority on the survival of a diversity of life on earth, or on the viability of the planet as a life-support system with or without humankind. Nor are these diverse visions, nor even the appreciation of their diversity, distributed, in any simple way, among groups and individuals who define their own perspectives as broadly environmentalist. For some the environmentalist quest is simple and clear cut, for others it is complex and contradictory.

Within what have been called 'contemporary complex cultures' (Hannerz 1992: 6), environmentalism impinges on public consciousness through many channels; through press reports and television documentaries, through government policy statements and pressure-group campaigns, through commercial advertising and charity appeals. Sometimes it appears as a preservationist, conservative influence (Cotgrove 1976: 24), sometimes as a radical challenge to established political and economic principles (Porritt and Winner 1988, Dobson 1990), sometimes as a spiritualist vision (Spretnak 1985, Luhrmann, below).

But environmentalism is not confined to 'contemporary complex cultures'. It is found both in the institutionalized practices of non-industrial peoples, and in their responses to external threats. The Australian Aborigine who avoids hunting animals on sacred sites, and performs ceremonies to ensure the continued existence of edible species, is, like the Greenpeace campaigner, implementing environmental responsibilities. The rubber-tappers of Amazonia, the Penan of Borneo, the subsistence farmers of northern India and many other communities have attempted to defend their traditional patterns of resource-use against what they see as the destructive consequences of large-scale commercial exploitation (Weber 1988, Revkin 1990).

ANTHROPOLOGY AND THE QUEST FOR A VIABLE FUTURE

A preliminary consideration suggests three main ways in which anthropological knowledge might contribute to the environmentalist cause. These are closely interrelated and overlap considerably with each other, but are worth distinguishing for the exploratory purposes of this introduction. First, environmental problems are almost always defined as ecological problems and anthropologists have, for many years, been students of human ecology. Second, the understanding of environmental problems and the implementation of solutions are often trans-cultural operations, and interpretation across cultural boundaries is recognized as a distinctive speciality of anthropologists. Third, through the analysis of environmentalism itself, anthropology, along with other social sciences, can help to refine the process of environmental advocacy.

Anthropology as human ecology

For many anthropologists, ecology has been an explicit and prominent component of their work.[2] Others have approached it 'from the shadows' (Croll and Parkin 1992: 4), through the study of various cultural traditions. If one accepts the anthropological cliché that culture is *the* mechanism through which human beings interact with (or, more controversially, *adapt to*) their environment (Ingold 1992: 39), then the whole field of cultural anthropology can be characterized as human ecology. Studies of people's religious beliefs and practices implicitly, if not explicitly, address their understanding of natural processes and their responses to environmental hazards. Studies of kinship systems and power relations almost invariably touch on the control and distribution of resources.

In its guise as human ecology, anthropology has embraced divergent theoretical perspectives. Ecological determinism – the view that cultural phenomena exist to serve the needs of ecological adaptation – was prominent through the 1950s and 1960s. Its limitations are well known (Moran 1990) and were exposed not least by the observation that some cultural practices are clearly maladaptive (Keesing 1981: 163–5). The insights offered by ecological determinism might have appeared more useful, in a practical sense, had the biological model been followed more closely; in other words, had it been assumed that cultures, like species, can become extinct. On the basis of this assumption, instead of striving to demonstrate that all cultural practices are adaptive, cultural ecologists could have addressed the question of which are adaptive and which are not, in specific environments. This is an important question, given that the quest for a viable future is seen by many environmentalists as a search for a sustainable culture – one whose fundamental principles, and the practices that follow from them, are environmentally benign.

Cultural determinism – the view that the world is defined through cultural perceptions – has been the more pervasive anthropological perspective over the past thirty years or so. At its most extreme, it can appear to deny the very existence of objective reality (Keat and Urry 1982: 5). Sapir's contention that 'the worlds in which different societies live are distinct worlds, not merely the same world with different labels attached' (1961: 69) was addressed and often reinforced through early studies of ethnoscience (Tyler 1969). The less extreme view, that culture brings order and meaning to an otherwise disordered world (Douglas 1966), has underpinned the study of cultures as symbolic systems (Geertz 1973, Leach 1976).

The potential value of human ecological studies in the quest for a viable future is clear. Human interaction with the environment is widely perceived both as the source of environmental problems and as the key to their solution. The importance of cultural anthropology in this context rests on the assumption that such interaction takes place through the medium of culture. Many of the contributions to this volume address directly the cultural perspectives through which people frame their interaction with the environment.[3] These studies raise questions concerning the variability of such perspectives. What circumstances, for instance, generate different representations of environment – as globe or sphere (Ingold), as lover, namesake or parent (Bird-David) – and what implications do these representations hold for environmental use and protection? What factors dictate whether social relations or natural history (Richards) will form the basis of symbolic representations?

Environmentalism and cultural interpretation

The distinction between more and less extreme forms of cultural determinism, referred to above, has implications for communication across cultural boundaries. The assumption that different societies live in distinct worlds implies that translation, and therefore cross-cultural communication, is theoretically impossible. If, on the other hand, it is not reality itself that varies across cultural boundaries but the meanings imputed to reality, translation remains possible, and indeed becomes an important function in a world where differences in perception and understanding can be damaging.

The nature of cultural boundaries is variable and complex. It is no longer appropriate (and probably never was) to treat cultures as discrete systems of meaning. Contemporary communication media transcend the barriers of distance, language, nationality and ethnic origin, creating dimensions of cultural complexity which challenge established anthropological models of social reality (Hannerz 1992). Differences in perceptions, meanings and values can arise in virtually any social arena. Several contributions to this volume address the implications of cultural variability for environmental issues. In particular, Einarsson discusses the potential for conflict between environmentalist and utilitarian concepts of nature, and Warren reveals the potential for misunderstanding between scientific and legal expertise.

Environmental policies are often formulated, by both national governments and environmental NGOs (non-governmental organizations), in international arenas such as the United Nations Conference on Environment and Development (UNCED) and the European Community. Decisions made in these fora have consequences for local communities, who may find their everyday activities banned by international laws, or their economies undermined by the campaigning efforts of NGOs.[4] A greater understanding of the cultural barriers that are crossed when policies are implemented could make those policies more sensitive to local needs (Milton 1989). At the same time, a knowledge of how policies and their implementation privilege some cultural perspectives over others (see Prato and Peace, both below) could lead to a greater understanding of how environmental goals might be achieved.

Anthropologists as theorists of environmentalism

The third major way in which anthropology might serve environmentalist interests is through the study of environmentalism itself. Social commitments advance – gather momentum through intellectual and popular support – through the development and expression of ideas. Cultural revolutions invariably have their theorists who provide inspiration and direction. Environmentalists point to the works of Schumacher (1973), Lovelock (1979, 1988), Naess (1989) and others as significant influences in the development of their thinking. An important part of this process is the analysis of the ideas and practices which constitute the social commitment. By turning the spotlight on environmentalism itself, and applying 'systematic doubt' (Morgan 1991: 224) to its fundamental principles, analysts can help to refine concepts, expose and eliminate contradictions and ultimately improve the credibility of environmentalist ideas.[5] In this way, for instance, the work of Rudolf Bahro (1982, 1984) helped to crystallize the philosophy of the German green movement.[6]

But is the study of environmentalism an appropriate task for anthropologists? Has this territory not already been claimed by other disciplines? Sociologists have been studying environmentalism since the 1970s. Early studies developed the distinction between radical and conservative forms of environmentalism (Kruse 1974, Cotgrove 1976) and documented the social bases of environmental concern (Cotgrove and Duff 1980, 1981). In recent years, with some notable exceptions (for instance, Yearley 1991, Redclift 1984, 1987),[7] sociologists have tended to set the analysis of environmentalism within the broader study of social movements (Jamison et al. 1990, Scott 1990, Eyerman and Jamison 1991). Political scientists have focused on environmentalists' emerging political involvement and awareness (Lowe and Goyder 1983, Lowe and Flynn 1989, Rüdig 1990) and on the development of green thought as a distinctive political ideology (Paehlke 1989, Dobson 1990). Economists, meanwhile, have explored ways of incorporating environmental values into models of economic practice (Pearce et al. 1989, 1991). Can anthropologists add anything distinctive or constructive to this burgeoning body of theory? Here, I shall argue that anthropologists are well placed to become theorists of environmentalism, that cultural theory can offer a complement to the more established perspectives of social, political and economic theory.

ENVIRONMENTALISM AS AN OBJECT OF ANALYSIS

So far, this discussion has avoided confronting the issue with which it began, namely, the problematic nature of anthropology's relationship with its subject matter. In suggesting that anthropological knowledge might contribute, in any of the three ways outlined above, to the environmentalist quest for a viable future, I am acknowledging that the study of culture can feed back into the object of its analysis and help to direct cultural change. Many anthropologists have taken this for granted and, accordingly, have regarded a degree of social responsibility as an integral part of their discipline (Berreman 1968, Keesing 1981). Others have felt distinctly uneasy about the possibility of their studies contributing to cultural change. This unease has two principal (and seemingly contradictory) sources: cultural relativism and a concern for objectivity.

One of the early leaders of Greenpeace argued that commitment to a cause is weakened by an ability to see the other point of view (Hunter 1979). If so, it is understandable that anthropologists, who spend their professional lives studying other points of view, should fall victim to a degree of moral paralysis. Active involvement in cultural change requires moral judgements. Cultural relativism – the view that all cultures are equally valid 'in their own terms' – has been one of anthropology's most important contributions to social science, but has also had the effect of excluding moral judgements from the professional concerns of the discipline (Schensul and Schensul 1978: 128).

Anthropology's quest for objectivity stems from an earlier era, when anthropologists were concerned to establish the scientific nature of their discipline (Schensul and Schensul 1978: 127). Although a concern with objectivity might seem to run counter to a cultural relativist position, the two are, in fact, closely related. The more cultural views are seen as being embedded in their own context, the more pressure is placed on analysts of culture to employ models which are supposedly free from specific cultural associations.

Insight into the nature of objectivity has been provided by Morgan, following Berkeley's observation that an object gains its objectivity through being observed, and that science, consequently, is a process of interaction or *engagement* between scientist and object (Morgan 1983: 12–13).[8] Different kinds of scientific knowledge result from engaging an object of study in different ways. It follows from this, not that social scientists should abandon objectivity – this would be impossible, in any case, if it is conferred in the act of observation – but that we should understand exactly what it means to objectify the things we analyse. Different kinds of insight into environmentalism are gained by objectifying it in different ways; this is effectively what the different branches of social scientific theory (social, political, economic, cultural) do.

Discourse and culture

I have stated that environmentalism is experienced by those who espouse its principles as a quest for a viable future. It was appropriate to describe it thus, as a quest, a cause, a goal-oriented project, in order to argue that anthropological knowledge can contribute to it. But this is not necessarily the most appropriate characterization of environmentalism as an object of analysis. The focus on experience, which is necessarily personal and individual, is inconsistent with the need to generalize an object for analytical purposes. There are, no doubt, many ways in which environmentalism could be objectified as a subject of study. Here I suggest that it might usefully be seen as a trans-cultural discourse.

The term 'discourse' has multiple meanings derived from its ancestry in linguistics and in social theory, where its use has been shaped largely through the writings of Foucault (1972, 1979).[9] Discourse analysis is also emerging as a discipline in its own right (van Dijk 1985). In social theory, discourse carries implications both of process and of substance. In the first sense, discourse as process denotes how social reality is constituted by the organization of knowledge in communication (Fairclough 1992: 3). In the second sense, a discourse is a field of communication defined by its subject matter or the type of language used: environmental discourse is discourse *about* the environment, the discourse of science is the language used in science. Discourse in this sense does not carry implications of homogeneity or internal consistency. While it is often useful to refer to a field of communication as *a* discourse, such a field may, in turn, comprise several diverse and/or competing discourses. In many social scientific uses of the term, the processual and substantive senses are simultaneously implied. Thus, 'environmental discourse' is not just communication about the environment, but also the process whereby our understanding of the environment is constituted through such communication. It is in this dual sense that I use 'discourse' to describe environmentalism as an object of analysis.[10]

Discourse bears some similarity to the more familiar anthropological concept of 'culture'. Like discourse, culture is both substance and process. In a substantive sense, culture refers to the complex of ideas (norms, values, representations and so on) through which people understand the world and which form a basis for action (Keesing 1981: 68). In recent years, the work of theorists such as Habermas, Touraine and Giddens has given rise to 'an actionist model of culture' (Harries-Jones 1986: 240), which sees it as the process whereby social practice both constitutes and transforms itself. The principal mechanism through which this process operates is communication. Discourse in its processual sense is therefore entirely consistent with this concept of culture. Indeed, some might argue that it is coterminous with it, that discourse *is* the cultural process.

In their substantive senses, however, culture and discourse carry different connotations. Cultures, as entities, have been associated with particular societies or 'people within some social unit' (Hannerz 1992: 7). The effect of contemporary communication media, which commonly transcend established social boundaries (see above), has been to free cultural phenomena from their associations with particular social units, and has led to the understanding that culture is becoming 'globalized' (Hannerz 1992: 217–67). Nevertheless, the traditional connotations of boundedness are difficult to forget. Discourse carries no such connotations. It travels wherever the channels of communication take it, without evoking associations with bounded social entities. Thus the idea of a trans-cultural discourse, as a distinctive product of contemporary communication systems, is less counter-intuitive than the concept of a 'trans-cultural culture'.

Environmentalism as discourse

Environmentalism as a discourse, then, is the field of communication through which environmental responsibilities (those which make up the environmentalist quest for a viable future) are constituted. Of the myriad ways in which human activity and the natural world impinge upon each other, some are identified as problems.[11] Groups crystallize around the search for solutions, messages are articulated, responsibilities are defined and allocated. Depending on the perceived scope of the problem, this may happen within a local community or on the international stage. Any environmental problem may generate new individual responsibilities. Those defined as national or 'global' may generate new government policies or international agreements.

Environmental disputes arise when interests conflict over the use of resources. These typically take the form of struggles, between opposing interests, to assert their rights, or the rights of those they represent; the outcomes of disputes can be expected to reflect the distribution of power. In this volume, McCay shows how legally defined rights to resources were shaped by a series of disputes over their use. Peace and Prato analyse disputes in which local communities struggled to assert their environmental rights in opposition to commercial interests.

Those who most influence the definition of environmental responsibilities are those who can make the most effective use of the tools of discourse (see Harries-Jones, below). These tools will vary from one cultural context to another, but they typically include the news media, the mechanisms of formal and informal education, advertising, entertainment media and political lobbying. Environmental activism often takes the form of trying to empower groups and organizations by increasing their access to these tools. Local protest groups are empowered by their supporters to employ scientific and legal experts (see Peace, below). The larger NGOs are empowered by the funds they receive from their members and sponsors to engage in publicity campaigns, to produce films and education packs and to lobby decision-makers.

The trans-cultural character of the discourse is demonstrated by the activities of some of the most powerful NGOs. Organizations such as Greenpeace, and the World Wide Fund for Nature (WWF) have branches in many countries. In 1986, WWF initiated a conservation network based on an alliance of the major religions. In 1987, WWF-India used a traditional scroll, depicting the problems caused by upsetting the natural balance, to draw attention to the damaging ecological and economic consequences of the trade in frogs' legs (WWF 1991: 18). The Royal Society for the Protection of Birds (RSPB), based in Britain, runs conservation and education programmes in West Africa, to protect both local species (see Yearley, below) and species which nest in Europe and winter in Africa.

The flow of information in environmentalist discourse is not only from a technological centre to a non-industrial periphery. The environmental responsibilities embodied in the indigenous cultures of North America and Australia, for instance, have been drawn into the discourse by campaigners anxious to find legitimation for their own concerns in the wisdom of the 'noble savage'. The use of non-industrial cultures in this way has been addressed elsewhere by anthropologists (Ellen 1986), and is taken up in contributions to this volume (Ellen and Harries-Jones). The popularization of non-industrial cultures through the media has also become a bone of contention between organizations campaigning for their survival (Porritt 1992). But there are instances of non-industrial peoples entering into environmentalist discourse as self-advocates. Chico Mendes personally brought the plight of Amazonian communities to the attention of the Inter-American Development Bank, whose funds were paying for the destruction of the rainforest (Cowell 1990: 183ff.).

Nothing demonstrates the trans-cultural nature of environmentalist discourse better than the Chipko (tree-hugging) movement, which began in northern India in the 1970s. Sunderlal Bahuguna, Chipko's leading advocate, was inspired by the works of Schumacher, to which he was introduced through personal contact with the leading tree conservationist, Richard St Barbe Baker (Weber 1988: 67–8). Bahuguna, in turn, used his own writings, lectures and presentations at international conferences to spread the message of Chipko throughout the world. Tree-hugging is now commonly used as a gesture of environmental protest,[12] and has been incorporated into green spiritualist practice.

Environmentalism and cultural theory

In what way does the understanding of environmentalism as discourse offer a different perspective on it from those offered by other social science disciplines? Anthropology is typically a broadening influence. As noted above, sociologists, at least in recent studies, have seen environmentalism primarily as a social movement, and political scientists have analysed it as an ideology. Both these ways of conceptualizing environmentalism are narrower than that suggested here. Cotgrove, in drawing the distinction between conservative and radical forms of environmentalism, suggested that only the radical elements should be seen as constituting a coherent social movement (1976: 24). Dobson (1990) distinguished 'ecologism' from 'environmentalism', and suggested that only the former has the character of a political ideology. Environmentalism as I have described it incorporates all culturally defined environmental responsibilities, whether they are innovative or conventional, radical or conservative.

In this framework, social movements and political ideologies become specific cultural forms through which environmental responsibilities might be expressed and communicated. Instead of environmentalism being seen as a category of social movement or ideology, these forms of cultural expression become types of environmentalism. This enables us to ask under what circumstances the discourse of environmentalism will be expressed in the form of a social movement or an ideology. It is not difficult to envisage, for instance, that new environmental responsibilities will sit more easily in some cultural contexts than others. Where guiding values and social forms predispose people towards protecting other species or safeguarding their own long-term future, environmental concerns are less likely to be expressed through calls for radical change than where the conventional relationship with nature is one of exploitation for short-term gain.

Identifying environmentalism as part of the wider cultural process raises specific questions about its incidence and variability. What conditions promote the development of an environmentalist perspective? Why is it that some societies define environmental responsibilities in terms of protection or conservation, while others (such as those described by Ellen, Richards and Sillitoe, all below) apparently do not? What circumstances lead environmental responsibilities to be expressed through laws (as in the cases discussed by Warren and McCay, both below), through scientific arguments (Yearley, below) or through spiritualist goals (Luhrmann, below)? How do different cultural expressions of environmentalism come to be adopted by different groups, and how does their interaction shape the character of an environmental movement or lobby (Harries-Jones, below)? Answers to some of these questions have been suggested by analysts using Douglas' model of cultural diversity (Douglas 1970). Different institutionalized ways of thinking and acting have been related to different concepts of nature, and have been shown to generate diverse cultural responses to environmental risks (see Thompson and Tayler 1986, James *et al.* 1987, Douglas 1992).[13]

Another way of framing this kind of enquiry is to consider how discourses are related to each other. If culture is the process whereby social life is constituted through the communication of knowledge, the analysis of culture will focus on, among other things, how knowledge is made to count (Harries-Jones 1986: 234), on how particular discourses impinge on public consciousness and on how some discourses acquire precedence over others. In this volume, Harries-Jones demonstrates how several cultural forms interact to constitute environmentalism, while James demonstrates how environmentalism combines with other discourses to constitute the public debate on organic food. Several contributions deal explicitly with the relationship between environmentalism and science. Some areas of environmentalist discourse share the subject matter of science (global warming, biodiversity, pollution) and invoke its language. Yearley examines the role played by scientific knowledge and arguments in the practical strategies of environmental NGOs. Other areas appear to conflict with scientific discourse. The moral dimension of environmentalism, for instance, might be seen as presenting a challenge and an alternative to scientific orthodoxy (Grove-White). But, as Peace demonstrates, the moral dimension can be marginalized when scientific orthodoxy is built into the decision-making process.

ANTHROPOLOGY AND ENVIRONMENTAL ADVOCACY

Environmental advocacy is active involvement in the discourse of environmentalism, in the process of defining and implementing environmental responsibilities. In practice it has much in common with other fields of advocacy in which anthropologists and other social scientists engage. Anthropologists have often intervened in political discourse on behalf of disadvantaged communities, by speaking for them in legal proceedings and other disputes (see Paine 1986), or helping to establish mechanisms through which they can more effectively represent themselves (see, for instance, Cowell 1990: 169). In some instances, the needs of such peoples coincide with environmental needs. Protecting the rights of rainforest communities to pursue their traditional lifestyles contributes to the defence of the rainforest as an ecosystem, as a stabilizing influence on climate, and so on.

Environmentalists also speak for other categories whose needs might otherwise go unrepresented. In particular, they speak for non-human species, for 'nature' (see Yearley, below), 'mother earth' or some other personification of the biosphere, and for future generations of human beings. Environmental disputes often take the form of a struggle to establish the needs of these categories. With no voice (and no votes) of their own, non-human species and future generations are at the mercy of interests whose advocates compete for the right to define their needs – a motorway or a chalk downland, a prosperous chemical industry or a clean environment.

The moral imperative that leads any specialist to use his or her knowledge in support of a particular cause will always be a matter of personal conviction. Thus it has not been my intention here to argue that anthropology *should* contribute to the environmentalist quest for a viable future, but to suggest that it *can* do so, and that such an application of anthropological knowledge is consistent with the discipline's theoretical principles. One piece of this argument remains to be clarified: the nature of the relationship between anthropology and advocacy *per se*.

I have already referred to the unease felt by some anthropologists at the possibility of their research contributing to cultural change. This unease has led, at times, to 'applied' anthropology being treated almost as a maverick sub-discipline, and certainly as something distinct from mainstream, academic anthropology (Schensul and Schensul 1978). However, as Harries-Jones has argued (1986), this distinction is invalidated once we understand culture as a constitutive process which operates through communicative action. Once advocacy is identified as 'making knowledge count' (Harries-Jones 1991), it is shown to be a central part of the cultural process; the difference between 'applied' and 'academic' anthropology is seen as lying in what the knowledge is made to count *for*. Those who have argued against the participation of anthropologists in cultural change, on the grounds that it is inconsistent with scientific 'objectivity', have, through their very arguments, *advocated* a positivistic image for the discipline and helped to privilege the discourse of science over that of morality.

Specialists have only ever had limited control over the purposes for which their knowledge is used. Contemporary technology has weakened that control, by making published documents, bibliographic details and so on easily available. At most we can select the discourses in which we actively engage. We can publish our knowledge in prestigious academic journals in the hope that it will influence the development of the discipline. We can broadcast it through the media, where it might influence public debate,[14] or we can try to communicate more directly with a group of activists by publishing in their specialist journals (for instance, Milton 1989). What we cannot do, however, unless we keep our knowledge entirely to ourselves, is opt out of the cultural process in which advocacy plays a central part. Whether we are concerned primarily for the future of the planet or of the people whose lives we study, whether we want to further the development of anthropology, to contribute to the growth of human wisdom, or to promote our own academic careers, we are all engaged in the process of making our knowledge count. The only alternative is a role in which our knowledge counts for nothing.

ACKNOWLEDGEMENTS

I am grateful to Steven Yearley, Elizabeth Tonkin, John Stewart and Hastings Donnan for their comments on an earlier draft of this introduction, and to David Parkin for the use of his summary notes from the ASA Conference.

NOTES

1   An ecological approach within anthropology is, of course, well established and is discussed briefly later in this introduction. While an environmentalist

anthropology might ultimately have much in common with an ecological approach, I would not wish, at this stage, to assume a degree of overlap.

2   See, for instance, Steward (1955), Rappaport (1967), Bennett (1976), Moran (1982), Ellen (1982), Richards (1985), Ingold (1986), and many others.

3   All the contributions do this in some degree, but in particular see Grove-White, Ingold, Harries-Jones, Einarsson, Bird-David, Ellen, Richards, Sillitoe, James and Luhrmann.

4   For example, the campaign against the Canadian seal hunt, led by Greenpeace and other NGOs, damaged the economies of Arctic communities dependent on the hunt for their livelihood (Wenzel 1991).

5   On this point, it is worth quoting Morgan at greater length:

> The use of doubt can act as a defence against dogmatism; it can create insight in place of blindness; and it can provide the basis for an evolving, learning-oriented platform for the advocate's interactions with the problems to be addressed . . . In adopting the kind of scientific attitude which encourages us to identify both facts and counter-facts, arguments and counter-arguments, it is possible to build a rich and changing picture of the problems at hand, and to guard against the traps that often accompany the advocate's strong value-orientation.
>
> (Morgan 1991: 226)

6   In a similar way, the critical appraisal of feminist ideas by social scientists and philosophers (for instance, Richards 1980) helped the women's movement to gain credibility during the 1970s and 1980s.

7   The field of development studies, within which (as in Redclift's work) environmentalism has been addressed, is something of an anomaly, spanning the boundary between sociology and anthropology.

8   See also Harries-Jones (1986: 227). Morgan's understanding of science as a form of engagement is interesting in the light of Ingold's suggestion (below) that engagement with the environment is somehow antithetical to observation of it.

9   For a detailed analysis of the concept of discourse see Fairclough (1992).

10 It should not be assumed that other contributors to this volume who use a concept of discourse (Grove-White, Ingold, Einarsson, Bird-David, Prato, Peace, James) share my understanding of the term.

11 See Yearley (1991) for a discussion of the application of the social-problems approach in the analysis of environmental issues.

12 In the summer of 1990, for instance, protesters in Islington, London, hugged a tree that was about to be felled.

13 For an application of Douglas' model in interpreting environmental policy, see Milton (1991).

14 For instance, in January 1992, BBC Television broadcast a programme in its *Horizon* series, entitled 'In Search of the Noble Savage', in which anthropologists, in particular Tim Ingold, played a prominent role.

REFERENCES

Bahro, R. (1982) *Socialism and Survival*, London: Heretic Books.
—— (1984) *From Red to Green: Interviews with New Left Review*, London: Verso.
Bennett, J. (1976) *The Ecological Transition*, London: Pergamon.
Berreman, G.D. (1968) 'Is anthropology alive? Social responsibility in social anthropology', *Current Anthropology*, 9 (5): 391–6.

Bourdieu, P. (1977) *Outline of a Theory of Practice*, Cambridge: Cambridge University Press.

Cotgrove, S. (1976) 'Environmentalism and Utopia', *Sociological Review*, 24: 23–42.

Cotgrove, S. and Duff, A. (1980) 'Environmentalism, middle-class radicalism and politics', *Sociological Review*, 28 (2): 333–51.

—— (1981) 'Environmentalism, values and social change', *British Journal of Sociology*, 32 (1): 92–110.

Cowell, A. (1990) *The Decade of Destruction*, Sevenoaks: Hodder and Stoughton.

Croll, E. and Parkin, D. (eds) (1992) *Bush Base: Forest Farm – Culture, Environment and Development*, London and New York: Routledge.

Dobson, A. (1990) *Green Political Thought*, London: HarperCollins.

Douglas, M. (1966) *Purity and Danger*, Harmondsworth: Penguin.

—— (1970) *Natural Symbols*, Harmondsworth: Penguin.

—— (1992) 'A credible biosphere', in *Risk and Blame: Essays in Cultural Theory*, London and New York: Routledge.

Ellen, R.F. (1982) *Environment, Subsistence and System: The Ecology of Small-scale Social Formations*, Cambridge: Cambridge University Press.

—— (1986) 'What Black Elk left unsaid: on the illusory images of Green primitivism', *Anthropology Today*, 2 (6): 8–12.

Eyerman, R. and Jamison, A. (1991) *Social Movements: A Cognitive Approach*, Cambridge: Polity Press.

Fairclough, N. (1992) *Discourse and Social Change*, Cambridge: Polity Press.

Foucault, M. (1972) *The Archaeology of Knowledge*, London: Tavistock.

—— (1979) *Discipline and Punish: The Birth of the Prison*, Harmondsworth: Penguin.

Geertz, C. (1973) *The Interpretation of Cultures*, New York: Basic Books.

Hannerz, U. (1992) *Cultural Complexity: Studies in the Social Organization of Meaning*, New York: Columbia University Press.

Harries-Jones, P. (1986) 'From cultural translator to advocate: changing circles of interpretation', in R. Paine (ed.) *Advocacy and Anthropology: First Encounters*, St John's, Newfoundland: ISER, Memorial University of Newfoundland.

—— (ed.) (1991) *Making Knowledge Count: Advocacy and Social Science*, Montreal and Kingston: McGill-Queen's Press.

Hunter, R. (1979) *Warriors of the Rainbow: A Chronicle of the Greenpeace Movement*, New York: Holt, Rinehart and Winston.

Ingold, T. (1986) *The Appropriation of Nature: Essays on Human Ecology and Social Relations*, Manchester: Manchester University Press.

—— (1992) 'Culture and the perception of the environment', in E. Croll and D. Parkin (eds) *Bush Base: Forest Farm – Culture, Environment and Development*, London and New York: Routledge.

James, P., Tayler, P. and Thompson, M. (1987) *Plural Rationalities*, Warwick Papers in Management 9, Warwick University.

Jamison, A., Eyerman, R. and Cramer, J. (1990) *The Making of the New Environmental Consciousness*, Edinburgh: Edinburgh University Press.

Keat, R. and Urry, J. (1982) *Social Theory as Science*, London: Routledge and Kegan Paul.

Keesing, R.M. (1981) *Cultural Anthropology: A Contemporary Perspective* (2nd edition), New York: Holt, Rinehart and Winston.

Kruse, H. (1974) 'Development and environment', *American Behavioral Science*, 17 (5): 676–89.

Leach, E. (1976) *Culture and Communication*, Cambridge: Cambridge University Press.

Lovelock, J.E. (1979) *Gaia*, Oxford: Oxford University Press.
—— (1988) *The Ages of Gaia*, Oxford: Oxford University Press.
Lowe, P. and Flynn, A. (1989) 'Environmental politics and policy in the 1980s', in J. Mohan (ed.) *The Political Geography of Contemporary Britain*, London: Macmillan.
Lowe, P. and Goyder, J. (1983) *Environmental Groups in Politics*, London: Allen and Unwin.
Milton, K. (1989) 'Anthropology: a conservationists' science', *Ecos*, 10 (1): 29–33.
—— (1991) 'Interpreting environmental policy: a social scientific approach', in R. Churchill, L. Warren and J. Gibson (eds) *Law, Policy and the Environment*, Oxford: Blackwell.
Moore, H.L. (1988) *Feminism and Anthropology*, Cambridge: Polity Press.
Moran, E.F. (1982) *Human Adaptability: An Introduction to Ecological Anthropology*, Boulder: Westview Press.
—— (1990) 'Ecosystem ecology in biology and anthropology: a critical assessment', in E.F. Moran (ed.) *The Ecosystem Approach in Anthropology*, Michigan: The University of Michigan Press.
Morgan, G. (ed.) (1983) *Beyond Method: Strategies for Social Research*, Beverly Hills: Sage.
—— (1991) 'Advocacy as a form of social science', in P. Harries-Jones (ed.) *Making Knowledge Count: Advocacy and Social Science*, Montreal and Kingston: McGill-Queen's Press.
Naess, A. (1989) *Ecology, Community and Lifestyle: Outline of an Ecosophy*, trans. and rev. D. Rothenberg, Oxford: Oxford University Press.
O'Riordan, T. (1981) *Environmentalism* (2nd edition), London: Pion.
Paehlke, R.C. (1989) *Environmentalism and the Future of Progressive Politics*, New Haven: Yale University Press.
Paine, R. (ed.) (1986) *Advocacy and Anthropology: First Encounters*, St John's, Newfoundland: ISER, Memorial University of Newfoundland.
Pearce, D., Markandya, A. and Barbier, E.B. (1989) *Blueprint for a Green Economy*, London: Earthscan.
Pearce, D., Barbier, E., Markandya, A., Barrett, S., Turner, R.K. and Swanson, T. (1991) *Blueprint 2: Greening the World Economy*, London: Earthscan.
Porritt, J. (1992) 'Facts of Life', *BBC Wildlife*, 10 (11): 69.
Porritt, J. and Winner, D. (1988) *The Coming of the Greens*, London: Fontana.
Rappaport, R. (1967) *Pigs for the Ancestors*, New Haven: Yale University Press.
Redclift, M. (1984) *Development and the Environmental Crisis: Red or Green Alternatives?*, London and New York: Methuen.
—— (1987) *Sustainable Development: Exploring the Contradictions*, London and New York: Methuen.
Revkin, A. (1990) *The Burning Season: The Murder of Chico Mendes and the Fight for the Amazon Rain Forest*, London: Collins.
Richards, J.R. (1980) *The Sceptical Feminist: A Philosophical Enquiry*, Harmondsworth: Penguin.
Richards, P. (1985) *Indigenous Agricultural Revolution*, Boulder: Westview Press.
Rüdig, W. (ed.) (1990) *Green Politics One*, Edinburgh: Edinburgh University Press.
Sapir, E. (1961) *Culture, Language and Personality: Selected Essays*, ed. D.G. Mandelbaum, Berkeley: University of California Press.
Schensul, S.L. and Schensul, J.J. (1978) 'Advocacy and applied anthropology', in G.H. Weber and G.J. McCall (eds) *Social Scientists as Advocates: Views from the Applied Disciplines*, Beverly Hills: Sage.
Schumacher, E.F. (1973) *Small is Beautiful: A Study of Economics As If People Mattered*, London: Blond and Briggs.

Scott, A. (1990) *Ideology and the New Social Movements*, London: Unwin Hyman.

Spretnak, C. (1985) 'The spiritual dimension of green politics', in C. Spretnak and F. Capra, *Green Politics: The Global Promise*, London: Paladin.

Steward, J. (1955) *Theory of Culture Change*, Urbana, Illinois: University of Illinois Press.

Thompson, M. and Tayler, P. (1986) *The Surprise Game: An Exploration of Constrained Relativism*, Warwick Papers in Management 1, Warwick University.

Tyler, S. (1969) *Cognitive Anthropology*, New York and London: Holt, Rinehart and Winston.

van Dijk, T. (ed.) (1985) *Handbook of Discourse Analysis*, 4 vols, London: Academic Press.

Weber, T. (1988) *Hugging the Trees: The Story of the Chipko Movement*, Harmondsworth: Penguin.

Wenzel, G. (1991) *Animal Rights, Human Rights: Ecology, Economy and Ideology in the Canadian Arctic*, London: Belhaven.

WWF (1991) *Annual Review*, Godalming, Surrey: WWF (UK).

Yearley, S. (1991) *The Green Case: A Sociology of Environmental Issues, Arguments and Politics*, London: HarperCollins.

Chapter 1

Environmentalism

A new moral discourse for technological society?

Robin Grove-White

The rise of 'the environment' as a social and cultural phenomenon was a striking feature of the 1970s and 1980s around the world. And if now, in 1993, it has begun to lose its sheen as the focus of an emergent social movement, that development too is a reflection of how widely its forms and perspectives have begun to penetrate into the common consciousness. Rhetorically at least, the problems of global climatic change, of waste and the motor car, of ozone holes and endangered species are now elements of the shared vocabulary in cultures like the UK's. Communiqués on common environmental aspirations have become almost routine in the currency of summit gatherings of world leaders. We have entered an era in which not only marginal social groups but also political parties, industrialists, religious leaders, scientists of all descriptions, even the legal and accountancy professions, all seek to reflect a sensitivity to 'environmental' priorities, whatever the other commitments they may aver.

The concern of this chapter is to make a small contribution to helping explain the apparent social purchase of 'environmental' discourse in societies like that of the UK. As numerous sociologists (including Beck 1986, Lash and Urry 1987, Giddens 1990, Bauman 1991) have argued, we are in the throes of convulsive 'post-modern' social change on a number of fronts, with 'risk' a cultural theme of growing significance. It would be surprising if the rise of 'the environment' as a central problematic were not bound up in such developments. Yet there is little recognition of such a perspective in the official world or in the research circles from whom advice on such matters is usually sought. That fact too demands explanation.

The nub of the argument developed below is that the dominant version of what constitutes 'environmentalism' is seriously incomplete. This is because it omits to recognize key social and cultural dimensions of what has driven the discourse into public prominence. These are dimensions on which Mary Douglas first offered initial anthropological insight more than twenty years ago (1970). Nor is the omission fortuitous. The frequently overlooked social and cultural dimensions constitute some of the most distinctive features of 'the environment'. They permit us to recognize in the arguments about it elements of a new form of moral discourse. However, such dimensions are extremely difficult for our social institutions to digest, because of their potential implications for a range of commitments, epistemological as well as institutional and economic, throughout society. So they have been sidelined, by and large. This calls into question whether 'environmentalism' can be thought of as a *successful* moral discourse.

To express the matter in this way may seem somewhat portentous. To keep the argument in bounds I consider the general problem through the experience of a specific culture, that of the UK.

THE EMERGENCE OF AN ORTHODOXY

Most commentators on the development of environmental politics in Britain point to Prime Minister Margaret Thatcher's speech to the Royal Society of 22 September 1988 as a crucial watershed (Thatcher 1988). Given Britain's highly centralized political institutions, the speech and the energy with which its contents were promoted in backstage media briefings and subsequent official initiatives were taken rightly to represent an official conversion to the reality of environmental problems. The effect of the speech was to unlock a new level of interest and commitment in officialdom and the media, legitimizing in Whitehall the depth of public concern which had been building up over the previous two decades. Following the publication of the UN-sponsored Brundtland Report, *Our Common Future* (Brundtland 1987), and in parallel with other initiatives in 1988 by senior political leaders in other countries – Gorbachev, Mitterrand, Bush and Kohl among them – the speech and the events it triggered helped vault environmental concerns into 'that rarefied zone where national leaders are the principal players' (Burke 1989). What had previously been seen politically in the UK as 'minority', or marginal, concerns were now affirmed as of central significance.

Rapidly, following the Prime Minister's lead, the official environmental agenda began to consolidate around a cluster of major issues – the greenhouse effect, ozone depletion, toxic wastes, wildlife and habitat losses, pollution of sea and rivers among them. Overwhelmingly, such issues have come to command consensus amongst politicians, industry, the news media and key environmental pressure groups as *the* significant issues, to which all efforts need to be directed to find solutions.

What features have characterized this 'orthodox' consensus? First, and overwhelmingly, the most pressing problems have been seen as existing objectively in nature, mediated through the natural sciences. Environmental problems worthy of the name are thus regarded as *physical* problems, arising from specific human interventions in natural systems; their character and boundaries are, so to speak, given to us from nature, their authenticity guaranteed by natural scientific investigation and confirmation (with global population pressures adding a chronic extra dimension). This being the case, the argument continues, what are now needed are 'solutions', to mitigate these physically identified 'problems' – solutions which may be found in persuasion or regulation, in technological innovation, in international agreements or in the application of economic instruments. In each of the international agreements so far established – on CFCs (chlorofluorocarbons), on sea-dumping of industrial wastes, on sulphur dioxide emissions and so on – there are implicit commitments to beliefs about the physical limits of the 'problems', and about the restorative effects of the particular actions agreed for limiting the pollutants in question.

Clearly, the problems captured by this overall description are immensely important. They have huge implications for equity between North and South, as well as for the quality of life in East and West. The scientific consensus on issues like global climate change and ozone depletion is impressive and alarming; so too is the evidence of accumulations of toxic wastes and other pollutants in our soil and water. Public opinion and the environmental pressure groups (non-governmental organizations – NGOs) are also seen as having a significant potential role: while the 'rationality' and 'responsibility' of the NGOs may be seen as suspect, because of their supposedly myopic partisanship, nevertheless 'solutions' to the principal problems will not come without their cooperation, in helping shape and mobilize public opinion.

This characterization of the prevailing orthodoxy is drawn most immediately from UK experience – the recent White Paper, *This Common Inheritance* (HMSO 1990), embodies broadly this view – but variants of it are now influential in most Western countries. The environmental problematic is now becoming defined and understood as a set of discretely identifiable physical problems with human ramifications, some of them acknowledged as deep-rooted in our economic practice and very difficult to address. 'Solving' the most intractable of them, it is suggested, will require major achievements of regulation, fiscal innovation and international diplomacy, as well as good-will of a kind almost without precedent. There is no time to be lost: partnerships of industrialists, politicians, NGOs and scientists are vitally needed to help develop realistic instruments to this end.

This description seems so self-evidently true, I suspect, that it may seem odd to question it at a fundamental level. However, it is far from adequate as an account of what has been going on. Here are four of its shortcomings.

Trivialization of the public's role

The orthodoxy – with its assumption that the key problems are those identifiable by natural scientific investigation – fails to account convincingly for the startling fact that almost all of the most significant environmental issues, global or domestic, were crystallized first not by governments responding to or using 'science', but by poorly resourced NGOs and sundry individual environmentalists in the period between the late 1960s and early

1980s. Indeed, too often over this period, the role of scientists and official scientific institutions was to patronize so-called 'emotional' and 'irrational' expressions of public environmental concern – on issues much later acknowledged by official scientific bodies and institutions to be indeed genuine and serious problems. Almost all of the arguments, and most of the solutions, now advocated by environment ministries and agencies have a long history – whether in the fields of energy, transport, agricultural policy or even industrial policy. In most of their outlines and much of their detail, the analyses and prescriptions which now increasingly underpin official thinking focus on much the range of issues on which environmental groups have been banging the drum since the early 1970s – physical excesses of trajectories of industrial society, the inadequacy of present regulatory processes for controlling such 'externalities', and the need for new approaches which recognize and take advantage of the inherently malleable nature of such concepts as 'economic growth' and 'consumer demand'. To a striking extent, the 1970s analyses of UK NGOs like Friends of the Earth, Greenpeace, the International Institute for Environment and Development (IIED), the Council for the Protection of Rural England (CPRE) and others have been vindicated – down to such diverse and specific *causes célèbres* as the economics of nuclear power; the need for, and feasibility of, major programmes of energy conservation and improved end-use efficiencies; the arguments against ever-increasing proliferation of the private car; the links between environmental degradation in Third World countries and poverty and famine; and the impacts on vegetation and wildlife of modern agriculture.

The point of this observation is not to score points by demonstrating the prescience of NGOs compared with governments and their advisers. Rather, it is to ask how a plausible account of this social reality can be derived from the 'orthodox' description of the environmental phenomenon given above. That model sees NGOs and 'public opinion' as essentially captious and irrational, given to 'unscientific' outbursts. These organizations are acknowledged to have had social importance, in having helped bring issues to political attention (Ashby 1978); but according to the orthodoxy, it has been science, particularly scientific enquiry conducted within an official framework, which has provided the true litmus test for whether or not issues are indeed issues.

The oddity remains. How and why 'the public' (reflected in the NGOs) understood the issues in advance of the arrival of official 'science', or why their 'intuitions' should have resonated so powerfully with wider social attitudes, is not considered a matter of significance, and these days tends to be set to one side in official circles.

Inflation of the role of science

A second shortcoming of the prevailing orthodoxy concerns precisely its view of the authority of the natural sciences, in providing the criteria for what constitutes 'fact' in the most significant areas of the environmental domain. Though the 1990 White Paper and recent international agreements on issues like North Sea pollution have laid new emphasis on the occasional need for action ahead of scientific 'proof' of damage, the so-called precautionary principle, the implicit underlying official conception of science remains a positivistic one. That is to say, scientific procedures are held up publicly as providing 'proof' and as therefore able to define and identify 'fact' in this field.

However, growing understanding by sociologists (in the wake of Popper, Kuhn, *et al.*) of the ways in which scientists actually conduct their business continues to undermine this reassuringly solid picture. Far from providing a fixed, objectively verifiable body of knowledge of nature's workings – through privileged access to essential physical reality – science itself exists as a social construct, in which doctrines of 'objective' practice rest on a web of conventions, practices, understandings and 'negotiated' indeterminacies (Wynne 1987).

The corollary is that scientific 'proof' or 'certainty', in the real world of non-laboratory circumstances in which *environmental* science has to be conducted, is a chimera. Uncertainty and indeterminacy in this arena are not simply provisional; they are all but endemic. Most scientists are responsible to institutions (industry, government, research councils). They are necessarily as selective in their identification of 'problems', and the relevant parameters that need to be considered, as are individuals or institutions using other modes of perception or understanding. What is more, society's concerns and the actions of an infinity of other actors are in constant, and unpredictable, flux. This helps explain why it is that controversy is so recurrent in politically sensitive fields in which science is used by official environmental agencies to underwrite inaction or to provide political reassurance. Quite simply, the scope for redefining issues 'scientifically', to embrace ever more new, real-world variables, or to refocus the significance attached to those already acknowledged, is to all intents and purposes infinite. It follows that the same is true also of the scope for criticism and disagreement, over much more fundamental matters than simply whether any specific scientific claim is 'accurate' or not.

So here too the prevailing orthodoxy is far less robust than it purports to be.

The perverse dominance of 'interests'

A third failing of the orthodoxy lies in its distorted reliance on the notion of 'interests' as the central tool for explaining environmental concern or value, and justifying corrective measures. This tendency flows from the conception of the sovereign individual, which has been at the centre of the British liberal political tradition since Locke; the picturing of most human motivation in terms of interests has been a natural corollary. It now dominates public political discussion of environmental matters in Britain, whether in the form of argument about straightforward conflicts involving individual 'interests', or talk of 'interests' of generations as yet unborn, or advocacy of the 'interests' of other (non-human) species.

There are two objections to this tendency. In the first place, it is simply not true that *all* environmental concern can be characterized appropriately in terms of interests. In my own experience, and contrary to appearances, individuals who have most shaped the environmental movement have been drawn together quite as much by openness and a groping sense of shared, or potentially shared, identity – forged against the prevailing social ortho-doxy – as by the pursuit of predefined policy objectives. As continental sociologists like Melucci (1989) have recognized, such individuals have been seeking and perhaps finding a better, more fruitful collective engagement with, and exploration of, reality, discovering it through simple human inter-action with one another, against a background of tension and argument with the prevailing social ethos. Such processes are of their nature open-ended and indeterminate. They cannot be represented usefully in terms of interests, other than *ex post facto*, since even the individuals concerned are by defini-tion unable to articulate fully what they are seeking. Indeed, part of their inspiration has lain in discomfort at, and the wish to find alternatives to, precisely the manipulation of political discourse entailed by the dominance of the 'interests' mentality.

This points to the second objection. While obviously in many circum-stances environmental concerns *do* involve interests, the present dominance of this way of looking at questions of value has developed a manipulatively self-fulfilling dynamic of its own. NGOs, recognizing that this is the discourse in which our political and legal culture now frames issues most comfortably, have tended to reduce what are frequently more inchoate concerns into terms consistent with the discourse, in their pursuit of advantage in contro-versies over issues as different as nuclear safety, global climate change, habitat protection or green belts. But necessary though this may be, its effect is further to reinforce the vocabulary's worst procrustean tendencies. Like all specialist discourses, it has difficulty in bringing to light or representing perspectives on reality which do not readily fit its own particular framing.

All of this points to a striking irony – that the supposedly detached and objective language of interests embodies crucially important *normative* com-mitments. And in environmental controversies, in practice, it is frequently encountered, and resented, as a moral rather than a neutrally descriptive discourse – and a thoroughly inadequate one at that.

No place for mystery

A fourth respect in which the present orthodoxy on environmental questions is inadequate is in its superficial treatment of the mysteriousness and open-endedness of existence itself. There is little sign in the official descriptions of environmental problems or methodologies of the radically unknown character of the future, or of humankind's place in creation.

The tendency in such exercises to characterize the future so far as possible in terms of sets of familiar and 'predictable' parameters – in which, for example, markets can flourish and corporate planners can plan – places at the centre of public discussion an artificially sterile and deterministic conceptualization of existence itself. It is a picture in which the indeterminacy, mystery, apparent capriciousness, open-endedness and ambiguity of life acknowledged by the classical philosophers and religious traditions, and the moral challenges these realities present to men and women encountering them in history, are drained of public significance, or at least 'privatized' by being driven to the margins of public culture.

Such processes have been by-products of the ways in which Western industrial culture has developed since Descartes; they have occurred during the success and hegemony of liberalism from Locke onwards and with the rise of the outstandingly effective set of scientific practices which, linked to liberal political institutions, have helped so to transform Western culture over the past three hundred years.

Their grip can be seen in the way in which the orthodox model now deals with 'the unknown' in environmental matters – reducing it wherever possible to merely provisional 'scientific' uncertainty or imprecision. Not only is this perverse in its own, explanatory, terms, as sociologists of science like Wynne have shown, but it also profoundly misrepresents reality at a deeper level.

Indeed, against a contemporary background of fundamental intellectual friction about the nature of scientific knowledge and the status of uncertainty, it is at least a reasonable hypothesis that some of the deeper shades of recent 'green' and 'new-age' religiosity are best understood as cultural symbolizations of just these tensions. They can be read (as Grove-White *et al.* (1991) have argued) as creative, if still dualistic, reactions against the hubris of still-dominant modernist expectations of scientific epistemology – challenging the way in which, in institutional practices of many different varieties, such expectations dominate not only our social identities and current political priorities in the environmental sphere, but also the definition of boundaries between the fixed and the tractable, between humankind and nature.

Nor are such tensions present only at the rarefied level of environmental science and policy. More prosaically, the tendencies towards the atomizing of human experience, and its representation in 'objective' behavioural terms, lead to a persistent trivialization at the everyday level of areas of human experience which may in fact bear on the mysterious depths of the individual person's relations with nature and the cosmos. This could be confirmed in discussion with individuals involved in many everyday disputes about land-use planning or nature conservation issues.

The persistent political misrepresentation of human experience, of the kind embodied in the conceptions of (positivistically conceived) 'uncertainty', 'amenity' and 'recreation', constitutes a form of imposed hegemony, which is not itself subject to choice, other than in terms which, arguably, intensify mistrust in engaged individuals in environmental and other NGOs, with increasingly disruptive, unpredictable political consequences. This results directly from the fact that the concepts – and *ergo* the models in which they rest – are frequently inadequate for reflecting the full dimensions of felt experience. To be sure, people use, and even manipulate successfully, such reductionist languages. But the consequential mistrust is corrosive, and capricious in its manifestations. Indeed, as is argued below, much of the drive behind environmental politics on the NGO side (and their resonances with wider publics) may well have arisen from it.

So far, this chapter has pointed to several respects in which the prevailing dominant representation of the environmental problematic seems seriously inadequate. It is unable to account for, or to encompass coherently, key realities of the political and social phenomenon of environmentalism, as they have actually arisen. Nor are these trivial realities; the importance of the worldwide grass-roots concern, the basis of the social authority of scientific knowledge, the complex character of human purposes and identities in environmental argument, and the need to address authentic human concern about deeper mysteries of existence – these are far from insignificant matters. Yet the orthodox model has little or nothing to say about them, in ways which can command respect.

None the less, few could deny the strengths of this overall model. It has contributed to clarification of the structure of certain kinds of problem, global as well as regional and local – not least because the relevant social, political and regulatory institutions, being embedded in the same cultural matrix, are framed to respond to the way of looking at problems that the model prescribes. Traffic engineers, economic analysts, risk-assessment specialists and the like operate within much the same assumptions about human behaviour implied by the model, to considerable effect on behalf of the limited communities for whom they work. But the wider constraints on thought imposed by the model are still more striking. For it leads to a picture of the overall environmental 'agenda' described at the outset of this chapter, as a set of visible and discrete problems, which present themselves objectively in the form of 'externalities' from economic processes. As we have seen, such a description is achieved only at the cost of dangerous over-simplifications and omissions.

AN 'ALTERNATIVE'

Consider now a sharply different hypothesis to that offered in the 'policy world' orthodoxy, to explain the way in which environmental issues have become socially defined.

Particular industrial societies like the UK have become progressively more locked into a vast range of commitments, which have developed over decades – commitments which are economic, industrial, infrastructural, geopolitical, technological and social. These have been underpinned by, and work to reinforce, a dualistic picture of humankind and nature. Most of the commitments (to individual motorized mobility, to ever higher levels of energy use, to social, moral and cultural norms encouraging increasing levels of material consumption) have tended to be producer-led. They have been entered into *without* prior public analysis or publicly taken decisions about their cumulative potential impacts. Yet they are commitments which help define and shape our collective social and political identities.

These commitments have helped determine the parameters not only of the physical but also of the social domain. Many of the most widely diffused technologies (the telephone, the word-processor, etc.) have few obvious deleterious impacts; but many (the internal combustion engine, civil nuclear power, pesticides, chemicals producing toxic wastes, etc.) do have adverse impacts, the significance of which becomes recognized retrospectively, but only gradually and with difficulty. Moreover, the *social* arrangements needed to make them 'work' (itself a disputable achievement) may be at least as significant, and arguably as negative, as their physical/biological impacts.

In our own time, these cultural configurations have become more and more dominant. Crucially, in the societies in which they are present, they have been producing their own distinctive patterns of social anxiety and response. The discourse of 'environmental' problems, expressed in terms of the same humankind–nature dualism as industrialism itself, is one key manifestation of this. Environmental pressure groups and green parties have derived their (paradoxical) political potency from the fact that they have been the agents of ways in which particular land-use or pollution controversies have come to symbolize, and resonate with, these widely shared, deeply rooted but previously inchoate and unfocused concerns. Not only do they focus on the conspicuous physical dimensions of the changes wrought by the social commitments (as these have become more and more pervasive). But, quite as crucially, they also focus on the increasingly problematic new relationships with the political and regulatory agencies responsible for monitoring what are now effectively scientific experiments imposed on society as a whole (as Krohn and Weyer have pointed out (1989: 15–18)), and for providing social reassurance that any side effects are being kept under control.

Seen in this light, three points about 'the environment' as a social phenomenon emerge. First, environmentalism in its grass-roots forms has been a vector for the selection and definition of the particular risks which have become magnets for social anxieties aroused by vulnerabilities inherent in the technological commitments in which our societies are, willy-nilly, embedded. These processes have occurred largely outside the nexus of 'formal' political and research institutions. In particular, seen in anthropological terms, it is environmental groups – for an adventitious mixture of reasons, moral, institutional and cultural – who have helped give definition to the risks and dangers which British society now recognizes as part of its description of the 'natural'; hence their immense resonance and credibility with the public at large over the past few years.

It is through social processes like these that the political agenda of environmental concern has become defined. The particular concatenation of concrete issues – water quality, whales, wastes and so on – on which the agenda came to focus in the 1970s and 1980s had a somewhat arbitrary, opportunistic character, the product more of a set of political and social contingencies than of any magisterial advance of more 'objective' processes of understanding.

In the second place, the successes of environmentalism in its pre-1988 phase reflected *realistic* intuitions – vivid in the case of NGOs and green parties, more attenuated in the case of wider groups – about the ways in which life in modern complex societies is now shaped and dominated by technological and corporate-bureaucratic systems outside the agency of formal political institutions in which there is any genuine sense of shared public control (Winner 1977, Giddens 1990). Indeed, in the UK's case it is no coincidence that the gap between 'reality' and constitutional 'fiction' in this regard has become so striking that it is a topic of routine concern to such political scientists as David Marquand (1988). The relationship of the environmental movement to these phenomena can be pictured, as Ron Eyerman and Andrew Jamison (1991) have suggested recently, as one of tacitly generating 'new knowledge' about such matters for society as a whole, through processes of 'cognitive praxis' in real-life, day-to-day arguments with the prevailing orthodoxies. However, to repeat a point made earlier, the partial and selective way in which this 'knowledge' has come alive has reflected important social and cultural contingencies.

Hence the third point is that because our public culture gives greatest recognition epistemologically to factors defined in objective 'scientific' terms, it has been on the *physical* manifestations of the wider social anxieties – that is, on individual abuses of or incursions into the 'natural' environment – that attention has focused most dramatically. What is more, in the Anglo-Saxon world, the pervasive, individualistic language of 'interests' has added what might be seen as a further filter: it has tended to disguise from view the fact that, as Melucci (1989) and other theorists of new social movements have begun to point out, grass-roots processes of reconfiguration of a refreshed sense of communitarian concern have been under way within the environmental movement. Paradoxically, the discourse of individualism may be being used to reconstitute, however partially, collectivities and a state of mutual interdependency previously articulated for society in the idioms of a now-tattered socialism.

Reductionisms of such kinds are omnipresent in political cultures like that of the UK. Here they have obliged participants in public 'environmental' debate to lean on the languages of individual 'interests' and unambiguous physical 'fact' at a workaday level – for example, when arguing within the context of the land-use planning system (the Town and Country Planning Acts), within the official vocabularies of nature protection (SSSIs – Sites of Special Scientific Interest – and the like), or within those of environmentally related forecasting tools. Cumulatively, the reductionist, utilitarian discourses in such fields actually lead to further processes of selection and attenuation of the environmental agenda. Subtly and unintentionally for the most part, they compound the inability of the engaged citizen to give explicit public expression to concerns which often relate to profoundly important moral, existential realities – simply because there is a lack of arenas in which such realities are granted public significance, unless reduced to the terms of a procedurally acceptable discourse.

Overall then, this more 'cultural' representation of the environmental problematic in complex societies like the UK's suggests that there is much more to it all than is implied in the now prevailing orthodoxy on the matter (described in the first half of this chapter). The physical dimensions of the environmental 'crisis' may be indeed quite as serious as is being suggested. But crucial human, social and cultural dimensions need also to be included and accorded the significance due to them.

This suggests a final question. What were the processes by which the post-1988 orthodoxy consolidated as it did in apparent neglect of such realities? A straightforward answer suggests itself. In 1987–8 the groundswell of public opinion, coupled to accumulated tensions between Britain and European Community institutions (Haigh 1990), attained such a level that minds had to be concentrated on it politically. The Prime Minister's September 1988 Royal Society speech was the most crucial result. However, the specific choice of problems on which that speech focused was deliberate and highly significant; they were global and scientifically defined (global climate, the ozone layer, biodiversity). The speech gave no trace of recognition that the social relations of technological society nearer home might be part of the issue. Subsequently, within Whitehall and the plurality of departments and public agencies with widening 'environmental' responsibilities, methodologies and vocabularies resting on instrumentalist, rational-choice foundations (economic tools; rationalistic risk-assessment techniques; performance 'indicators' relying on artificially unambiguous definitions of phenomena) have been brought increasingly into play. Ironically, these echo the kinds of method and approach which helped feed the arguments defining the environmental *Weltanschauung*, and on which the cultural tensions to which the NGOs were attuned focused in the 1970s and 1980s.

Part of the explanation for the fact that government (and its agencies) has moved seamlessly to entrench such discrete, 'objective' characterizations of issues in this domain is that these enable it to shift control of the political initiative on such matters from the effectual level, dominated by media images generated by NGOs and green parties, to itself and its own politically 'rational' priorities. If a consensus can be established that the issues are best understood in more precise, unambiguous terms, they lend themselves to being addressed, in principle at least, by the limited instrumentalities at government's disposal (these being themselves embedded in such forms).

But the short-term gains from such an 'innocently' intended progression may involve a high price later on, in terms of policy incoherence and public inconsistency.

At the heart of the problematic lies a troubling paradox. Opinion polls confirm that many people now accept the significance of the crisis we call environmental, acknowledging that the industrial societies of which Western countries have been exemplars have become locked into trajectories which bode long-term ill, unless they can be altered. Yet individually, relatively few people do anything significant about this recognition in their personal lives. Can it be that such inconsistency reflects in part the inauthenticity of the largely 'physicalist' descriptions of what is at stake, which our society's epistemological commitments have given us? If, as this chapter has groped to suggest, a crucial dimension of environmentalism is moral, human and relational, it would not be surprising if the scientism of the orthodoxy (even in its radical 'deep green' forms) was failing to engage people's full beings, however much the opinion polls may continue to report public 'concern'.

The question of how 'environmentalism' is to be characterized most appropriately is not one of simply historical or conceptual interest. It is of the greatest potential moment for society itself. Without a richer sense of the nature and extent of the human concerns embedded in the phenomenon, public policy processes in this sphere will continue to operate un-convincingly. Crucial lessons will not be learnt, and we will continue down increasingly confusing, inequitable and dangerous paths.

ACKNOWLEDGEMENTS

The author is especially grateful for continuing collaboration and discussion with Brian Wynne on ideas and approaches in this paper. He also acknowledges with appreciation the Economic and Social Research Council's support of the related research programme at Lancaster University's Centre for the Study of Environmental Change.

REFERENCES

Ashby, E. (1978) *Reconciling Man with the Environment*, Cambridge: Cambridge University Press.
Bauman, Z. (1991) *Intimations of Post-Modernity*, London: Routledge.

Beck, U. (1986) *Risikogesellschaft*, Frankfurt: Suhrkampf (translated [1992] as *The Risk Society: Towards an Alternative Modernity*, London and Newbury Park, California: Sage).

Brundtland, Gro H. (1987) *Our Common Future*, Oxford: Oxford University Press.

Burke, T. (1989) 'The turning green tide', *Marxism Today*, 33 (4): 43–5.

Douglas, M. (1970) 'Environments at risk', in *Implicit Meanings*, London: Routledge and Kegan Paul.

Eyerman, R. and Jamison, A. (1991) *Social Movements: A Cognitive Approach*, Cambridge: Polity Press.

Giddens, A. (1990) *The Consequences of Modernity*, Cambridge: Polity Press.

Grove-White, R., Morris, P. and Szerszynski, B. (1991) *The Emerging Ethical Mood on Environmental Issues in Britain*, Report to the World Wide Fund for Nature, Godalming, Surrey: WWF(UK).

Haigh, N. (1990) *EEC Environmental Policy and Britain* (2nd revised edition), Harlow: Longman.

HMSO (1990) *This Common Inheritance: Britain's Environmental Strategy*, Cm 1200, London: HMSO.

Krohn, W. and Weyer, J. (1989) 'Society as laboratory: the production of risks by experimental research', unpublished ms, Bielefeld, Germany.

Lash, S. and Urry, J. (1987) *The End of Organised Capitalism*, Cambridge: Polity Press.

Marquand, D. (1988) *The Unprincipled Society: New Demands and Old Politics*, London: Fontana.

Melucci, A. (1989) *Nomads of the Present*, Philadelphia: Temple University Press.

Thatcher, M. (1988) *Speech to the Royal Society*, London: Conservative Party.

Winner, L. (1977) *Autonomous Technology: Technics-out-of-Control as a Theme in Political Thought*, Cambridge, Massachusetts, and London: MIT Press.

Wynne, B. (1987) *Risk Management and Hazardous Waste: The Dialectics of Credibility*, Berlin, London, New York: Springer-Verlag.

Chapter 2

Globes and spheres

The topology of environmentalism

Tim Ingold

My purpose in this chapter is no more than to try out a rather embryonic idea. It concerns the significance of the image of the globe in the language of contemporary debate about the environment. Though the image has long been deployed in geopolitical contexts, and even longer in connection with navigation and astronomy, my impression is that its use as a characterization of the *environment* is rather recent. I have in mind such phrases, which slip so readily off the tongues of contemporary policy-makers, as 'global environmental change'. One is immediately struck by the paradoxical nature of this phrase. An environment, surely, is that which surrounds, and can exist, therefore, only in relation to what is surrounded (Ingold 1992: 40). I do not think that those who speak of the global environment mean by this the environment surrounding the globe. It is *our* environment they are talking about, the world as it presents itself to a universal humanity. Yet how can humans, or for that matter beings of any other kind, possibly be surrounded by a globe? Would it not be fairer to say that it is we who have surrounded it?

My idea is that what may be called the global outlook may tell us something important about the modern conception of the environment as a world which, far from being the ambience of our dwelling, is turned in upon itself, so that we who once stood at its centre become first circumferential and are finally expelled from it altogether (Figure 2.1). In other words, I am suggesting that the notion of the global environment, far from marking humanity's reintegration into the world, signals the culmination of a process of separation.

The image of the globe is familiar to all of us who have gone through a Western schooling and are used to studying models upon which are drawn, in outline, the continents and oceans, and the grid-lines of latitude and longitude. We are taught that this is what the earth looks like, although none of us, with a handful of significant exceptions, has ever seen it. By and large, life is lived at such close proximity to the earth's surface that a global perspective is unobtainable. The significant exceptions comprise, of course, that privileged band of astronauts who have viewed the earth from outer space. In a sense, the astronaut's relation to the real globe seen through the

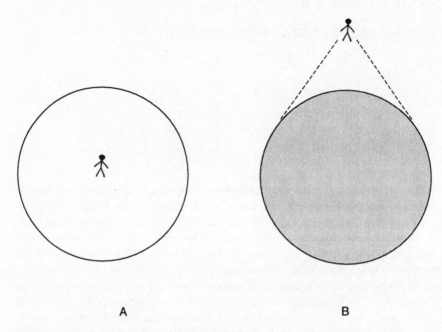

A   B

Figure 2.1 Two views of the environment: (A) as a lifeworld; (B) as a globe

window of the spacecraft mirrors the schoolchild's relation to the model globe in the classroom: in both cases the world appears as an object of contemplation, detached from the domain of lived experience. For the child the world is separately encapsulated in the model; for the astronaut life is separately encapsulated, albeit temporarily, in the space module. My point with this comparison is a simple one: with the world imaged as a globe, far from coming into being in and through a life process, it figures as an entity that is, as it were, presented to or confronted by life. The global environment is not a lifeworld, it is a world apart from life.

Before pursuing the implications of this view, I should like to introduce an alternative image of the world which, at least in European thought, is of far more ancient provenance. This is the image of the sphere. Something of the difference in connotation between 'globe' and 'sphere' is suggested in their very acoustic resonance: 'globe' is hard and consonantal; 'sphere' soft and vocalic. A globe is solid and opaque, a sphere hollow and transparent. For the early astronomers, of course, the cosmos itself was seen to be comprised of a series of such spheres, at the common centre of which stood man himself. The idea was that as man's attention was drawn ever outward, so it would penetrate each sphere so as to reach the next. This is illustrated in Figure 2.2, taken from the *Scala Naturale* of Giovanni Camillo Maffei,

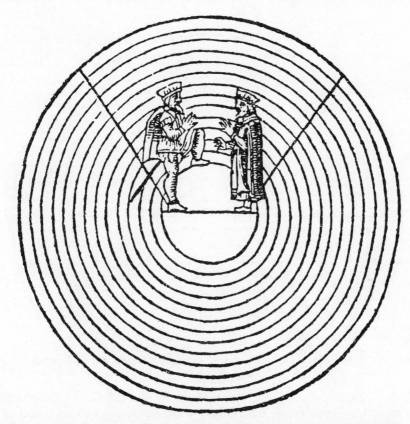

Figure 2.2 The fourteen spheres of the world, as drawn by Giovanni Camillo Maffei of Solofra in his *Scala Naturale* (Venice, 1564). Giovanni's patron, the Count of Altavilla, is shown beginning his ascent through the spheres

published in Venice in 1564, and dedicated to the Count of Altavilla. Here there are fourteen concentric spheres which – Maffei tells us – may be envisaged to form a giant stairway, the ascent of which affords, step by step, a comprehensive knowledge of the universe. In the picture, the Count is shown taking the first step, under Maffei's direction (see Adams 1938: 58–9).

Unlike the solid globe, which can only be perceived as such from without, spheres – as is clear from this figure – were to be perceived from within. The global view, we might say, is centripetal, the spherical view centrifugal. Nor is it any accident that the perception of the spheres was imaged in terms of listening rather than looking. Visual perception, depending as it does on the reflection of light from the outer surface of things, implies both the opacity and inertia of what is seen and the externality of the perceiver. The spheres, being transparent, could not be seen, but undergoing their own autonomous rotations about the common centre, they could be heard: thus the motion of

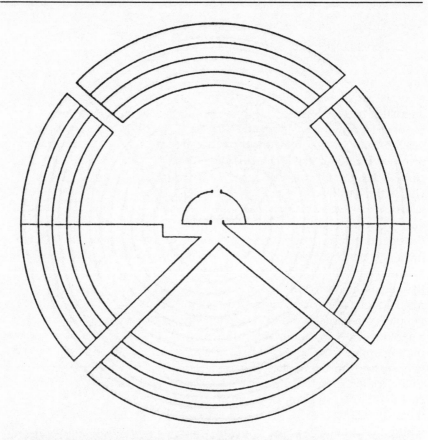

Figure 2.3 Yup'ik cosmology in cross-section
Source: *Eskimo Essays* by Ann Fienup-Riordan 1990: 111; copyright © 1990 by Ann Fienup-Riordan. Reprinted with permission of Rutgers University Press

the spheres was supposed to make a harmonious sound that could be registered by the sufficiently sensitive ear.

The idea of the spherical cosmos is by no means exclusive to the history of European thought. Let me present one further example, taken from Fienup-Riordan's (1990) account of the lifeworld of the Yup'ik Eskimos. Her cross-sectional depiction of the cosmos as perceived by the Yup'ik, reproduced in Figure 2.3, bears an uncanny resemblance to Maffei's diagram. At the centre is the dwelling, from which roads lead in various directions through the several surrounding spheres.

A person journeying far enough in any direction would eventually arrive at a point where the earth folded back up into the skyland, the home of the spirits of the game . . . Not only was the earth encompassed by a canopy from above, but below its thin surface resided the spirits of the

dead, both animal and human, each in separate villages. Four or five
'steps' separated these two distinct but related domains.

(Fienup-Riordan 1990: 110)

Notice how in this image the surface of the earth, far from bounding the
world externally, is but a thin and permeable membrane dividing the world
internally, between upper and lower hemispheres.

What I hope to have established, at least in outline, is that the lifeworld,
imaged from an experiential centre, is spherical in form, whereas a world
divorced from life, that is yet complete in itself, is imaged in the form of a
globe. Thus the movement from spherical to global imagery is also one in
which 'the world', as we are taught it exists, is drawn ever further from the
matrix of our lived experience. It appears that the world as it really exists can
only be witnessed by leaving it, and indeed much scientific energy and
considerable resources have been devoted to turning such an imaginative
flight into an achieved actuality. One consequence is the alleged discrepancy
between what, in modern jargon, are called 'local' and 'global' perspectives.
In so far as the latter, afforded to a being outside the world, is seen to be both
real and total, the former, afforded to beings in the world (that is, ordinary
people), is regarded as illusory and incomplete. Retrieving from my shelves
a geology textbook published in 1964 – two years before the earth was first
photographed from space – I read on the very first page that 'races of men
[whose] horizons are limited to a tribal territory, the confines of a mountain
valley, a short stretch of the coast line, or the congested blocks of a large city'
can have no conception of the true nature and extent of the world about
them (Putnam 1964: 3). If true knowledge is to be had by looking *at* the
world, this statement is self-evidently valid. My point, however, is that this
visualist assumption is precisely what has given us the imagery of the world
as a globe. And it is this assumption, too, that privileges the knowledge we
get from school by looking at model globes over the knowledge we get from
life by actively participating in our surroundings.

Do not misunderstand me. I am not some latter-day flat-earther or pre-
Copernican. I do not mean to deny that the earth takes the form of a globe –
something that has been known, if not universally accepted, at least from the
time of Pythagoras – or that it is one of a number of planets revolving around
a rather insignificant star. My question is how it came to pass that this globe,
the planet we call earth, was taken to be an environment, or what my
geology textbook called 'the world about us'.

We can take a cue from the writings of Kant who, in his *Critique of Pure
Reason*, drew a sophisticated analogy between the topological form of the
earth and that of the universe as a whole – that is, the 'world' conceived as
the domain of all possible objects of knowledge. Kant first places himself in
the shoes of one ignorant of the fact that the earth is global in form:

If I represent the earth as it appears to my senses, as a flat surface, with a circular horizon, I cannot know how far it extends. But experience teaches me that wherever I may go, I always see a space around me in which I could proceed further.

(Kant 1933: 606)

One is thus in the hapless position of realizing that one's knowledge is limited, but of having no way of knowing just how limited it is. Once it is recognized, however, that the earth is a globe, and given a knowledge of its diameter, it is immediately possible to calculate, from first principles, its surface area. And so, even though – as we traverse the surface – new horizons are always opening up, not only can we work out, by subtraction, how much there remains to be discovered, but also every fresh observation can be slotted into position, in relation to each and every other, within a complete, unifying spatial framework. Thus, to obtain a comprehensive knowledge of the environment, we must already have in mind an image of the globe, or come pre-equipped with what Kant called 'an extended concept of the whole surface of the earth', on to which may be mapped the data of experience (see Richards 1974: 11). Moreover, the same applies to knowledge in general, which the mind sees as arrayed upon the surface of a sphere, at once continuous and limited in extent:

Our reason is not like a plane indefinitely far extended, the limits of which we know in a general way only; but must rather be compared to a sphere, the radius of which can be determined from the curvature of the arc of its surface.

(Kant 1933: 607)

In this analogy, the topology of the earth's surface comes to stand for the fundamental idea, which the mind is said to bring to experience, of the unity, completeness and continuity of nature. Here, surely, is to be found the very essence of the global outlook.

Let us, then, compare an imaginary Kantian traveller, journeying across the globe in search of new experiences to fit into his overall conception, with the Yup'ik Eskimos, in whose cycles of everyday and seasonal movement the cosmos, as they see it (Figure 2.3), is continually being re-created (Fienup-Riordan 1990: 110–11). For both, the earth provides the ground on which they move, but whereas for the Yup'ik, this movement is conducted *within* the world, the Kantian traveller, for whom the world is a globe, journeys upon its *outer surface*. It is at this surface, the interface between world and mind, sensation and cognition, that all knowledge is constituted. Not only is the surface a continuous one, it also lacks any centre. Anywhere upon it can serve, in principle, equally well as a point of origin or as a destination. Thus if the 'world about us' is the globe, planet earth, it is not a world *within* which we dwell, as is the Yup'ik world depicted with the house at its centre, but one *on* which we dwell. The globe, of course, *does* have a centre, yet a journey to the centre of the earth, as immortalized in Jules Verne's celebrated novel, is a voyage into the unknown, a domain of strange and terrifying primordial forces.

In short, from a global perspective, it is on the surface of the world, not at its centre, that life is lived. As a foundational level of 'physical reality', this surface is supposed already to have been in existence long before there was any life at all. Then somehow, through a series of events of near-miraculous improbability, there appeared on it first life and then, very much later, consciousness. These appearances are commonly pictured in terms of the addition of extra layers of being to that basic layer represented by the earth's surface: hence the tripartite division into lithosphere, biosphere and noosphere, corresponding respectively to the inorganic substance of rocks and minerals, the organic substance of living things and the superorganic substance of human culture and society.

Although spherical imagery is employed here, the spheres are defined as layered surfaces that successively *cover over* one another and the world, not as successive horizons disclosed from a centre. And the outer wrapping is none other than the human mind and its products. This picture (see Figure 2.4) is the complete obverse of the medieval conception illustrated in Figure 2.2. The difference may be considered in relation to the genesis of meaning. The world which the Count of Altavilla is setting out to explore in Maffei's diagram is itself a world of meaning which, through a kind of sensory attunement, an education of attention, will be gradually revealed to him as he proceeds from one level of understanding to the next. This world has properties of both transparency and depth: transparency, because one can see into it; depth, because the more one looks the further one sees. By contrast, the world depicted in Figure 2.4, in so far as it corresponds to 'planet earth', consists of pure substance, physical matter, presenting an opaque and impenetrable surface of literal reality *upon which* form and meaning is overlaid by the human mind. That is to say, meaning does not lie in the relational context of the perceiver's involvement in the world, but is rather inscribed upon the outer surface of the world by the mind of the perceiver. To know the world, then, is a matter not of sensory attunement but of cognitive reconstruction. And such knowledge is acquired not by engaging directly, in a practical way, with the objects in one's surroundings, but rather by learning to represent them, in the mind, in the form of a *map*. We discover, here, a direct connection between the notion of the world as a solid globe and the idea, commonly encountered even in anthropological literature, of the environment as a *substrate* for the external imposition of arbitrary cultural form. The world becomes a *tabula rasa* for the inscription of human history.

The familiar globes of geography classrooms provide a vivid example of such inscription or covering over. Though the sea is painted blue, the

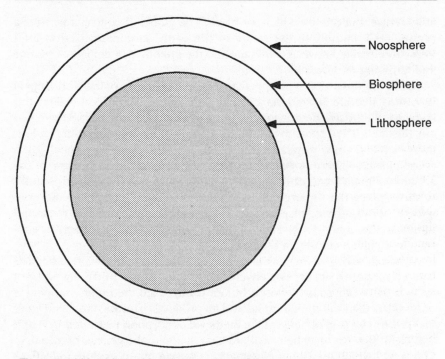

Figure 2.4 Lithosphere, biosphere and noosphere

continental landmasses are frequently painted in a mosaic of contrastive colours, representing the territories of nation states. Thus, we are led to think, has the order of human society wrapped itself around the face of the world. Yet that order, we know, has its roots in the history of colonialism, and the attendant voyages of (principally maritime) discovery and exploration. The image of the world as a globe is, I contend, a colonial one. It presents us with the idea of a preformed surface *waiting to be occupied*, to be colonized first by living things and later by human (usually meaning Western) civilization. Through travel and exploration, it is said, mankind has *conquered* the globe, everywhere – in Engels' (1934: 179) imperialistic phrase – impressing 'the stamp of his will upon the earth'. Having now filled it up, and still multiplying in numbers at an alarming pace, we are urgently searching around, not just in fantasy but also in fact, for new worlds to colonize. Not only, then, does it appear that the world existed prior to life; it also appears that life can hop from world to world and even – like a parasitic vector flying between successive hosts – exist temporarily in worldless suspension.

The idea that the world exists prior to the forms of life that come to occupy it, and hence that each of these life forms is itself separately encoded in a context-free vehicle, a kind of free-floating capsule that can carry form from one site of occupation to another, is deeply entrenched in both biological and anthropological thought. In biology it appears as the doctrine of genetic preformation, according to which every organism may be specified, independently of the environmental context of its development, as a unique configuration of self-replicating elements (genes). Through a process of variation under natural selection, organisms are supposed to evolve in ways that make them better adapted to the conditions of their environments, yet the very notion of adaptation implies that these conditions are given in advance as a set of exogenous specifications, quite distinct from the endogenous, genetic specifications of the adapting organisms. There is thus one set of specifications for life, and another set for the world (see Lewontin 1983). In anthropology, cultural information is made to play much the same role as is played by the genes in biology. Again, there is one set of specifications for the forms of life that are carried around – as it used to be said – 'inside people's heads'. And there is another set for the environment, often identified with 'nature' or 'the physical world', upon which these forms are inscribed. And if we ask 'What kind of world is this, that is an environment for every form of life yet external to all of them?', the answer, as we have seen, is planet earth, the globe.

Moreover, once the world is conceived as a globe, it can become an object of appropriation for a collective humanity. In this discourse, we do not belong to the world, neither partaking of its essence nor resonating to its cycles and rhythms. Rather, since our very humanity is seen to consist, in essence, in the transcendence of physical nature, it is the world that belongs to us. Images of property abound. We have inherited the earth, it is said, and so are responsible for handing it on to our successors in reasonably good condition. But like the prodigal heir, we are inclined to squander this precious inheritance for the sake of immediate gratification. Much of the current concern with the global environment has to do with how we are to 'manage' this planet of ours. That it is ours to manage, however, remains more or less unquestioned. Such management is commonly described in the language of intervention. But to intervene in the world, as Raymond Williams (1972: 154) has pointed out, implies the possibility of our choosing not to do so. It implies that human beings can launch their interventions from a platform above the world, as though they could live *on* or *off* the environment, but are not destined to live *within* it. Indeed, this notion of action towards the environment as planned intervention in nature is fundamental to the Western notion of production. History itself comes to be seen as a process wherein human producers, through their transforming reaction on nature, have literally constructed an environment of their own making.

The idea is epitomized in the title of an influential volume, published in 1956, called *Man's Role in Changing the Face of the Earth* (Thomas et al. 1956). There are two points about this title to which I wish to draw attention. The first is that with the world envisaged as planet earth, it is its *face* that is presented to humanity as the substrate for the latter's transforming interventions. This recalls my earlier observation that in the global outlook, life appears to be lived upon the outer surface of the world rather than from an experiential centre within it. The world does not surround us, it lies beneath our feet. The second point concerns the notion of change. It is not of course the case, as was believed by some of the early advocates of uniformitarianism, that the earth has persisted since the beginning of time in homeostatic equilibrium, at least until humans came along to upset the balance. On the contrary, it has been – and continues to be – racked by geological forces acting on such a scale as to make the most impressive feats of human engineering seem puny by comparison. These earth-shaping processes, however, are considered to be immanent in the workings of nature. They are what the world *undergoes*. But in speaking of the role of humanity, the world appears as an *object* of transformation. Change figures as what is *done to* the planet by its present owner-occupiers, human beings. It is thus exogenous rather than endogenous, not nature transforming itself, but nature transformed through the imposition of non-natural, human design.

This is what is meant when, in 'changing the face of the earth', the universal agent – 'man' – is said to have replaced the natural environment with one which is, to an ever-greater extent, *artificial*. Thus the construction of the human order appears to entail the destruction of the natural one, as production entails consumption. We are, today, increasingly concerned to limit what are perceived to be the destructive consequences of human activity. My point, however, is that the very notions of destruction and damage limitation, like those of construction and control, are grounded in the discourse of intervention. That is to say, they presume a world already constituted, through the action of natural forces, which then becomes the *object* of human interest and concern. But it is not a world of which humans themselves are conceived to be a part. To them, it is rather presented as a spectacle. They may observe it, reconstruct it, protect it, tamper with it or destroy it, but they do not dwell in it. Indeed, what is perhaps most striking about the contemporary discourse of global environmental change is the immensity of the gulf that divides the world as it is lived and experienced by the practitioners of this discourse, and the world of which they speak under the rubric of 'the globe'. No one, of course, denies the seriousness of the problems they address; there is good reason to believe, however, that many of these problems have their source in that very alienation of humanity from the world of which the notion of the global environment is a conspicuous expression.

This point brings me back to the distinction, mentioned earlier, between 'local' and 'global' perspectives. The difference between them, I contend, is not one of hierarchical degree, in scale or comprehensiveness, but one of kind. In other words, the local is not a more limited or narrowly focused apprehension than the global, it is one that rests on an altogether different *mode* of apprehension – one based on an active, perceptual engagement with components of the dwelt-in world, in the practical business of life, rather than on the detached, disinterested observation of a world apart. In the local perspective the world is a sphere, or perhaps a nesting series of spheres as portrayed in Figures 2.2 and 2.3, centred on a particular place. From this experiential centre, the attention of those who live there is drawn ever deeper *into* the world, in the quest for knowledge and understanding. It is through such attentive engagement, entailed in the very process of dwelling, that the world is progressively revealed to the knowledge-seeker. Now different centres will, of course, afford different views, so that while there is only one global perspective, indifferent to place and context, the number of possible local perspectives is potentially infinite. This does not mean, however, that they are in any sense incomplete, or that they represent no more than fragments of a total picture. It is only when we come to represent local differences in terms of a globalizing discourse that the centre from which each perspective is taken is converted into a boundary *within* which every local view is seen to be contained. The idea that the 'little community' remains confined within its limited horizons from which 'we' – globally conscious Westerners – have escaped results from a privileging of the global ontology of detachment over the local ontology of engagement.

To the extent that it has been used to legitimate the disempowerment of local people in the management of their environments, this idea has had serious practical consequences for those among whom anthropologists have conducted their studies. To adopt a distinction from Niklas Luhmann (1979), it might be argued that the dominance of the global perspective marks the triumph of technology over cosmology. Traditional cosmology places the person at the centre of an ordered universe of meaningful relations, such as that depicted by Maffei (Figure 2.2), and enjoins an understanding of these relations as a foundation for proper conduct towards the environment. Modern technology, by contrast, places human society and its interests *outside* what is residually construed as the 'physical world', and furnishes the means for the former's control over the latter. Cosmology provides the guiding principles for human action *within* the world, technology provides the principles for human action *upon* it. Thus, as cosmology gives way to technology, the relation between people and the world is turned inside out (Figure 2.1), so that what was a cosmos or lifeworld becomes a world – a solid globe – externally presented to life. In short, the movement from spherical to global imagery corresponds to the undermining of cosmological certainties and the growing belief in, and indeed dependence upon, the technological fix. It is a movement from revelation to control, and from partial knowledge to the calculated risk.

Let me add one further comment in conclusion. I have written throughout as though the characterizations of the environment, respectively, as globe and sphere were irrevocably opposed, and thus mutually exclusive. But this is not really so, since each view contains the seeds of the other. To regard the world as a sphere is at once to render conceivable the possibility of its logical inverse, the globe; and of course vice versa. We could say that both perspectives are caught up in the dialectical interplay between engagement and detachment, between human beings' involvement in the world and their separation from it, which has been a feature of the entire history of Western thought and no doubt of other traditions as well. Concretely, this is perhaps most clearly manifest in the architectural form of the dome (Smith 1950). A sphere on the inside, a globe on the outside, this form has a cosmic resonance of near-universal appeal. But for any society, at any period of its history, we may expect one perspective to be ascendant, and the other to be associated with its more or less muted undercurrent. And my sense of the contemporary discourse on the environment in the West is that it continues to be dominated by global imagery associated with the triumph of modern science and technology, but that it is under increasing threat from those – including many anthropologists – who would turn to local or indigenous cosmologies of engagement for sources of insight into our current predicament.

ACKNOWLEDGEMENTS

For ideas on the original draft of this paper, several of which I have incorporated into the present version, I am particularly grateful to Paul Richards, Gisli Palsson and Raymond Firth, as well as to the many participants in the ASA Conference who raised comments in discussion.

REFERENCES

Adams, F.D. (1938) *The Birth and Death of the Geological Sciences*, London: Baillière, Tindall and Cox.
Engels, F. (1934) *Dialectics of Nature*, Moscow: Progress.
Fienup-Riordan, A. (1990) *Eskimo Essays: Yup'ik Lives and How We See Them*, New Brunswick: Rutgers University Press.
Ingold, T. (1992) 'Culture and the perception of the environment', in E. Croll and D. Parkin (eds) *Bush Base: Forest Farm – Culture, Environment and Development*, London: Routledge.
Kant, I. (1933) *Immanuel Kant's Critique of Pure Reason*, trans. N.K. Smith, London: Macmillan.
Lewontin, R.C. (1983) 'Gene, organism and environment', in D.S. Bendall (ed.) *Evolution from Molecules to Men*, Cambridge: Cambridge University Press.
Luhmann, N. (1979) *Trust and Power*, Chichester: Wiley.
Putnam, W.C. (1964) *Geology*, New York: Oxford University Press.
Richards, P. (1974) 'Kant's geography and mental maps', *Transactions of the Institute of British Geographers* (N.S.), 11: 1–16.
Smith, E. Baldwin (1950) *The Dome: A Study in the History of Ideas*, Princeton, New Jersey: Princeton University Press.
Thomas, W.L., Sauer, C.O., Bates, M. and Mumford, L. (eds) (1956) *Man's Role in Changing the Face of the Earth*, Chicago: University of Chicago Press.
Williams, R. (1972) 'Ideas of nature', in J. Benthall (ed.) *Ecology, the Shaping Enquiry*, London: Longman.

Chapter 3

Between science and shamanism

The advocacy of environmentalism in Toronto

Peter Harries-Jones

The environmental movement is a global phenomenon, of necessity, and Toronto is only one of many localities. Toronto houses most of the better-funded and most publicized environmental advocacy groups, including Green-peace with a Canadian membership of about 350,000 and the World Wildlife Fund (Canada) (WWFC), a branch of the World Wide Fund for Nature, which has more than two hundred thousand Canadian members. During the period under discussion in this chapter (1990), which covered the public consultation phase of the Canadian Green Plan (see below), environmentalism became the nation's primary political issue, though displaced later by economic and constitutional questions. Almost 90 per cent of Canadians are concerned about some environmental issues; more specifically, 87 per cent of those questioned in a Decima poll in the spring of 1991 expressed concern about the quality of the environment in and around their homes.

In all, Canada has about two thousand organizations which consider themselves to be 'environmental groups'. Some 400 of these are resident in the Province of Ontario. This number might indicate solid and continuing active support for environmentalists, but as the same Decima poll revealed, only 20 per cent of Canadians are firmly committed to making lifestyle changes in order to protect the environment and their health (Macleans 1991: 52). From this 20 per cent a much smaller number, perhaps 2–5 per cent, contribute funds to 'environmental groups'. The small number giving continuing support to environmental non-governmental organizations (ENGOs) has crucial repercussions for their funding.

The ENGOs with which I am concerned in this chapter are the better-funded, long-term organizations which are also the most influential in Ontario. For reasons to be considered below, 'influence' is coincident with media coverage of their activities. But even influential ENGOs face a large gap between concern and activism, between recognition of a need to change and reluctance to oppose vested interest, between an acceptance of or acquiescence in an overall green point of view and a rejection of specific green proposals. A city of two million which responds enthusiastically to recycling of trash balks at the next step, re-use of bottles and other packaging; a province whose members were prime movers in organizing the 'Earth Summit' on the environment at Rio de Janeiro in June 1992 is unable to enforce anti-pollution legislation passed some years ago.

ADVOCACY AND ENVIRONMENTAL NGOs

ENGOs are organizations for social advocacy. They share common features with other social advocates in Canada – the women's movement, the human rights movement, the peace movement and various other ethnic or subnational advocacy groups. I would define social advocacy as a positive form of protest carried out by a defined network or group. It distinguishes itself from advocate–client relations in the legal sense of the term, as it does from straightforward political dissent, although one form of advocacy may interweave with another.

Unlike political dissenters, advocates do not aim to overthrow other political parties or capture state power. Rather, social advocates challenge the reality of dominant beliefs and values through protest. They are 'armed' with new cultural or scientific knowledge which they advertise in various forms of political engagement. Advocacy is a major communicative process in modern democracies by which alternate forms of knowledge enter into the construction of society (Touraine 1985, Harries-Jones 1991: 5).

ENGOs are extra-parliamentary but non-violent. Rather than inducing social crisis, a primary avenue for advocacy is consciousness raising through communication media. Consciousness raising combines with political empowerment, but the empowerment which advocates seek is not specifically tied to a type of political party; rather they seek to embarrass parliamentary legislatures through catching public interest.

The major exception to the non-violent, mass media approach lies in the response of some Canadian Indian bands (First Nations). For the First Nations an environmental threat is almost always linked to threat of abrogation of their rights to land. In several instances, including the Oka incident which received worldwide publicity in 1989, failed negotiation about land rights has led to political militancy.[1] I will return to consider the case of First Nations and environmentalism below.

FINANCE AND ORGANIZATION

In Toronto grass-roots environmental advocacy takes three forms. The most important is legal advocacy – securing court injunctions or environmental reviews. A second form is political lobbying of provincial, federal and international agencies; the third form is advocacy through media presentations. Legal advocacy is a most successful route for environmentalists in that ordinary taxpayers cannot pursue legal action against large, wealthy corporations. Class action on pollution and other related environmental issues is not permitted as yet. The Canadian Environmental Law Association has established an Environmental Defence Fund which enables grass-roots organizations to overcome the disadvantages of their smallness, by parlaying local disputes through the courts. Winning legal precedents on criteria for environmental reviews ensures that a strict accounting of 'sustainability' will become valid throughout the nation (interview, Canadian Environmental Defence Fund, 26 July 1990).

Responsibility for environmental policy is split between federal and provincial jurisdictions.[2] Split jurisdiction is complicated by a turf-war between ministries and departments in Ottawa which actively resist any possibility that Environment Canada becomes a super-ministry monitoring the environmental appropriateness of government policies. All environmental activists interviewed say that they spend much of their time attempting to get government to do something – anything – and point out that often roadblocks to environmental action have nothing to do with absence of support for environmental initiatives but rather require major change in the decision-making procedures of government bureaucracy.

In recent years the much-mentioned Brundtland Commission has been a 'charter' for ENGO activity in Canada as a whole.[3] Through its auspices the Ontario Round Table on Environment and Economy was established in 1988. The Round Table was predicated on a 'partnership principle' for 'sustainable development'. Partnership in this context means a three-way decision-making procedure involving ENGOs, government and business. As will become evident, government adoption of 'sustainable development' and 'the partnership principle' has been a two-edged blessing for environmental advocates. The deliberations of the Round Table have been inordinately slow in ENGO eyes, so much so that 'participation' is just a rhetorical gesture. Many activists have become exhausted by a process of procrastination and non-response by governmental ministries (interview, Ontario Environmental Network, 25 July 1990). For this reason ENGOs will often operate in opposition to government policies rather than in partnership with them.

Their oppositional strategy is modified by the fact that most environmental advocacy in Toronto is 'co-opted advocacy'. It is co-opted in the sense that most advocacy organizations do not have a sufficiently large membership base to be autonomous, and therefore have to rely upon direct government financing. Others are helped financially through government-awarded consultant contracts.

Yet even those awarded government contracts, such as Pollution Probe, cannot rely upon a safe annual income, especially in times of recession. This means that advocacy groups spend most of the organizational time combating recurrent financial crises. Greenpeace is an exception in that, after the lean years of the early 1980s, it is able to rely entirely on grass-roots donations.

All environmental advocacy groups, including Greenpeace, suffer from rapid attrition of personnel. Greenpeace has countered this turnover of personnel by separating its executive board from day-to-day fund-raising, telephoning and local action committees. Most other Toronto-based advocacy organizations are too under-funded to adopt this solution. Their executives are responsible for all aspects of mobilization, and they are constantly having to choose between alternative demands – fund raising or research; public education through newsletters or political opposition; organization of 'community' activities or networking with other environmental organizations. The perpetual problem is to rise above the primary demands of organizational survival to maintain their position as effective lobbyists.

Poor funding, over-extended commitments on time, and the enticement of better salaries and conditions on 'the other side' of the fence are a powerful combination for constant shifts in personnel. As may be imagined, this situation tends to reduce a whole range of advocacy organizations to key actors. Privately some ENGO activists will acknowledge that only between twenty-five and fifty key social actors hold the co-opted organizations together.

FIVE SHADES OF GREEN

Toronto's environmentalists have little trouble defining who they are against, though they have difficulties in presenting a united platform of what they are for. Part of the reason for this is that, while their members are mostly middle class, they come from several political persuasions ranging from left wing (social democrats, Marxists and anarchists) to right of centre. They therefore have widely different perspectives on how to pursue an activist stance. Their common opponents are neo-conservatives, who in the United States would be identified with the right wing of the Republican Party and in Great Britain with the Thatcherite wing of the Conservative Party. In Toronto neo-conservatives can be found at national level in the ruling Conservative Party and its supporting councils of business interests; in the populist Reform Party and in the Nationalist Citizens Coalition, a populist reform business group; and in a variety of right-wing 'think-tanks' such as the C.D. Howe Institute.[4]

Authors from different countries have noted distinctions in political orientation among members of environmental organizations. McCormick speaks of the conservationists in the environmental movement and the 'new environmentalists', the post-1970 activists (McCormick 1989: 47–68, 125–48). Diani and Lodi provide a useful contrast between 'conservationism', 'environmentalism' and 'political ecology' in Milan (1988: 103–24). I would prefer 'five shades of green' to categorize the Toronto situation, in which two shades of 'light green' symbolize conservationist-type advocacy, while two shades of 'dark green' are associated with radical advocacy or militant activism. (The fifth shade is discussed in the next section.)

The 'light greens' in Toronto are primarily 'pragmatist reformers'. They have a common but loose-linked set of ties through the Ontario Environmental Network, which results in some discussion about joint plans. They are also linked electronically through WEB-net. The pragmatist reformers are exemplified by WWFC. The level of professionalism in WWFC suggests comparison with a successful entrepreneurial firm.[5]

Another shade of 'light green' is represented by the Conservation Council of Ontario (Diani and Lodi's 'conservationists'). This umbrella organization embraces 31 member organizations and claims a combined membership of more than one million (a heavy percentage of which must be accounted for by the Ontario Federation of Labour). Unlike other pragmatist reformers, the Conservation Council operates with very little public outreach or even interest in ordinary citizens. It represents professional organizations close to environmental planning, such as the Ontario Professional Foresters Association, together with environmental 'users' such as the Bruce Trail Association. Members of the Council are basically establishment power-brokers who, if anything, seek to reduce the influence of the grass-roots ENGOs by making aspects of centralized decision-making through ministries much stronger (interview, Conservation Council of Ontario, 27 August 1990).

Pragmatist reformer greens, such as WWFC, have a strong sense of the entrenched power of the establishment, and are prepared to adopt a policy of flattering business if it will lead to positive action on environmental questions.[6] At the same time, several leaders of the 'light greens' claimed in interviews that they were 'Greenpeacers' at heart.

Occasionally the papering over of tensions, cynicism at government inaction and pragmatic pandering to industry will affect the running of an organization. The most notable case was that of Pollution Probe when its director, Colin Issacs, decided to endorse the 'green consuming' campaign of a major supermarket chain. The members insisted on his resignation, after which Pollution Probe underwent a total reorganization. Issacs had always sought to push Pollution Probe from grass-roots advocacy into a high-profile policy-making group for the Ontario government. The new board of directors shifted direction. While Pollution Probe continues to maintain a research policy function, its new directors give far more attention to the public aspects of information sharing (interview, Pollution Probe, 17 August 1990).

Greenpeace is the radical spokes-organization of the 'dark greens'. By 'radical' I mean that Greenpeace constantly challenges the cosy relationship established between government and business, calling for the government to recognize the necessity for citizen involvement. The radical challenge requires government to commit itself to public support for ENGOs and to establish committees to monitor the impacts of existing policies and agreements on environmental issues, and targets individual companies or ministries refusing to comply with environment-related decisions.[7]

One organization in the Toronto area which has been able to match Greenpeace is the Temagami Wilderness Society (TWS, now called Earthroots). One of its most successful coups was to blockade logging operations at Temagami in November 1989, causing 300 well-publicized arrests. Among those arrested was the then leader of the Opposition and current Premier of Ontario, Bob Rae.

The society was founded in 1984 as a typical grass-roots organization of three or four people operating out of a basement on a highly sensitive issue – that of increased incursion of logging in one of the last great stands of original or old-growth trees in Ontario. From humble beginnings, the organizers were soon able to count on a membership of 14,000, enough for them to consider carrying out spectacular examples of 'eco-drama'. During the 1990 election they moved around Ontario with a large model of a chain saw suspended in the back of a truck. Wherever the former Liberal Premier of Ontario, David Peterson, was about to give a public address, they turned on a tape, a highly amplified endless-loop recording of the sound of a chain saw. This caused the Premier to 'say a few things that could not be repeated in most newspapers' (interview, Temagami Wilderness Society, 19 July 1990).

In addition the TWS had two people camping under trees at Queen's Park (the grounds of the Provincial Legislature) in order to express its objections to the failure of the then Provincial Minister of the Environment to respond to an Environmental Assessment Inquiry into Temagami. On Earth Day in April 1990, Toronto residents awoke to find the whole of the downtown area plastered in white-paint slogans from the TWS.

For a time Greenpeace was divided between two shades of 'dark green' – 'radical advocacy' and 'militant activism'. Paul Watson, one of the founders of Greenpeace, organized a campaign to ban sealing off the coastal waters of Newfoundland. The 1983 campaign was planned in conjunction with animal rights organizations. Though a triumph for Greenpeace in the European Community, the campaign was a membership disaster at home and led to Watson's dismissal several months later. He went on to found the Sea Shepherd Conservation Society which, among other things, engaged in militant opposition to vivisection (Manes 1990: 110). Watson then moved to the US to establish Earth First!, a political action group which has claimed responsibility for several acts of 'ecotage', sabotage on behalf of ecological advocacy. Earth First! operates mainly in the US and British Columbia but has some support in Ontario universities.

FIRST NATIONS AND ENVIRONMENTALISTS

The fifth shade of green links environmental activists to First Nations land claims. This is a special feature of environmentalism in Canada. In British Columbia and Quebec, links between the two have achieved some success. In the case of the South Moresby dispute in British Columbia, joint action changed the political framework of the province. The cosy relations between the logging industry and the Provincial Government were irrevocably cut (May 1990). In Quebec, the outcome of joint action on the proposed second stage of the James Bay project is unclear, but the chances of the Quebec government's realizing its original plans to transform an area the size of France with only scant attention to environmental reviews have been considerably curtailed.

In Toronto and Ontario generally, joint action is far more hesitant. Communication between aboriginal rights groups and environmental activists is generally poor, partly as a result of the absence of unified environmental policy among First Nations and partly as a result of personality conflicts between environmentalists and Indian leaders.[8] There is also a clash of cultural aspiration. Indian leaders object to environmentalists seeing the struggle of First Nations as a sort of surrogate wish-fulfilment of the new environmental age. In an interesting cultural turn-about, the First Nations accuse environmentalists of being 'shamanistic' in the wrong sense of that term.

Indian leaders believe environmentalists perceive Indian opposition to development in Ontario in an inappropriate framework. Spokespeople for the environmentalist movement have transformed Indian respect for land and communitarianism into a cult-like vision of new-age 'spirituality'. Traditional forms of respect among First Nations in placing the good of the group before the individual are misappropriated and translated into an entirely different set of understandings. The modern poverty of the First Nations has little to do with white suburban antagonism to industrialism or with the cult of Aquarius.[9]

Nor can a solution to Indian poverty be won through a joint, heroic stand against the consumer-industrial society as environmentalists might wish, says the Union of Ontario Indians. It can only be won through sustained political support for land claims over a large area which would enable the First Nations to proceed with self-government. Self-government would permit them to articulate and implement a sound, alternative environmental policy (interview, Union of Ontario Indians, 7 August 1990).

The difference in perspective between Ontario Indians and environmentalists was evident in the Temagami protest. Chief Gary Potts of the Tema-Awaugame mounted two blockades quite separate from those organized by the TWS. His reason for doing so, he said, was that TWS had only concerned itself with the protection of trees on Crown land, while the aim of his own band had been protection for all its resources. If anything, his own band's protest had been more 'ecosystemic' than that of the environmentalists (interview, 'Holding the Balance', Television Ontario, 4 June 1992).

ICONIC PRAXIS

As already indicated, a striking observation about environmentalism in Canada, as in all North America, is that articulate environmentalists are to be found all along the left–right political spectrum (Paehlke 1989: 190). Friendly critics have despaired about the unfocused political 'all-over-the-placeness' of ENGOs. Nevertheless, despite differing political orientation, the various shades of green tend to avoid competition over resources and instead create a network of environmentalists, which links the larger environmental groups – the ENGOs with big, high-profile projects – with smaller environmental groups which promote local issues.

It is not unusual to find that environmental supporters have memberships in several environmental groups and that ENGO activists themselves do not belong exclusively to one organization. Key executives in the present list of ENGOs have either served on executives of other groups, or have aided the fund-raising, education and general consciousness-raising activities of other groups. Some executives of one ENGO were founders of other environmental organizations, and veteran activists are usually able to wear several hats in the movement. There is a conscious effort, notwithstanding occasional personality clashes, to build relationships which will celebrate each other's successes and which will offer a shared body of information to the public.

Compared with this higgledy-piggledy patchwork of environmental activism, Eyerman and Jamison speak of a contrasting situation in Europe in which 'movement intellectuals' become key actors integrating environmentalism into 'a living cognitive praxis' (Eyerman and Jamison 1991: 66). On the basis of their experience in Scandinavia, they identify movement intellectuals as disenchanted establishment advisers or bureaucrats (Eyerman and Jamison 1991: 118). They argue that movement intellectuals combine three 'knowledge interests' into an integrative environmental movement which has a quasi-autonomy of its own. The three knowledge interests are cosmological, technological and organizational.

Toronto is not without its movement intellectuals, such as those described by Eyerman and Jamison, but it cannot compare with the density of linkage and quasi-autonomy they describe.[10] The best-known movement intellectual derives his influence from TV and newspaper columns. David Suzuki has been both a peace activist and a champion of ecological thinking since leaving his university position in British Columbia. His TV series *The Nature of Things* has strongly supported the Cree Indians in their fight against the vast hydroelectric project known as James Bay Two.[11]

The prominence of David Suzuki, I would argue, is not mere happenstance. 'Iconic praxis' replaces 'cognitive praxis' as the predominant form of knowledge interest in Toronto. The distinction reflects a difference of political space in Canada and Europe. In Canada 'political space' is so highly mediated through TV, radio and print that the impact of environmental issues is, like all forms of political campaigning, congruent with photo opportunities and image-making. The interventions of the media, especially TV, are crucial for the formation of a *Gestalt* about environmentalism.[12]

Since knowledge interests are largely framed through images, this, in turn, has affected the organization of ENGOs. Environmentalists have learned from the brilliant successes of Greenpeace in this regard. Almost from the start Greenpeace began to organize for iconic praxis. In a recent Canadian TV production celebrating their twentieth year, Greenpeace executives spoke of the way in which their use of media meshed with their organizational aims. The major aim of Greenpeace, they said, was to 'bear witness' to a variety of untenable situations. By pointing to them in the most dramatic fashion they could conceive, they would be able to make visible those effects of ecological degradation which otherwise would remain invisible.

There is an interesting script to be written on how Greenpeace moved from planning 'real' eco-drama, against formidable odds, to a simulation of eco-drama. The first strategy resulted in armed assault on the *Rainbow Warrior* by French commandos in August 1973, and the sinking of that ship in Auckland harbour, 10 July 1985. From then on, simulation of eco-drama became a better way for both conserving organizational resources and protecting the safety of its activists. It is just as effective for 'witnessing' if spokespersons are trained to present complex environmental issues through it: instead of the real voyage against armed gunboats, Greenpeace members can do just as much by climbing towers and bridges, unfolding banners of protest.

In iconic praxis,

> The territory no longer precedes the map, nor survives it . . . it is the map that engenders the territory . . . It is the real, and not the map, whose vestiges subsist here and there, in the deserts which are no longer those of the Empire, but our own.
>
> (Baudrillard 1983: 2)[13]

The simulated eco-drama is successful when the journalist or video-recorder is able to engender the territory – to evoke the complex local issues of environmental policy, without citing all its details, in an image-friendly manner.

Images evoking a 'map' are joined to various forms of advertising. One crucial factor in the success of WWFC is the way it has been able to persuade media organizations, including prestigious advertising firms, to provide free advertising as a 'public service'. More than seventy magazines and newspapers and more than fifty radio and television stations donated either print space or air time in 1988 to this organization. In addition WWFC has found out that if it can be seen as an organization which contributes towards a scientific understanding of nature, or promotes a value-free contribution to environmental improvement, then this potent mix of science and advocacy can be sold as a private consumption good. Its 'Guardians of the Rainforest' and 'Guardians of the Amazon' campaigns, in which the public was urged to purchase 'an acre of rainforest', doubled WWFC's contributor and funding base in 1989–90. A spin-off was to get private corporations to promote the same campaign through window displays, T-shirt promotion and purchase of regular advertising space, and then to make the commercial promotion of their campaign an item of newspaper interest. In a double switch, the newspaper interest in the commercial promotion of WWFC enabled WWFC to promote a 'donate-while-you-shop' routine in those commercial stores promoting 'purchase' of 'an acre of rainforest'.

For Eyerman and Jamison, in contrast, the presence of the media is important but not crucial to the discussion of cognitive praxis (Eyerman and Jamison 1991: 139).

BETWEEN SCIENCE AND SHAMANISM

Eyerman and Jamison refer in their European study to 'environmental cosmology'. They define environmental cosmology as 'basic assumptions or beliefs derived from systems ecology, which all environmental activists took more or less for granted' (Eyerman and Jamison 1991: 66). From cosmology derives ideology which movement intellectuals try to implement within political frameworks.

It could be argued that environmental advocates in Toronto have a joint list of things they want done, an agenda which indicates a common set of values and which is, therefore, a precursor of recognizable ideology. One of their main integrative strategies has been to press government for an Environmental Charter of Rights. The proposal has been presented separately to both federal and provincial governments. The concept of a charter could be said to be ideological, much as the social Chartists of a hundred and fifty years ago in England could be said to be ideological. On the other hand, environmental Chartism is a very recent phenomenon deriving partly from the federal government's desire in 1990 to constitute a formal Green Plan.[14]

It is possible to speak of a political ideology of environmentalism in Toronto only in the future tense. Most grass-roots advocates seek to translate their environmentalist perspective into new rules, and anticipate that these will act as precursors to a new set of cultural premises or values with regard to the environment. But their notions of systems ecology are scattered. At one end are those organizations who can promote themselves as science-for-nature, since there is a well-founded public understanding that scientists and naturalists were the first to give warning of the need for a conserver society. As Paehlke points out (1989), environmentalism still remains a perspective derived from findings in the sciences – ecology, toxicology, epidemiology and the assessment of energy supply and demand. The problem is that the scientists in Environment Canada and the National Scientific Research Council balk at the moral and political transformation their studies of conservation and 'sustainable development' require. Their official documents usually argue that environmental change must not impede the competitive position of Canada in the twenty-first century (Science Council of Canada 1988: 16). At the other end are the tiny number who seek 'spirituality' in ecosystem concepts, through no-compromise environmentalism. As already mentioned, their ventures into shamanism are rejected by the Union of Ontario Indians in so far as they evoke analogies to Indian communitarian life.

Paehlke, who served on the National Advisory Committee of the Canadian Environmental Defense Fund, is among the first to construct a list of environmental values which link scientific findings to an identifiable political platform for the future. He sees his task as constituting environmentalism within a revived progressive political platform (Paehlke 1989). For the moment, environmental cosmology in the urban setting of Toronto tends to be reduced to change in lifestyle, rather than transformation of lifeworld. The public is urged to extend concern for food and dietary habits, and to monitor the environmental quality of products bought. Both government and industry encourage the belief that if enough people decide to change their consumption patterns, then industry will respond and this will be the solution to ecological crisis.

Government appeals to the public are based on the assertions of environmental 'choice' and the muddy proposition of 'responsible' and 'irresponsible' consumers:

> You are in charge of your own actions and you are responsible for what you do or do not do. You are also responsible for keeping our environment clean and healthy and for not wasting our natural resources. Here are 25 things you can choose to do to clean up and protect our environment.
>
> (Environment Canada 1990)

In short, individual consumerism is placed ahead of ecosystemic understanding.

CO-OPTATION

An ecosystems approach implies entirely different concepts from those offered by 'stakeholder participation'. The veterans of the environmental movement, who are responsible for publications on this theme, know this well. As the authors of one Pollution Probe document put it, 'the difference between environment and ecosystem [is] equivalent to that between house and home. House implies something external, home, something that we see ourselves in even when we are not there' (Cooper and Millyard 1986: 55).

The ecosystem concept is integrative, argues Pollution Probe. It requires the implementation of a coordinated monitoring system which has legally enforceable controls and to which 'the public must have access, and the public must be consulted when decisions are made' (Cooper and Millyard 1986: 54–5). It also stresses the cosmological nature of 'interlock' between human beings and their environment in a pointed fashion.

Yet at a meeting the Ontario Environmental Network convened to develop a response to the Federal Green Plan, alternative propositions based on a dialectic of 'ecosystem' and 'class' received lukewarm enthusiasm. In fact, the environmental activists felt unable to raise any issue of economic redistribution, or any which would replace 'partnership' and 'sustainability' by integrative aspects of an ecosystemic approach.

Co-optation is one of the major processes used by modern democratic governments for the absorption of radical protest – and because co-optation is successful, leaders of social movements generally settle for much less than they initially demand (Etzioni-Halevy 1990: 221). As ENGO participation in the Green Plan demonstrated, the outstanding question for all members of the Ontario Environmental Network is whether co-optation will undermine environmentalism as a social movement or whether, in the long run, it will bring about the sort of transformation of values environmentalists seek.

The evidence is inconclusive, but turns on how ENGOs construe the notion of 'stakeholder'. While the Federal Green Plan identified grass-roots environmentalists as 'stakeholders' and encouraged them to write up agendas for combating ecological crisis, ENGOs understood that their position as 'stakeholders' in any political decision-making was marginal. They all understood the process of public consultation was largely a distraction – and 'stakeholding' an exercise ensuring that genuine consultation would not occur. They knew that decision-making processes would revert quickly to the coterie of bureaucrats and science advisers who have always been responsible for government initiatives on the environment.

Greenpeace was quite open in its opposition to the whole exercise, for it realized that the whole process of co-optation stacked the cards against environmental advocates. On the one hand, the rhetoric of 'participation' and 'stakeholding' in the Green Plan enabled corporate business to establish its place as partner in the implementation of a government agenda about 'sustainability'. On the other hand, ENGOs were unable to challenge government on their piecemeal, crisis-based management approaches of the past.

As might be expected, Greenpeace and WWFC showed diverging positions on the consultation process. Greenpeace's strategy remained that of 'iconic praxis', advocating the social construction of environmentalism in a collage of images either embarrassing government for its inaction or provoking public dialogue through local eco-drama. WWFC became the umbrella organization for Greenprint (Greenprint for Canada Committee 1989), the ENGO collective response to the Green Plan.

The umbrella group which brought out Greenprint hailed its own document as 'a new vision of Canada's ecological security based on a sustainable economy'.[15] The agenda it presented tended to mirror the format of governmental decision-making on the environment, a highly departmentalized approach to environmental issues, stressing the tightening of existing legislation and repeating proposals for an Environmental Charter of Rights.

On the political level Greenprint said very little. A noticeable absence in Greenprint was any call for redistribution of factors of production. At the same time, it is evident that the vision of stakeholding which pragmatist reformers hold is not the same as that derived from political economy. The 'stakes' are the money and the freedom – the social space – to pursue communicative strategies in order to transform society's perspective of its relationships with nature. Their view seems to be that zero-sum political gaming is only part of a wider process of civil and cultural decision-making about the environment. Ultimately pragmatist reformers believe their 'stake' lies not at the level of state power, but in a process of continuing reciprocal legitimation – any move which will bring about the perspective of nature's intrinsic value and the transformation of 'nature-as-machine'.[16]

ACKNOWLEDGEMENTS

Funding for this project was provided by a Sabbatical Leave Fellowship and a Teaching Development Grant from York University, Ontario. I wish to thank Victoria Heftler for information on WWFC and Colin Gomez for interviewing fifteen other grass-roots environmental advocacy organizations. I also acknowledge the valued suggestions of Colin Gomez and Peter Timmerman for improving this chapter.

NOTES

1 The Oka incident concerned a band of Mohawk Indians, the Akwasasane, whose territory straddled the border of New York State and the Province of Quebec. When the mayor of Oka threatened to take over band burial sites in order to extend the town's golf course, the band set up roadblocks. The confrontation lasted about a month; the uneasy stand-off between 'Warriors' and units of the Canadian army almost erupted into a shoot-out.

2 Conservatism at national level is balanced by a provincial government in Ontario which, in recent years, has been centre or left of centre. The current Minister of the Environment for the New Democratic Party, Ruth Grier, is the first minister with experience in grass-roots environmental activism. The metropolitan and city governments are mixed.

3 The Report of the World Commission on Environment and Development (the Brundtland Commission) acknowledged the role of NGOs and citizens' groups in pioneering and maintaining public and political awareness of environmental dangers, and in promoting practical measures to deal with them (Brundtland 1987: 326).

4 The corporate sector seeks to outflank environmental activism by various means. For instance, neo-conservative columnists on two of the three main newspapers frequently condemn environmentalists as 'eco-freaks', and commercial interests have succeeded in converting middle-of-the-road environmental uneasiness into profitable commodity consumption by promoting 'green products'.

5 WWFC has British royal patronage and strong corporate support. In 1990 it was supported by Environment Canada with a sum of Can $4 million over six years. Its most ambitious schemes include 'debt-for-nature' swaps (for example, at Monteverde in Costa Rica) of the kind undertaken in many parts of the world by its parent body, WWF International.

6 For example, WWFC has established a Wildlife Toxicology Fund, 'to fund research to protect wildlife from harm caused by toxic chemicals, and to enhance funding of such work by the private sector'. A spokesperson for WWFC acknowledged, 'Some of the worst polluters [in Canada] are major investors in this fund' (interview, World Wildlife Fund (Canada), 4 April 1990).

7   The call for citizen involvement is general among both 'light greens' and 'dark greens' and was the first subject discussed in the Ontario Environmental Network's (OEN) 'Environmental Agenda for Ontario'. OEN stated that all Canadian governments consult behind closed doors with powerful interests before making major decisions. In theory Canadians live in a democracy but in practice, 'the concentration of economic and political power in our society limits citizens' ability to participate in their own government, including protection of the environment' (Ontario Environmental Network 1990).

8   For example, some band leaders in Ontario have welcomed nuclear power facilities to electrify their reserves in order to provide employment, while others have deliberately rejected this alternative and committed themselves to a lifestyle of 'modern poverty' (interview, Union of Ontario Indians, 7 August 1990).

9   The Ontario Green Party has made 'spirituality' one of their seven guiding principles (*Globe and Mail* 1990). The party claims 500 members.

10 Indeed, one cannot even compare support for environmentalism with support for the women's movement, which comes much closer to demonstrating a quasi-autonomous public space.

11 Despite his impeccable scientific credentials, Suzuki was 'let go' from *The Globe and Mail* for presenting, in his science column, dissenting views against corporate intransigence on environmental issues. He later reappeared in *The Toronto Star*.

12 As I have pointed out elsewhere, the university in Canada is also an important source for 'movement intellectuals', and plays a more prominent role in policy research and social advocacy than in the US, where ENGO activity is heavily supported by professional lobbyists (Harries-Jones 1991: 97–8). In Canada the university has played a prominent part in supporting some advocacy organizations such as Pollution Probe, Probe International and the Coalition Against Acid Rain, but its reaction to grass-roots environmentalism has been tempered by 'co-optation' in the form of grants favouring university–business partnerships for environmental action.

13 The quote from Baudrillard at greater length is:

> Abstraction today is no longer that of the map, the double, the mirror or the concept. Simulation is no longer that of a territory, a referential being or a substance. It is the generation by models of a real without origin or reality: a hyperreal. The territory no longer precedes the map, nor survives it. Henceforth, it is the map that precedes the territory . . . it is the map that engenders the territory . . . . It is the real, and not the map, whose vestiges subsist here and there, in the deserts which are no longer those of the Empire, but our own.
>
> (Baudrillard 1983: 2)

Baudrillard introduces an important theme for environmental advocacy which adds depth to themes of 'betweenness' examined here; advocacy lies 'between' an appeal to an aesthetic sense of beauty beyond utilitarianism and the 'hyperreal', a simulation of aesthetic appreciation.

14 For a short time during the spring and summer of 1990 the federal government adopted a new framework of consultation. It decided to promote an action-learning formula as part of its Green Plan. In this process, bureaucrats and technical staff within the environmental field (such as deputies to ministers, weather forecasters or professors with research grants to study environmental issues) became 'information officers' and 'facilitators' for the purpose of leading public workshops on sustainable development. Output from the workshops was then taken back to ministries. ENGOs were recognized as important 'stakeholders' and asked to submit formal agendas for environmental change.

15 The Assembly of First Nations were signatories to Greenprint. The Sierra Club of Ontario refused to sign and brought out its own document, as did the Conservation Council of Ontario.

16 As Touraine has put it, 'The utilitarian tradition is the main limit and obstacle to social movements today, as religion was in more traditional cultures' (Touraine 1985: 779). Among writers on social movements, Touraine has been foremost in pointing out that new social movements are about reform of people's perceptions rather than overthrowing the state.

REFERENCES

Baudrillard, J. (1983) *Simulations*, New York: Semiotext(e), Columbia University.

Brundtland, Gro H. (1987) *Our Common Future* (World Commission on Environment and Development), Oxford and New York: Oxford University Press.

Cooper, K. and Millyard, K. (1986) *The Great Lakes Primer*, Toronto: Pollution Probe.

Diani, M. and Lodi, G. (1988) 'Three in one: currents in the Milan ecology movement', in B. Klandermans, H. Kriesi and S. Tarrow (eds) *From Structure to Action: Comparing Social Movements Across Cultures*, Greenwich and London: JAI Press.

Environment Canada (1990) 'The Green Scene'.

Etzioni-Halevy, E. (1990) 'The relative autonomy of élites: the absorption of protest and social progress in western democracies', in J.C. Alexander and P. Sztompka (eds) *Rethinking Progress: Movements, Forces and Ideas at the End of the 20th Century*, Boston: Unwin Hyman.

Eyerman, R. and Jamison, A. (1991) *Social Movements: A Cognitive Approach*, Cambridge: Polity Press.

Globe and Mail, The (1990) Toronto, 5 February, p. A.11.

Greenprint for Canada Committee (1989) 'Greenprint for Canada: A Federal Agenda for the Environment', Ottawa, June.

Harries-Jones, P. (ed.) (1991) *Making Knowledge Count: Advocacy and Social Science*, Montreal and Kingston: McGill-Queen's Press.

Macleans (1991) 104, 50, 16 December, pp. 52, 54.

Manes, C. (1990) *Green Rage: Radical Environmentalism and the Unmaking of Civilization*, Boston: Little, Brown.

May, E. (1990) *Paradise Won: The Struggle for South Moresby*, Toronto: McClelland and Stewart.

McCormick, J. (1989) *The Global Environmental Movement*, London: Belhaven Press.

Ontario Environmental Network (1990) 'Environmental Agenda for Ontario' (draft), 18 July.

Paehlke, R.C. (1989) *Environmentalism and the Future of Progressive Politics*, New Haven: Yale University Press.

Science Council of Canada (1988) *Environmental Peacekeepers: Science, Technology and Sustainable Development in Canada*, Ottawa: Ministry of Supply and Services.

Touraine, A. (1985) 'An introduction to the study of social movements', *Social Research*, 52 (4): 749–87.

Material derived from interviews with the following organizations

Canadian Environmental Defence Fund, 26 July 1990.
Citizens for a Safe Environment, 7 September 1990.
Conservation Council of Ontario, 27 August 1990.

Greenpeace (informal interviews June–August 1990).
Greenplan: Workshops, Toronto, 1 June 1990.
Nuclear Awareness Project, 16 August 1990.
Ontario Environmental Network, 22–4 June (Annual Meeting), 25 July 1990.
Pollution Probe, 17 August 1990.
Recycling Council of Ontario, 10 July 1990.
Temagami Wilderness Society, 19 July 1990.
Union of Ontario Indians, 7 August 1990.
World Wildlife Fund (Canada), 4, 5, 6 and 12 April 1990. (These interviews
    resulted in an unpublished memorandum by Victoria Heftler entitled 'Securing
    spaces, social and natural: World Wildlife Fund and redefinition of value'.)

Chapter 4

Standing in for nature

The practicalities of environmental organizations' use of science

Steven Yearley

The Ulster Wildlife Trust, a leading nature conservation group in Northern Ireland and one of the environmental organizations to be discussed in this chapter, introduced a new slogan in 1989 to describe its work: 'Standing up for nature'. The essence of the analysis I wish to put forward can usefully be understood through an adaptation of this slogan; I am interested in the way in which environmentalists stand in for nature.

Environmentalists or 'greens' are in the business of arguing that the natural world has needs which are being threatened by human activities, including commerce and economic development. Yet, by and large, nature has no way of speaking directly to us about these issues. In some very special cases – if whole forests seem to die or if lakes are filled with sick fish – virtually anyone can read the signs. But once the signs can be interpreted by 'just anybody' it can be too late to intervene: the woods have already been reduced by acidification or fish stocks have been over-fished. Environmental groups stand in for nature by claiming special competence in reading the signs vouchsafed by the natural world and by claiming to possess a stock of background knowledge about nature's needs. These groups can make such claims in an authoritative manner because they can invoke scientific knowledge about nature. Thus, plant biology and ecology are the keys to knowing what vegetative life needs, while the requirements of birds are understood through ornithological study. On a larger scale, it is through scientific study of the atmosphere that we have come to learn of the world's need for a protective ozone layer and of the vital influence of greenhouse gases in maintaining (and now probably disrupting) the climate.

Often, it is rather esoteric scientific expertise which allows environmentalists to identify the subtle ways in which wildlife or the environment is threatened. We may all be fond of butterflies and dragonflies but only an expert in natural history would know the favoured foods of the larval stages of butterflies or the specific requirements of infant dragonflies; yet if these particular foodstuffs are imperilled, so are the species. Equally, environmental scientists will understand the ironic consequences of some apparently benign human interventions in nature; they will know that to eliminate certain farm weeds will endanger well-loved butterflies or that to kill off crop pests will threaten the birds and small mammals which feed on them. In these ways conservation scientists can claim to hear the voice of nature while it is still a whisper and respond before the danger is too advanced.

It would therefore appear necessary for scientific considerations to occupy a central position in green arguments, arguments which are now coming to have an indisputable popular appeal. Consequently, green groups and campaigners must devise some way of mobilizing the appropriate scientific skills and knowledge. As we shall see, the job of putting this knowledge and expertise to practical use is far from straightforward. It is from details of putting science to work that we can learn how environmentalists go about standing in for nature.

LIMITATIONS ON SCIENCE AS A 'STAND-IN' FOR NATURE

The authoritative position of scientific experts in the current environmental debate is not as clear and as straightforward as the above (brief) account might suggest. For one thing, many of the leading ecological problems can be seen as the result of our technological civilization. For example, it was scientific research which first produced the pesticides which have posed such a threat to wildlife since the 1960s (see Nicholson 1987: 46–51). Similarly, ozone-eating CFCs (chlorofluorocarbons) are not naturally occurring chemicals; they were synthesized in scientific laboratories. In these ways, scientists can be seen to have been collaborators in much of the ecological destruction associated with our high-technology society. Many individual scientists are also closely associated with particular projects which are frequently viewed as environmentally damaging, such as nuclear power generation or intensive farming practices. There is at least a potential contradiction for greens who may experience a scepticism about the supposed benefits of scientific progress but who are asked to accept that scientists must play the role of nature's representatives.

In the face of these problems some environmentalists have been attracted to versions of the green argument which are principally founded on non-scientific forms of authority. For example, it is possible to seek to underpin an ecological worldview in conventionally religious or other spiritual ways. People can claim to gain a knowledge of nature's purposes and needs through this sort of enquiry (see Spretnak 1985). But in secular Western societies these appeals can exercise only a limited attraction, and the principal form of legitimation in the leading environmental organizations remains that of scientific expertise. Even a celebratedly anti-establishment organization such as Greenpeace is increasingly drawing on scientific authority, having appointed an academic scientist as its director of science in London in 1989 (*Times Higher Education Supplement*, 7 April 1989: 8) and equipped itself with the 'most sophisticated mobile laboratory in Europe' (Brown and May 1989: 150).

To argue for the indispensability of scientific legitimations for environmental judgements is not, however, to minimize the importance of moral justifications for green activism, particularly in relation to the conservation of wildlife. During the late 1980s the vocabulary of animal rights and animal welfare rapidly entered everyday language, indicating a fundamental change in common ways of considering animals and signalling an expansion in the kinds of being held to have moral rights (see Warren 1983, Dobson 1990: 38). But talk of rights has been most effective in promoting change in those cases where humans deliberately inflict suffering on individual animals; for example, during hunts or in the course of *in vivo* experiments. Moreover, for all the power of such arguments they have pragmatic limitations. For one thing, rights are not yet widely seen as extending to all kinds of animal (laboratory rats maybe, but not sewer rats) and certainly not to plants and micro-organisms. Second, rights make most sense when applied to individuals rather than abstract entities such as species or even the habitats which support species. Arguments about rights may prevent cruelty to particular golden plovers, but they do not translate easily into firm guidance about the development of the bogs on which these birds like to breed (see Clark 1983: 192–3). Finally, even if we take just those animals to which rights may well be granted, one still needs to know what it is that those animals want to use their rights for; once again, it is scientists who are in a position to say what animals need and want.

The common ambivalence about the authority to be accorded to science may even tend towards antipathy among groups which are ideologically opposed to features of our current technological civilization and among animal welfare activists who find that their campaign targets include research scientists. In these cases, green activists and supporters have often come to have a distrust of experts and of scientific pronouncements. They are aware that reputable scientists have supported policies to which these groups are opposed (such as nuclear power) and also that governments and established interests often use demands for scientific proof as a way of delaying practical action. In the UK the most conspicuous example of this strategy was its use by the Central Electricity Generating Board (CEGB) and – initially at least – government spokespersons as well, to argue that there was no certain proof that acid emissions from UK power stations were responsible for the acidification of lakes and the death of trees in continental Europe. Official agencies could protest that they were as concerned as anyone but, until there was conclusive evidence that it was their power stations' waste gases which caused the pollution, it would be irresponsible to spend taxpayers' money on reducing emissions (see Rose 1990: 124).

Once ambivalence shades into opposition, green groups face a serious difficulty. They have good grounds for distrusting scientific authority but have no other place to turn for universalistic, definitive answers. Their own occasional impatience with scientific procedures, arising from a desire to take prompt practical action and from a distrust of the motives behind delays in arriving at officially recognized scientific conclusions, opens them to attack from outside observers on the grounds that they lack objectivity (for an example see North 1987).

VARIATIONS IN THE ROLE OF SCIENCE AS A 'STAND-IN'

In the light of these difficulties, it is only to be expected that the status accorded to science by different green groups varies. Much of this variation can be understood by referring to a distinction, made by some commentators, between 'environmental' groups and 'conservation' organizations (for example, Dobson 1990: 3). Typically on this view, the former (such as Greenpeace) work through campaigning to 'confront the negative effects on the environment of late-twentieth-century society and [to] try to ameliorate them' (Dobson 1990: 3). For their part, the latter (including the Royal Society for Nature Conservation – RSNC) aim to conserve and enhance existing habitats and species. In many respects this dichotomy is exaggerated. The Royal Society for the Protection of Birds (RSPB), a clear candidate for the second group, could none the less justly be said to have been established to confront the 'negative effects on the environment' of late-nineteenth-century society.[1] In any case, bodies such as the RSNC and the RSPB are increasingly adopting a policy of campaigning, in part because they recognize that more land or habitats can possibly be saved by, for example, pressuring MPs and MEPs (Members of Parliament and Members of the European Parliament) to alter the Common Agricultural Policy than by raising money for the purchase of reserves. This is also true of the smaller conservation groups such as Plantlife and the Marine Conservation Society.

However, the dichotomy is revealing in one way: conservation groups typically had a background in natural history and their membership has generally been dominated by enthusiasts or scientists. As a result, their ethos was different from that of the environmental groups which started off in the late 1960s and early 1970s as groups critical of contemporary Western society (for all practical purposes Greenpeace was founded in 1971 and Friends of the Earth in 1970; see Lowe and Goyder 1983: 124–37, Yearley 1992).

This difference in background and ethos has significant implications for these groups' approach to science and scientific authority. Let us start by taking the RSNC as an example of a nature conservation group and examine the part played by science in its ethos and its practice.

The RSNC originated just before World War I as the Society for the Promotion of Nature Reserves (SPNR), with a restricted and self-consciously elite, scientific membership. Its initial objective was to encourage other organizations, such as the National Trust, to acquire sites of importance for natural history. Such reserves were for 'the enjoyment of lovers of wild nature, the pursuit of scientific knowledge, and the well-being of the community in general' (SPNR, cited in Sheail 1976: 62). Early tensions between those who wanted to preserve rare and wild natural places and those who valued reserves chiefly as 'outdoor workshops' for the study of ecological science (the ecologist W.B. Crump, cited in Lowe 1983: 341) were gradually resolved in favour of the latter. Subsequently the SPNR was encouraged by the government to assist in developing a strategy for nature conservation and in drawing up a list of proposed nature reserves and, according to Lowe (1983: 342), it was during this period that 'ecologists gradually assumed the leadership of the conservation movement'. The government acted on the advice of the appointed Committee and established an official body, the Nature Conservancy, the 'first official *science-based* environmental conservation agency in the world' (Nicholson 1987: 95, emphasis added).

The SPNR (subsequently the RSNC) and Nature Conservancy (subsequently the Nature Conservancy Council – NCC – until 1991, when it was divided into national bodies for each of Wales, Scotland and England) have remained close ever since, in particular sharing an emphasis on the use of scientific criteria in assessing conservation merit. The flavour of legislation has also been decisively shaped along these lines, with the most ubiquitous conservation designation in the UK being the Site of Special Scientific Interest (SSSI).

The other major institutional development of the SPNR gathered pace in the late 1950s and early 1960s. This was the rapid growth in the number of county Wildlife Trusts, local bodies concerned with nature conservation, reserve acquisition and site management. The SPNR became the national coordinating body for these groups and accordingly changed its name (by a two-stage process in 1977 and 1981) to the RSNC. These Trusts took on much of the ethos of the central body, being dominated in the early stages by natural historians, scientists and enthusiasts. Although not as closely bound to the science of ecology as the RSNC and NCC, the Trusts retained a scientific ethos. Initially run by volunteers, they were dominated by people with a scientific understanding of, and interest in, wildlife. They shared the conservation goals of the RSNC and NCC and were keen to run activities of interest to members, such as field trips. These features lent the Trusts important strengths but also weaknesses.

PRACTICALITIES OF A SCIENTIFIC ETHOS

It is useful to start with the strengths associated with these groups' scientific ethos. As Trusts began to grow they tended to take on scientifically trained staff. Scientifically trained civil servants or academics were well represented on their voluntary governing bodies. This staffing meshed closely with their early activities, acquiring and managing reserves and assessing the local needs of wildlife. With this composition the Trusts were well placed to interact with local authorities, the Department of the Environment (DoE) and the NCC. The authorities had confidence in the groups' abilities and saw them as the responsible face of environmentalism. Often the groups shared many of the objectives of the official agencies – getting more sites assessed for declaration as SSSIs, managing the sites and so on. The official agencies could count on the Trusts to perform these tasks competently and in a manner of which they would approve. There were good informal contacts between the Trusts and the official agencies, and it was far from unknown for people to move from jobs in the voluntary sector to the official sector and, occasionally, vice versa. Nicholson observed this potential for mutual support early on since he believed that voluntary agencies 'could benefit by the Conservancy's official status, contacts and information, while it could gain no less advantage from their ability overtly to campaign against mis-behaving official bodies, and to whip up political and other support' (Nicholson 1987: 98).

Even on those occasions when the Trusts were in disagreement with the NCC or DoE, their scientific credentials meant that they could engage in proficient debate with the official agencies and that their views could not be swept aside as 'ill informed'. Still, their relationship with official bodies was mostly characterized by closeness and cooperation. Adapting the term intro-duced earlier, it could be said that the Trusts, as well as standing in for British wildlife (by representing its needs to the state), often stand in for the state in its dealings with nature.

In particular, their closeness to government provided a means for the Trusts to derive financial support. Precisely because they could be expected to be carrying out reserve management and site conservation duties, just the things which the NCC and aspects of the DoE are in business to do, and doing these things competently and cheaply, the groups were eligible for substantial funding, which supported both capital expenditure (on equip-ment and so on) and a small number of salaried posts. Having established this degree of cooperation, the Trusts were well placed to benefit from the government-financed job creation schemes of the high unemployment years of the early-to-mid-1980s; the Community Programme and, in Northern Ireland, the ACE scheme (Action for Community Employment) were par-ticularly important in providing labour for conservation tasks.[2] And in Northern Ireland, where the Ulster Wildlife Trust (UWT) is the local RSNC-affiliated Trust, the Province's persistent employment problems boosted the importance of this factor even more. The ACE scheme lasted longer than that operated elsewhere in the UK; the UWT even obtained employees with science degrees and, rarely, doctorates through this scheme (see Yearley and Milton 1990).

The second major strength which this scientific basis and ethos has lent is the ability to earn money. While the ethos permits the Trusts to be seen by official agencies as trustworthy and competent – and thus to merit grant aid

– it allows other bodies to see them as authoritative. Trusts affiliated to the RSNC have been among the leaders in developing consultancy services, whether providing environmentally sensitive landscaping advice to schools and hospitals or preparing environmental statements for developers. Of course, the customers are attracted by the green 'imprimatur' associated with advice from an environmental charity, but the work they carry out is also valued for its scientific standing.

Their scientific expertise can yield profits in other ways too; for example, through the organization of wildlife holidays led by natural history experts, and occasional lectures and scientific entertainments. The ability to earn money in these ways is important to environmental charities, not simply because it adds to their total income but because it lessens their dependence on government largess and thus frees them to be more outspoken in their campaigning if they feel it is necessary. Environmental consultancy is a doubly important area of work for green groups. It earns them good, 'free' money – especially since green groups currently enjoy a favourable market position as firms and developers are keen to be seen as green, while some commercial consultants do not yet have the necessary expertise. Second, the Trusts and similar groups believe that, if they perform the work themselves, this will maximize benefits to the environment, since they view their own consultancy advice as single-mindedly wildlife-friendly.

PRACTICAL DRAWBACKS OF A SCIENTIFIC ETHOS

While the scientific ethos and credentials of the Trusts have lent them significant strengths, there are corresponding pragmatic weaknesses. First, the ethos may lead to scientific tasks and objectives receiving priority. As I mentioned earlier, many nature conservation objectives may be achieved more readily through lobbying policy-makers than by trying to do the conservation oneself. For example, through fund raising, purchase and subsequent management a group may be able to conserve an example of peatland. If, on the other hand, government agencies can be pressured into declaring peatlands as protected sites, or if green consumerism can lead to a large reduction in the demand for horticultural peat, rather larger amounts of bog habitat can be saved. In practice the debate may be more complicated than this. If a conservation group acquires peatland it has greater control over it than if it succeeds simply in getting it declared an ASSI.[3] Certainly, official designations are revocable and an ASSI is not a guarantee that development will never take place. In each case a practical judgement has to be made about the competing advantages of the alternative strategies.

Still, it is sufficient for my overall argument to make the general point that the scientific heritage of the Trusts has led them to feel more at ease in acquiring reserves than in mounting campaigns. Furthermore, the scientific work involved in surveying and inventorying a reserve is considerable whereas campaigning often involves less intensive use of field skills. Campaigning might therefore be thought to confer advantages of economy or efficiency, but in so far as surveying is what scientists like doing, the lobbying route is less appealing to them.

A similar tension arises over other kinds of skill which organizations need but which natural scientists are not necessarily trained to possess. For example, as conservation groups grow in terms of both income and staff they develop needs for new kinds of leadership. Within a group culture dominated by practising scientists, specifically scientific skills may well be rated more highly than others. Even at the level of volunteer workers it may be difficult to mobilize people with managerial or financial skills, if only because they are not commonly involved in the same informal and friendship networks as the initial core members.

This disjunction between a primarily scientific and an organizational outlook arises acutely with regard to fund raising and publicity, particularly in the matter of campaign priorities. Natural historians will typically have their own conservation priorities, perhaps based on rarity or on scientific interest (and therefore sometimes linked to typicality). These priorities will not necessarily coincide with the issues best calculated to excite public interest and media attention; put bluntly, while a drab bird may be endangered, majestic and colourful birds offer the best photo opportunities.

Occasionally such disparities can be used to humorous effect. *The Independent* ran a story about a rescue mission to save the giant earwig of St Helena, an eight-centimetre monster of the tropics under threat from accidentally introduced rats. In defence of these insects, the scientist from London Zoo was quoted as saying that the earwigs had an 'attractive family life-style . . . The females make extremely good mothers' (*The Independent*, 9 February 1988: 1). In a similar vein, members of the scientific committee of the UWT, discussing which issues to highlight in promotional material, moved on from considering suggestions for badger week and otter campaigns to muse on the possibility of slug week and rat year. These jokes are a symptom of an anxiety that promotional needs – the organizational requirement to find a popular, newsworthy campaign target – will be elevated above scientific priorities. Similar concerns may arise in the case of publicity material. While those with a marketing and design interest may evaluate logos and slogans on the basis of supposed public appeal, naturalists are prone to insist on their biological accuracy. Thus posters for a wildlife campaign run by the UWT displayed a charming stoat drawn by an English art student; a prominent Irish biologist subsequently pointed out that the posters were misleading – and possibly insulting – since the picture showed an English, not an Irish, stoat. Such concerns are further attested to by naturalists' humour, in this case a proposal that the UWT's slogan should be: 'protecting your local biotopes'.

Such tensions between different aspects of these organizations with contrasting objectives are likely to be intensified by current trends in the environmental movement. Increasingly, environmental organizations are having to compete with each other to gain public attention and support, and for this reason it is important to be associated with leading, newsworthy issues. The background to this competition is clear enough. The pressure groups are not quite like businesses competing for market share: they cooperate a good deal, and members are not exactly like customers since many supporters are willing to join more than one group. Of course, ordinary members will limit their subscriptions at some point but the real competition is for major sponsors – increasingly companies but also charitable trusts – which have specified budgets to disburse. Under these competitive conditions, fund-raising and publicity success is to some degree self-perpetuating: firms will fund campaigns which have a high profile, a profile further heightened by this backing. No groups can afford to miss out on these important market opportunities. Moreover, such competition operates to concentrate more attention on the highest-profile issues (such as the rainforests, the conservation of attractive species and so on) and can leave other environmental issues 'orphaned'.

The RSPB is well known as a highly successful fund-raising group, and aspects of its strategy are instructive here. Although mostly concerned in recent years with British birds, the RSPB has lately followed migrating species overseas and developed campaigns outside of its usual territorial limits (see Samstag 1988: 144-7). From migrating birds it is a short step to a concern with birds which never visit the UK at all. A recent campaign concerns the birds and bird habitat of rainforest areas of Sierra Leone, particularly one characteristic, endangered species, the white-necked picathartes. Such a move imaginatively combines demands for species and habitat conservation with the attractive organizational achievement of linking the RSPB to the task of rainforest conservation.

In short, environmental charities are having to acquire managerial skills and styles more characteristic of big business. The pursuit of increasingly market-oriented strategies cannot be expected to lead to the same policies and objectives as would have followed from scientists' priorities. Recent trends have thus had a large impact on scientifically dominated nature conservation groups.

GREEN GROUPS WITHOUT A SCIENTIFIC ANCESTRY AND ETHOS

My analysis of the groups which Dobson and others would label 'environmental' is essentially that they lack both the weaknesses and the strengths outlined above. Thus, even had they wished to, they could not have enjoyed such close, practical cooperation with official agencies as has the RSNC. Nor have they been able to earn their green pounds in the same way. They have, however, been more able to respond to certain market forces, particularly the 'markets' of public opinion and of media coverage. Crucially for my argument, they have been freer to be critical of scientific opinion and of expertise more generally. This is not to say that they have been free of campaigning constraints; Friends of the Earth (FOE), for example, have been studied in their avoidance of party-political partisanship (Yearley 1992: 97). But, since scientific study of the natural world is of less inherent appeal to their supporters, since the organization's work depends more on campaigning than on surveying and management, and since these groups refuse to engage in consultancy work, they can retain some distance from science.

In turn this distance may result in difficulties. In some cases, the information necessary for campaigning can be straightforwardly derived. Thus, in the celebrated case of (UK) FOE's popular and successful campaign against CFC-driven aerosols in 1988–9 (Friends of the Earth 1989), it was enough to argue that, if American firms could withdraw CFCs from deodorants and other spray-can products, then so could British ones. An exactly similar argument was used by Greenpeace against Ford's failure to fit catalytic convertors or other emission control systems on its British models. Borrowing the company's own slogan ('Ford gives you more'), the Greenpeace campaign pointed out that a Ford car in Britain gives vastly more toxic pollution than one bought in the USA because of the company's response to the different pollution control regulations (*The Guardian*, 27 October 1988: 5). Essentially in both cases the argument is one about double standards. If something is technically possible in one developed country, it must be equally possible in Britain. The argument is, so to speak, an immanent one.

When it comes to contested scientific information these groups are in a less comfortable situation. Thus, on 12 August 1990 a programme was broadcast on Channel 4 in the UK casting doubt on the reality of global warming. It implied that climate scientists might be led into making exaggerated claims about warming because the existence of such a threat would make it easy to acquire the resources for their research programmes: 'It may not quite add up to a conspiracy, but certainly a coalition of interests has promoted the greenhouse theory: scientists have needed funds' (Channel 4 1990: 27).

In the FOE *Local Groups Newsletter* a staff member attacked this programme by appealing to the weight of majority scientific opinion. The testimony of 'around a dozen dissident scientists' had to be weighed against the views of the three hundred or so scientists who 'wrote and peer reviewed' the report to the Intergovernmental Panel on Climate Change (IPCC) (Dilworth 1990). The article went on to bolster this argument by rhetorically pointing out that the IPCC scientists could hardly be portrayed 'as a raving bunch of eco-anarchist nutcases. Some would say they are a cautious bunch, wary of hard-won scientific reputations and not prone to wild exaggeration'. The droll use of the expression 'some would say' seems to imply that this opinion is universally shared, rather than just being the view of FOE.

No doubt it is quite reasonable for FOE workers to argue in this way. But the point arising from this example is that FOE have no scientific evidence of their own to use in settling this controversy, nor any comparable expertise. Their best argument is just that the most well-informed scientific opinion is on their side. They find themselves invoking the 'consensus of scientific opinion' to overcome the TV journalists' deconstructive arguments – exactly the opposite of arguments environmentalists have themselves employed in other contexts (for example, against the official consensus on the supposed safety of nuclear installations).

We have already seen how those organizations with a scientific ethos have been altered by the growing demands of competition. We can anticipate a corresponding change in this second type of environmental group which is likely to be affected by growing scientific and technical competence. As technical expertise increases, confidence grows in one's ability to win arguments through persuasion. A corresponding relaxation of former, strident campaign styles can be anticipated. In their authorized history of Greenpeace, Brown and May allude to this process:

> [T]here is a current media cliché that Greenpeace is turning its back on such tactics [as direct action] and is becoming a more bureaucratic, softer version of its earlier radical self. This is demonstrably untrue; the number of direct actions continues in an upward spiral.
>
> (Brown and May 1989: 5)

No doubt Greenpeace's commitment to radical environmental campaigning remains. But the concern expressed in this passage appears to me an oblique acknowledgement of the potential conflict between professionalization and radicalism.

STANDING IN FOR SCIENCE

We have seen the potential drawbacks which surface when environmentalists are dependent on others' (for example, the IPCC's) science. At this point, attention should also be drawn to practical limitations which arise when groups seek to use their own scientific expertise for campaigning work. Even groups which have a large scientific staff or can count on assistance from sympathetic academic researchers find that they cannot gain access to all the information they would like. They do not have the budgets to subscribe to all the publications they might desire, and they cannot maintain extensive libraries. Worse, academic science – even in ecology – will not necessarily generate the kinds of research they would like to see done; after all, much academic science is addressed to problems formulated within the scientific community rather than by outside bodies.

Furthermore, environmental groups often need to respond to urgent queries about, for example, the environmental impact of spilled chemicals. Even if they had the resources (which they typically do not), they would not have the time to conduct original research on such issues. As Cramer observes: 'The opportunity to base advice on new ecological research is therefore rare, which means that the ecological experts try to gather as much relevant published material as possible. This material can vary widely both in quality and in quantity' (Cramer 1987: 50).

Even the larger organizations, ones which have sufficient resources to fund some research, find themselves in a dilemma. For example, the RSPB has obligations to spend money on its reserves and on practical bird conservation while Greenpeace needs to fund its campaigns and its ships. Against such practical and pressing expenditures, a research budget is hard to justify.

In consequence, such organizations are dependent on scientific knowledge produced by other persons or agencies, knowledge which is suited to the objectives and agendas of those other groups. Even if it is attractive for environmental groups to try to stand in for science, they are confronted by severe practical restrictions.

CONCLUDING DISCUSSION: THE IMPACT OF OUTSIDE INSTITUTIONS ON GREENS' USES OF SCIENCE

Since the natural environment and wildlife are perceived as unable to speak up for themselves, they need a stand-in. In modern industrialized societies science is the only stand-in capable of commanding widespread legitimacy. Scientific knowledge also plays an important practical role for conservation groups, in tasks such as reserve management and, increasingly, in relation to income generation. But science does not assume the role of stand-in easily. In the case of nature conservation organizations a dominant scientific ethos has tended to lead to managerial and administrative difficulties while, for campaigning groups, increasing reliance on scientific expertise is likely to imply changes in their campaign style.

For all these groups it is a major practical challenge to work out how to treat scientific knowledge claims and how to deal with scientific expertise. Fortunately, for most purposes it is up to the groups themselves to figure out their standpoint on scientific issues. Thus, Wildlife Trusts can make their own judgements about the scientific value of their nature reserves; FOE can formulate their own stance on the conflicting evidence about global warming. However, in certain significant institutional contexts they have much less control over the handling of, say, scientific evidence on the emission of acidic gases or on threats to indigenous wildlife. Foremost among these contexts is the representation of green issues in the mass media, where presentational conventions often demand a balance between competing 'sides' and where there is a premium on the photogenic or picturesque (see Lowe and Morrison 1984, Lowe and Flynn 1989: 296).

In this way, outsiders' views and practices will exercise an influence over the value attached to scientific considerations and scientific authority within the green movement. Institutions such as the mass media, but also the law (see Yearley 1989), will act as a filter, affecting the public prominence of scientific aspects of the green case. None the less, science remains singly authoritative as a stand-in for nature. And, as we have seen, it is in the groups' own management of scientific expertise and use of scientific legitimations that the workings of this stand-in can be most fully appreciated by social scientists.

ACKNOWLEDGEMENTS

The research reported in this chapter was supported by an award (A0925 0006) from the ESRC and Science Policy Support Group under the Public Understanding of Science Initiative. Many thanks are due to Kay Milton for her editorial guidance in the preparation of this chapter.

NOTES

1 The RSPB, which celebrated its centenary in 1989, originated as a campaigning organization opposed to the needless killing of birds for the feather trade. By the middle of this century it had turned into the body for bird enthusiasts which essentially it still remains.
2 It is significant that the employees on these schemes were mostly doing un-contentious conservation and maintenance tasks; the government was not funding people to organize campaigns to protest against its own policies on, say, nuclear power or road transport. Thus, only some environmental groups benefited from these schemes.
3 In Northern Ireland, SSSIs are termed Areas of Special Scientific Interest (ASSIs). Furthermore, the NCC did not operate in the Province; its approximate functions were carried out by a branch of the DoE(NI).

REFERENCES

Brown, M. and May, J. (1989) *The Greenpeace Story*, London: Dorling Kindersley.
Channel 4 (1990) *The Greenhouse Conspiracy*, London: Channel Four Television.
Clark, S.R.L. (1983) 'Gaia and the forms of life', in R. Elliot and A. Gare (eds) *Environmental Philosophy*, Milton Keynes: Open University Press.
Cramer, J. (1987) *Mission-Orientation in Ecology: The Case of Dutch Fresh-Water Ecology*, Amsterdam: Rodopi.
Dilworth, A. (1990) 'Global warming', *FOE Local Groups Newsletter* 186, September: 19.
Dobson, A. (1990) *Green Political Thought*, London: Unwin Hyman.
Friends of the Earth (1989) *The Aerosol Connection*, London: Friends of the Earth.
Lowe, P. (1983) 'Values and institutions in the history of British nature conservation', in A. Warren and F.B. Goldsmith (eds) *Conservation in Perspective*, Chichester: Wiley.

Lowe, P. and Flynn, A. (1989) 'Environmental politics and policy in the 1980s', in J. Moran (ed.) *The Political Geography of Contemporary Britain*, London: Macmillan.

Lowe, P. and Goyder, J. (1983) *Environmental Groups in Politics*, London: Allen and Unwin.

Lowe, P. and Morrison, D. (1984) 'Bad news or good news: environmental politics and the mass media', *Sociological Review*, 32: 75–90.

Nicholson, M. (1987) *The New Environmental Age*, Cambridge: Cambridge University Press.

North, R. (1987) 'Greenpeace: still credible?', *The Independent*, 21 September: 15.

Rose, C. (1990) *The Dirty Man of Europe: The Great British Pollution Scandal*, London: Simon and Schuster.

Samstag, T. (1988) *For Love of Birds*, Sandy, Bedfordshire: RSPB.

Sheail, J. (1976) *Nature in Trust: The History of Nature Conservation in Britain*, Glasgow: Blackie.

Spretnak, C. (1985) 'The spiritual dimension of green politics', in C. Spretnak and F. Capra, *Green Politics: The Global Promise*, London: Paladin.

Warren, M.A. (1983) 'The rights of the non-human world', in R. Elliot and A. Gare (eds) *Environmental Philosophy*, Milton Keynes: Open University Press.

Yearley, S. (1989) 'Bog standards: science and conservation at a public inquiry', *Social Studies of Science*, 19: 421–38.

—— (1992) *The Green Case: A Sociology of Environmental Arguments, Issues and Politics*, London: Routledge.

Yearley, S. and Milton, K. (1990) 'Environmentalism and direct rule: the politics and ethos of conservation and environmental groups in Northern Ireland', *Built Environment*, 16: 192–202.

Chapter 5

All animals are equal but some are cetaceans

Conservation and culture conflict

Niels Einarsson

> It quickly became apparent that the panda symbol was a totally strange visual concept for these African villagers. They were curious to know what it was, where it lived, did it exist in their country, and could it be eaten.
>
> (Zalewski, quoted in Pearce 1991: 87)

> I am a twelve year old who has seen what you do to whales. I cannot call you sir as I should for you are worse than godless beasts. You are lazy savages who do not wish to work at other things but prefer to kill innocent creatures. You make civilized children sick. I am sure God hates you all.
>
> (Letter from an American child to the Icelandic Government, 1990)

Many people worry about environmental issues. Global environmental degradation, including wildlife destruction, has taken the place of nuclear war as the greatest perceived threat to humankind, at least in those countries where people do not have to worry about food for the day. Apocalyptic messages are abundant, and so is a variety of literature on 'how to save the world'. Even small children are becoming aware that our planet may, slowly but surely, be turning into a reeking and lifeless rock. Recently my 7-year-old son came to me and reprimanded me for throwing away a piece of paper. 'If you do this all the trees die and the animals and we will have no air to breathe. Do you think that's good?' he said, in an accusing tone. He had learned this in the first grade at the Swedish school he attends, and he was worried. I tried to convince him that things were not all that bad. Although there were problems in some parts of the world, not all forests everywhere were disappearing. And what about the people who work as loggers and whose occupation and livelihood was based on cutting down the trees we then use? What would happen to them? He had not thought about that, and this had not been an issue in school. This short lesson in environmental ethics that I received from my son is quite relevant for the subject of this chapter as it has to do with how people relate to 'natural resources', in this case whales.[1]

It is probably fair to say that whaling has for some time, especially before the rainforests and the ozone layer gained international attention, been among the most high-profile environmental issues and for some environmental groups the main issue. Whales are not the relatively ordinary and uncomplicated natural resources they were some thirty years ago, when it was possible to publish a book in which commercial whaling could be portrayed as a fine and dignified profession (Ash 1962). There has been a profound shift in the perception of these animals. Today people who whale are often depicted by influential animal rights and environmental organizations as the worst of eco-criminals, barbaric and cruel. In campaigns against whaling it is also compared to slavery and cannibalism (Barstow 1991: 4). Even the Holocaust, a concept usually reserved for the fate of people, is considered a fit metaphor for describing the over-exploitation of former times.

In this chapter I am concerned with whales, which have become unusual resources indeed. This can, for example, be seen in a recent pamphlet published by a leading British cetacean protection agency in which a supporter, Her Highness the Begum Aga Khan, in a personal message, pleads, in the following terms, for a 'moratorium for the millennium':

> I imagine sometimes that in a Universe inhabited by sentient peoples, each planet might be judged on how well it treated its whales . . . those magnificent, intelligent and peaceful animals, who have been around so much longer than we and have always appeared, to me, so much wiser.
>
> (Aga Khan 1991)

And in an opening speech to the 1990 annual meeting of the International Whaling Commission (IWC), the Dutch minister of fisheries claimed that 'Whales are the roses in our garden and roses should bloom.' President Bush, in his address to an IWC meeting in San Diego the year before, had reminded the participants that 'Whales have become symbolic of all wildlife and precious natural resources that current environmental problems challenge us to protect', and had encouraged them to 'safeguard whales effectively in the years to come'.

Safeguarding whales can be done in a number of ways depending on whether the focus is on the welfare of individuals or the survival of species. A much-used argument in save-the-whales campaigns has been that they are unique and (despite the claims of some environmental groups that all animals are equally worthy), in fact, 'more equal' than other animals. This view is strongly expressed in a recent article in the *American Journal of International Law* entitled 'Whales: their emerging right to life'. The authors argue that it is time for what they call 'cetaceans' rights', as there already exists 'a broadening international consciousness about whaling amounting to an *opinio juris* – the psychological components of international customary law' (D'Amato and Chopra 1991: 22). The main justification for whale rights is their intelligence and other human attributes:

> Writers of science fiction have often speculated about what it would be like to discover, on a planet in outer space, a much higher form of intelligence. How would we react to these creatures? Would we be so

fearful of them that we would try to kill them? Or would we welcome the opportunity to attempt to understand their language and culture? Stranger than fiction is the fact that there already exists a species of animal life on earth that scientists speculate has higher than human intelligence ... They are sentient, they are intelligent, they have their own community, and they can suffer.

(D'Amato and Chopra 1991: 21–2)

ECOCENTRISM, ANTHROPOCENTRISM AND WHALES

At the beginning of the 1970s whales came into the focus of the environmental movement, an important turning point being the United Nations Conference on the Human Environment held in Stockholm in 1972, where the United States took the initiative in calling for a moratorium on all commercial whaling. Having been recklessly over-exploited, whales seemed to epitomize everything that was wrong with the relations of humankind with the environment. Whales became key symbols for the environmental movement, and during the subsequent years, the IWC moved away from being primarily a forum of whaling nations, as more and more nations without economic interests in whaling became members. In 1982 a majority supported an international moratorium on whaling, to begin in 1986 (see Cherfas 1989).

The moratorium reflects not only concern about the biological survival of whales (many of the seventy-four or so species of whales are not endangered), but a more fundamental issue, whether or not whaling can be justified morally. For the environmental movement whales have become uniquely special. The problem is, however, that for people such as Icelandic whalers and fishermen they are not uniquely special at all but simply like other natural resources.

For the Icelandic fishermen among whom I have worked, the ban on taking the relatively abundant minke whales around Iceland (which the IWC scientific committee has said are not endangered) seems very unfair and, for some of them, it has meant a drastic loss of income. The ban is contradictory to a worldview in which people have a self-evident right to take animals for their livelihood.

Icelandic fishermen see campaigns against the hunting of whales as threatening both a way of life and, in the longer run, their right to basic subsistence. A frequent answer to the question of why they do not give in concerning seals and whales is the belief that environmentalists will stop at nothing less than a total ban on the taking of any animal, whale, fish or fowl. Environmentalists are seen as basically fundamentalists and extremists. This image is strengthened by articles written in Icelandic newspapers by locally well-known animal rights people, such as the spokesperson for the Icelandic Whale-friends Society. He has argued against all killing of animals, including fish, on which fishermen depend for subsistence and which make up around three-quarters of Iceland's exports. In countries like contemporary Iceland it takes considerable civil courage to argue for such views and face the consequences (for a discussion of Icelandic nationalism and the whaling issue see Brydon 1990).[2]

While environmentalists tell stories about cetaceans rescuing people, Icelandic small-scale fishermen tell stories about whales sinking boats and causing deaths, apart from destroying gear and eating scarce fish otherwise caught by fishermen. Today the discussion is very much about the quantity of fish whales eat and how whales could, if not hunted, bring the fishing industry to its knees. When the fishing industry faces a drastic 30 per cent cut, at one fell swoop, of its catch of cod, with great consequences for all sectors of the industry, these are important issues for everyone.

The Icelandic small-scale fisherman's view of animals and nature is basically utilitarian and anthropocentric. Within such a framework there is little room for romantic experiences of oneness with nature. Perhaps a few examples of fishermen's encounters with animals will clarify this point. One late afternoon, while doing fieldwork in an Icelandic east-coast fishing village, I met an older fisherman who was returning from his daily trip. I helped him tie up his small boat and asked whether he had had any luck with the fishing. He said no, the sea had been totally 'dead', except for fish he was not interested in. When I asked him what he meant by that, he told me that, as he had been sitting with his handline, a minke whale had suddenly appeared, circling around the boat and diving under it. Then after a couple of minutes, the whale came swimming right up to the small boat and stopped with its head above the boat, apparently watching the man. 'I could have touched it with my hand', he said. The whale stayed in this position for a couple of minutes and then left. The fisherman had never seen a whale do this before, but he was not very impressed and not even particularly interested in telling me about this incident.

On another occasion I was fishing with another fisherman when a strange, shark-like fish appeared on the longline. I, the observing participant, had never seen a fish like that during the years I had been engaged in small-scale fishing. The fisherman did as he did with all fish that he could not sell, returned it immediately to the water. He had never seen such a fish either, but it was worthless, he said. I never found out what kind of fish it was except that it was classified as *drasl*, which in Icelandic means 'rubbish' or 'waste', or in the terms of fishermen's ethnoecology, fish that do not belong to valuable species such as cod or haddock.

Another fisherman told me how he had nearly had a heart attack when, in the dark of night, he had suddenly noticed a minke whale towering above his small boat. A few days later a minke whale was caught in a longline set by the same fisherman, dragging the boat for some time and causing the loss of much of the longline. When the perceived interests of fishermen and whales come into conflict it is evident in the fishermen's anthropocentric view that the animals have to be sacrificed. But this is only one possible way of looking at human–animal relations and the role of humans in nature.

Those who will accept no hunting of whales are guided by a fundamentally different view of nature and how humans should relate to it, a view which could be called an ecocentric one. An ecocentric view of nature questions the right of humans to do as they please in the natural world, and also the arrogant assumption that what are perceived as human interests should always come first even at nature's cost. Nature has a value and right of its own and humans are but a part of a much larger plan. In this view it is the grey, utilitarian and destructive ideology of industrial society that is responsible for the environmental ills of the planet. The following quote from a Greenpeace 1990 calendar summarizes that organization's ecocentric view of how we should treat whales:

> Save the whales. Whales and humans share a common enemy – humankind itself. Our blind greed has pushed the whale to the brink of extinction. We are arguably not far behind. Whales are beautiful and intelligent creatures, each of which has the innate right to survive. We must see to it that whales as a species continue to grace the ecological tapestry of our planet. The lessons we learn from saving whales can educate us in how to approach other global environmental problems. We must save the whales, not only for their sake, but for ours . . . Greenpeace is committed to ending all commercial whaling once and for all.

WHALE MYTHS AND METAPHORS

Metaphors and other tropes abound in the whaling conflict, and the study of these can contribute to an insight into the nature of that conflict. By pointing out the importance of looking at metaphors and how they give clues to and influence basic assumptions, I am by no means claiming that they govern the way people think about reality. If that is the strong version of metaphor theory (see, for example, Lakoff and Johnson 1980) then I would rather subscribe to a softer version which stresses the influence but not necessarily the ultimate rule of metaphors (see Keesing 1987, 1989, Fernandez 1991). I do, however, see metaphors as important in *revealing* structures of ideas, even if they may not themselves *be* those structures. (For example, I find it revealing when people say that whales are the roses of the sea.) Metaphor is culturally based and can be 'invoked to reason with' (Quinn 1991: 93). In this instance the choice of metaphors is conditioned by the paradigms of nature and reflects the perceived interests of the actors.

In the campaigns for saving whales, metaphors, as rhetorical devices, have been of great importance in their power emotionally to engage people for causes that might otherwise have passed relatively unnoticed, and, as I said above, I believe that the metaphors and tropes used in these campaigns can also tell us a great deal about the basic assumptions of the environmentalists and of their opponents.

One of the most powerful metaphors is that of anthropomorphism, changing what people in Western culture ordinarily classify as non-human and without self-evident rights into moral objects of sympathy and concern. In general, moralizing the natural world through humanizing metaphors has become a major rhetorical device in environmental campaigns in Western culture, where many question the rift between nature and culture, animals and humans. 'In this view humankind is part of nature and everything in the universe is connected with everything else . . . Western culture, it seems, is now in a phase that might almost be called neototemistic' (Willis 1990: 6).

In the whale mythology of contemporary environmental discourse, whales straddle the Cartesian divide between animals and humans, occupying a Pan-like role in these relations. The moral consequence of humanizing whales is great as it transforms them from being potential natural resources into a very different category of animals; they become 'uniquely special' (Barstow 1991). Within this axiom there is no possibility of allowing the hunting of whales, regardless of the humaneness of killing methods, or as biologist and campaigner Roger Payne puts it:

> Even if an entirely painless method could be found to kill them, it would not remove the immorality of killing whales. It would remove the wrong caused by the gratuitous suffering visited on whales by the current whaling techniques, but that would not make the killing of whales, to fill purposes that do not require their killing, any less wrong. If we were to take something that is morally wrong and make it less wrong, it is not made right. If you could find a way to kill someone so painlessly that it did not even disturb their sleep, it would not make it morally right to kill them.
>
> (Payne 1991: 22)

For people like Roger Payne, former president of the UK-based Whale and Dolphin Conservation Society, it is inherently wrong to kill whales. With this in mind it is possible to understand the rage felt by whale-saving activists such as Paul Watson when facing the raw reality of whaling operations:

> We have caught the whale butchers red-handed in the act of taking an undersized whale. Riding out on a Zodiac, I leap from the inflatable craft onto the slain whale, its skin warm and oily, the blood flowing from the gaping wound in its side, hot on my hand. I stroke the flipper, reach down toward the vacantly staring open eye and close the eyelid. I am lost and lonely upon the ocean with that dead whale child.
>
> (Quoted in Brown and May 1989: 37–8)

In this passage the whale involved is described as a child, an anthropomorphizing metaphor that serves to reduce the emotional distance between the reader and the fate of an animal.[3] I argue that an important part of the explanation of why whales are so potent as symbols and why so many find it easy to identify with them is their humanized image. It is the implicit and explicit projections of human motives on to the behaviour of cetaceans which has given rise to a whole body of cetacean mythology where the metaphor of anthropomorphism plays a major role. Take the example of dolphins saving people from drowning, often cited to show the superior and human-like moral consciousness of cetaceans. There is no doubt that dolphins have saved people from drowning by pushing them to the surface and towards the shore. They do this to their newborn offspring and seem in general to like pushing things around, but not always towards the shore, which may explain why most stories told are by people who have been pushed in that direction. There are also incidents of people being attacked by dolphins, of people drowning while nearby dolphins did nothing to help and of swimmers prevented from re-entering boats (Lockyer 1990, Klinowska 1992).

There has also been a difference between representation and reality in the case of whale songs, made famous by best-selling singles and the film *Star Trek IV*. The eerie sounds that humpback bulls make have been interpreted as whale language in which whales (i.e. the males) 'speak' to each other and which, if deciphered, could make it possible for humans to communicate with them in the future. Recent research has shown that whale songs or calls are much more likely to be connected to their reproductive behaviour (Cherfas 1989: 53).

As key symbols (Ortner 1973) whales, as endangered and over-exploited species, sum up and stand for everything that is wrong in the relations between humans and the natural world. They provide an analogy for thinking about the environment in general. As Lévi-Strauss has pointed out (1964), animals are good to think, and good to think with. This may be, as James Fernandez has suggested, because of

> mankind's ancient, virtually universal interest in animals . . . The various animals and objects of the natural world are . . . sensible images which can be predicated upon inchoate subjects . . . Is it not arguable that primordially animals are predicates by which subjects obtain an identity and are thus objects of affinity and participation?
>
> (Fernandez 1986: 32)

Whales have certainly become 'objects of affinity and participation', and as such have provided many people with a metaphor to think about otherwise complex environmental issues, making the choice of action easier by focusing on particular species of symbolic value: 'Men can be and are, through the diverse powers of culture, many things . . . If they can look around and find some lessons in cows and calves, bears and rats, their choices are made easier' (Fernandez 1972: 41).

When whales had become symbols for environmental organizations such as Greenpeace, the saving of the whales became the test of the ability of environmentalists to fight the forces of environmental destruction. As the former president of the Whale and Dolphin Conservation Society put it, in a slogan often cited by whale savers, 'If we can't save the whale, we can't save anything' (quoted in Whale and Dolphin Conservation Society 1991: 3). Whether or not whaling is ecologically sustainable is largely irrelevant when it comes to saving key symbols. According to former Canadian Greenpeace leader Patrick Moore,

> The scientific debate about whether whales really are in danger of extinction is nothing we want to get reduced to . . . The general public is not going to understand the science of ecology, so to get them to save the whale you have to get them to believe that whales are good.
>
> (Quoted in Pearce 1991: 27)

But it is one thing to postulate that whales are special and that animals should have rights, and another thing to condemn the cultural practices of people relating to the use of animals and attempt to force them to give up these practices. Animal rights transformed into practice easily turn into what might be called ethnocentric cultural imperialism (see Wenzel 1991). Most anthropologists will protest when 'their' people are subjected to ethnocentric treatment attacking their culture or even threatening their subsistence. Many anthropologists are suffering from 'species compassion fatigue' when they see this as threatening the way of life of people whom they have lived among and learned to appreciate.[4]

Icelandic minke whalers are not numerous; only some nine boats were involved in minke whaling during the years before the moratorium on whale hunting started in 1986. Neither are the boats large, ranging from 19 to 30 tonnes gross. Part of their income used to come from fishing, but 60–70 per cent came from whaling. After 1986 this income was lost. This happened at the same time as the quota allotted to fishing boats was decreasing fast as a consequence of government regulations. Minke whalers have been in a particularly vulnerable position as the fish quota allotted to each boat was based on records of previous catches, excluding whales. This means that the owners of minke boats received much smaller quotas than those who were solely occupied with fishing.

For Icelandic minke whalers and the villages they live in, the question of whaling or not whaling is more than philosophical speculation about the intrinsic value of animals, speciesism and so forth. It is a question of economic survival and the possibility of living in the village where you feel you belong. But these two things may be very difficult to combine with the loss of income from whaling. To fetch as high a price as possible for the remaining quota, it may be necessary to move to where the big fish markets are and where the price for fish can be twice as much as in the small villages. This usually means moving to Reykjavik, the capital. As one minke whaler said, 'I do not want to move to Reykjavik like my colleague did a couple of years ago. I was born here and raised, and it is here I have my family and relatives. But I may be forced to and that is sad.'

For every boat that disappears from a fishing village's fleet there are many jobs lost. In Icelandic fishing villages there are almost no alternatives to fishing. Such facts of life make people extremely bitter towards those who are seen as taking away their chances of existence. In the words of an Icelandic minke whaler:

> To me it is clear that if these people are going to force upon us what they think is right it can only end with a bloodbath. People have to realize that we want to live according to our customs and off what nature here has to offer or else we will simply die. We are living on the edge of the habitable world and there isn't anything else to live off. And if you do not live off what there is you will die. There are no alternatives. I am ready to fight. I feel that our right to exist and that of my offspring is threatened and I am willing to suffer to defend our rights. Whaling may not matter very much to the world, but to us it matters a great deal.

CONCLUSIONS

Conflicts concerning conservation often involve external influence on local resource-use, where conservationists from the outside and indigenous resource-users disagree on how, or even if, a resource should be used. The conversation of conservation (Kaus 1990, Gomez-Pompa and Kaus 1992) is often hampered by basically different cultural assumptions on how natural resources are to be viewed. Such conflicts are culture conflicts and not just a question of scientifically rational standards of resource utilization. In the whaling conflict the parties involved are not equal in terms of power, and in the *realpolitik* of international relations, ethnocentric assumptions can be forced upon cultures that deviate from what hegemonic cultural superpowers define as civilized and acceptable. But cultural and political hegemony entails a responsibility, or as Aron has pointed out in the case of whaling:

> If the concern is based largely on the need to correct abuses of the past and to restore marine mammal populations to former abundance levels, continuing the current sweeping policy of virtually total protection for all species is no longer required. If, however, the concern for marine mammals is essentially based on ethics or morality of their harvest, we probably should continue our current course. In doing so we must clearly recognize that there is a difference between imposing a moral or ethical standard on US citizens and imposing such standards on the international community.
>
> (Aron 1988: 107)

In my view people must be seen as a natural part of ecosystems and not as a foreign negative element, or even, as the most radical eco-warriors put it in a telling metaphor, a cancer on the environment. There is a serious need to include the plans local people have for their living and to show respect for their values and interests relating to natural resources, however unpalatable it may seem to outsiders.[5] To most anthropologists this may seem self-evident, which may be the reason why anthropologists sometimes have difficulty communicating with environmentalists, compared with the relative success they have had with the development community. But as Marianne Schmink has recently noted, 'environmentalists have a different culture. Many of them are unschooled in the social dynamics of resource use, tending to see people only as intruders who should be removed from pristine natural settings' (Schmink 1990: 8). In this respect environmentalists may sometimes be as naive as my 7-year-old who worried about the fate of the forest and the animals in it but entirely forgot that people, in their pursuit of making a living, may also be at risk.

ACKNOWLEDGEMENTS

Thanks are due to Peter Bretschneider, Gisli Palsson, Kay Milton, Roy Willis and Matthew James Driscoll for constructive advice.

NOTES

1 I think it is important to point out the ever-present problem concerning language when people discuss the conflict over marine mammals. There is no third, objective and intermediate language. For example, natural resources only exist as such because of human use and because they have been classified as such (Rayner 1989). From a fundamentally different point of view 'natural resources' are not natural resources at all and many people find it improper to talk about whales as natural resources, something which is more or less obvious to Icelandic fishermen. The paradigms of nature, our views of nature, restrict the kind of language we can use. In this chapter I will, quite consciously, be using the language of the Dominant Western Paradigm (Buttell 1987) even though it invites accusations of grey mindset, homocentrism and Cartesian dualism as these concepts are defined in a recent green dictionary (Johnson 1991).

2 This man has not led an easy life since he became known as the best friend of whales, having, among other things, survived an attempt on his life by an aggressive car driver.

3 'Lexical processes like synecdoche and metonymy are frequently involved in the manipulation of affective meaning . . . Other metaphorical processes have important affective dimensions' (Besnier 1990: 425).

4 It seems to me that, in general, anthropologists tend to be anthropocentric and sceptical towards including non-humans in the moral community. To quote Edmund Leach, 'Unless you are prepared to argue that Koko the gorilla might become a Christian, ethics concern rules which apply to human beings but not to non-human beings' (Leach 1982: 120). This may be the reason why moral philosopher Mary Midgley sees the need for extra-terrestrial anthropologists, i.e. not

those around her, to question the division of animals and people into separate moral categories: 'If anthropologists from a strange planet came here to study our intellectual habits and customs, they might notice something rather strange about the way in which we classify the living things on our planet' (Midgley 1989: 1). Leach's claim that the distinction between humans and non-humans is pan-human may not, however, be that obvious. At least there is great cross-cultural variation in the degree of that distinction. But even if the present paradigm in Western culture and anthropology may be that of the Cartesian division between humans and nature, there are anthropologists who question the feasibility of such a view, arguing for a more holistic, less arrogant, integrative view where humans are seen not as apart from and above, but as part of the whole of nature (Willis 1990).

5   The case of the conservation of whales has been a successful one in terms of putting an end to whaling by a total moratorium, irrespective of the possibility of local abundance of single species. Some of those who were engaged in the save-the-whale campaigns are now, victory having been won, moving to other problems such as the diminishing rainforests. But in the long run it may prove hazardous to overstate the plight of the environment, as by saying that all whales are endangered when this is not at all the case. For some of the eco-warriors this may not be an issue, or to quote recently resigned Greenpeace leader David McTaggart, 'You've got to be prepared to keep the No. 1 thing in mind: you're fighting to get your children into the 21st century, and to hell with the rules' (quoted in Brand 1989: 44). It is also questionable that powerful environmental organizations such as Greenpeace sometimes pick up problems for campaigns only if it is likely that they will be a success. According to international director Steven Sawyer, 'our philosophy on issues is extraordinarily pragmatic. We choose the ones we feel we might be able to win' (quoted in Pearce 1991: 40). Such attitudes are perfectly understandable if you are working by the metaphor of war, a global one for the environment, but as John Maddox put it at the beginning of the 1970s:

> The common justification is to say it is necessary to exaggerate to get people stirred, to get things done. But people are easily anaesthetized by repetition and there is a danger that, in spite of its achievement so far, the environmental movement could still find itself falling flat on its face when it is most needed, simply because it has pitched its tale too strongly.
>
> (Maddox 1972: 237)

REFERENCES

Aga Khan, Her Highness the Begum (1991) 'A personal message', in Whale and Dolphin Conservation Society, Why Whales?, Bath: WDCS.
Aron, W. (1988) 'The commons revisited: thoughts on marine mammal management', Coastal Management, 16: 99–110.
Ash, C. (1962) Whaler's Eye, New York: Macmillan.
Barstow, R. (1991) 'Whales are uniquely special', in Whale and Dolphin Conservation Society, Why Whales?, Bath: WDCS.
Besnier, N. (1990) 'Language and affect', Annual Review of Anthropology, 19: 419–51.
Brand, D. (1989) 'Profile: cutting his own path', Time, 21 August: 44–6.
Brown, M. and May, J. (1989) The Greenpeace Story, London: Dorling Kindersley.
Brydon, A. (1990) 'Icelandic nationalism and the whaling issue', North Atlantic Studies, 2 (1–2): 185–91.

Buttell, F.H. (1987) 'New directions in environmental sociology', *Annual Review of Sociology*, 13: 465–8.

Cherfas, J. (1989) *The Hunting of the Whale: A Tragedy That Must End*, London: Penguin.

D'Amato, A. and Chopra, S.K. (1991) 'Whales: their emerging right to life', *American Journal of International Law*, 85 (1): 21–62.

Fernandez, J.W. (1972) 'Persuasions and performances: of the beast in every body and the metaphors of everyman', *Daedalus*, 101 (1): 39–80.

—— (1986) *Persuasions and Performances: The Play of Tropes in Culture*, Bloomington: Indiana University Press.

—— (1991) 'Introduction: confluents on inquiry', in J.W. Fernandez (ed.) *Beyond Metaphor: The Theory of Tropes in Anthropology*, Stanford: Stanford University Press.

Gomez-Pompa, A. and Kaus, A. (1992) 'Taming the wilderness myth', *BioScience*, 42 (4): 271–9.

Johnson, C. (1991) *The Green Dictionary*, London: Optima.

Kaus, A. (1990) 'The conversation of conservation', paper given at American Anthropological Association meeting, New Orleans, 28 November–2 December 1990.

Keesing, R. (1987) 'Anthropology as interpretive quest', *Current Anthropology*, 28 (2): 161–76.

—— (1989) 'Exotic reading of cultural texts', *Current Anthropology*, 30 (4): 459–79.

Klinowska, M. (1992) 'Brains, behaviour and intelligence in cetaceans (whales, dolphins and porpoises)', in O.D. Jonsson (ed.) *Whales and Ethics*, Reykjavik: Fisheries Research Institute, University of Iceland Press.

Lakoff, G. and Johnson, M. (1980) *Metaphors We Live By*, Chicago: University of Chicago Press.

Leach, E. (1982) *Social Anthropology*, London: Fontana.

Lévi-Strauss, C. (1964) *Totemism*, London: Merlin.

Lockyer, C. (1990) 'Review of incidents involving wild sociable dolphins, worldwide', in S. Leatherwood and R.R. Reeves (eds) *The Bottlenose Dolphin*, San Diego: Academic Press.

Maddox, J. (1972) *The Doomsday Syndrome*, London: Macmillan.

Midgley, M. (1989) 'Are you an animal?', in G. Langley (ed.) *Animal Experimentation: The Consensus Changes*, London: Macmillan.

Ortner, S. (1973) 'On key symbols', *American Anthropologist*, 75 (5): 1338–46.

Payne, R. (1991) 'Is whaling justifiable on ethical and moral grounds?', in Whale and Dolphin Conservation Society, *Why Whales?*, Bath: WDCS.

Pearce, F. (1991) *Green Warriors: The People and the Politics Behind the Environmental Movement*, London: Bodley Head.

Quinn, N. (1991) 'The cultural basis of metaphor', in J.W. Fernandez (ed.) *Beyond Metaphor: The Theory of Tropes in Culture*, Stanford: Stanford University Press.

Rayner, S. (1989) 'Fiddling while the globe warms?', *Anthropology Today*, 5 (6): 1–2.

Schmink, M. (1990) 'Anthropologists and the global environment', *Anthropology Newsletter*, 31 (9): 8–9.

Wenzel, G. (1991) *Animal Rights, Human Rights: Ecology, Economy and Ideology in the Canadian Arctic*, London: Belhaven Press.

Whale and Dolphin Conservation Society (1991) *Why Whales?*, Bath: WDCS.

Willis, R. (1990) 'Introduction', in R. Willis (ed.) *Signifying Animals: Human Meaning in the Natural World*, London: Unwin Hyman.

Chapter 6

The making of an environmental doctrine

Public trust and American shellfishermen

Bonnie J. McCay

Anthropologists have given relatively little attention to the culture of the law in Euro-American settings. I do not mean that we have neglected study of the attitudes, values, class affiliations and so forth of attorneys and jurists. Nor do I necessarily mean the legal consciousness of people and their experiences with the formal institutions of the law. These are well defined as the proper domain of social scientists (e.g. Merry 1990), as have been the legal institutions and social and cultural dimensions of law in non-Western societies (e.g. Rosen 1989). What I mean is the set of symbolic constructs that makes up a particular body of law and that is used to underpin legal practice: concepts and doctrines and how they come about and change (see Starr 1989).

'Public trust' is one such construct. Its general meaning is self-evident: something is held in trust for the public. In law it has come to mean that certain kinds of property should be open to the public, subject to public rights of use, and managed for the public interest. Although the notion of public trust is sometimes used to support broad environmentalist claims, in precise renditions of the law it has an even more delimited referent: the foreshore and tidewaters.

The doctrine, which I will specify more fully below, has played a decisive ideological role in maintaining and changing structures of access to resources and responsibility for human impacts on nature. I am interested in how it has come about and how its changes and persistence are linked to the claims and contests of fishermen. My research into this topic has been organized around the court reports and rulings of shellfishery and fishery property cases heard in New Jersey's Supreme Court, federal district and circuit courts, and the US Supreme Court. It originated with studies of illegal fishing or 'poaching' in New Jersey and Europe (McCay 1981, 1984) and owes a heavy debt to the work of historians on rural crime and protests over enclosures in England (e.g. Thompson 1975, Reaney 1970, Archer 1990). It is part of my work on the human ecology of the commons (McCay and Acheson 1987). Similar stories can be told of Maryland (Power 1970, Kennedy and Breisch 1983) and Long Island (Gabriel 1921), although the federal public trust law arose specifically from the New Jersey conflicts.

THE PUBLIC TRUST DOCTRINE

According to the American public trust doctrine, the submerged lands of all navigable waters below high-tide mark are the property of the state, which holds this property in trust for the citizens of the state, who are the true owners. This hearkens to the English common-law understanding that the monarch owns such domains subject to public rights of navigation and fishing. By virtue of the American Revolution, the people became sovereign, and thus they own the muddy shores, the shifting sands, and the waters brushed and influenced by the tides. The states act as trustees on their behalf, and sometimes this is called 'state ownership'.

In legal theory the state does not own the fish and shellfish of those waters because they cannot be owned by anyone until captured, but US policy is that the individual states have management jurisdiction over the fisheries, shellfisheries and other extractive industries within three miles of the coastal baseline. Part of the public trust message is that the state governments should manage the waters for the benefit of the people. In addition, even if the resources are alienated from state 'ownership' or management, the 'public trust' remains in that the public continue to hold common rights for specific purposes, originally those of commerce, navigation and fishing, and now recreation. In English common law this is known as the *jus publicum*.

The doctrine is seen as an 'unusual legal doctrine' (Sax 1980: 485, Stevens 1980, Rose 1986) in continuing to support public interests and claims that are often vague, ill-defined and customary against private property claims that are definite and precise. Historically, as students of common rights in agrarian England have shown, the latter won out over the former in courts of law (Thompson 1976: 339–40).

Like much else symbolic and central to culture, the public trust doctrine is ambiguous and multivalent. As noted, it is peculiar in challenging the dominance of private property in ways that would seem to favour the relatively poor and powerless at a time when great fortunes and properties were being accumulated, during the rise of industrial capitalism, and legal institutions were bent and moulded to suit that process. On the other hand, a synonym for public trust is 'state ownership' (e.g. Territorial Sea 1982); this doctrine has been used as well to argue that the states are owners in fee, and that state legislatures and their administrative bodies can grant, sell and otherwise alienate the public trust to private owners.

Thus a central, difficult question concerns the meaning of proper stewardship or trusteeship: can the trustee sell off the resources of the trust or allocate them to private firms? Or are the public's rights inalienable? Negotiation over alternate meanings and their application to particular situations and bodies of fact is central to legal practice. In this chapter I offer instances of practice making culture, focusing on historical events through which the public trust doctrine was interpreted on the side of inalienability, which also, in its time (the nineteenth century), meant on the side of the poorer, fishing classes. The setting is the state of New Jersey, site of conflicts and legal decisions that were central to the development of the American public trust doctrine.

THE SHREWSBURY RIVER CASE

Clammers and oystermen of very humble circumstances in New Jersey were quick to turn to the law for redress of their complaints and support of their claims, suggesting that, whether rightly or not, they believed that the law could be impartial if not supportive (see Thompson 1975). The first fishing case to appear before New Jersey's supreme court is a case in point that also provides important context for the public trust cases, all of which included a claim to common right of fishery.

Oyster planting involves transplanting young oysters from their nursery beds to new ones, where they can be tended and kept until large enough to market. The method was just beginning in the northeastern region of the United States at the time of this case, but by 1808 it was well-enough established in the Shrewsbury area of New Jersey for a lawyer to note that, prior to the conflict to be described, the planters had exercised private property rights. However, these were only claims backed by local custom and by a gentlemen's agreement: 'recognized by a sort of tacit consent, and the property protected by mutual forbearance' (*Shepard* v. *Leverson* 1808: 373). Two oystermen, Shepard and Layton, upset this fragile applecart, we are told, because they were afraid that 'the whole of the river might be appropriated' by planters, destroying the right of common fishery (*Shepard* v. *Leverson* 1808: 270).

They took one thousand oysters that had been planted by one Leverson in a tidal river. Although the fine was only $3, the case was taken *on certiorari* to the state supreme court in order to 'try the right' because of its implications. The court held that Leverson was held to have no private property right. The court supported Shepard and Layton's claim to the planted oysters with the old English common-law test of 'abandonment'. By planting his oysters in a river that was clearly a 'public navigable river and highway, where the tide flowed and reflowed' (*Shepard* v. *Leverson* 1808: 274), and especially in a river where oysters naturally grew, Leverson had abandoned them to the public. Accordingly, before the law, men surely perceived as thieves and 'pirates' by an entrepreneur like Leverson were simply 'commoners' exercising their rights.

In arguing the case, the possibility was raised that by heavy harvesting, oystermen could create 'barren' oyster lands out of 'natural' ones and appropriate the whole river (*Shepard* v. *Leverson* 1808: 270). The argument underscores the class basis of the problem: people depending on wild fisheries were afraid of losing access because of the rise of planting, which was, and continued to be, dominated by people who had superior positions with respect to capital and markets.

'TO TRY THE RIGHT'

It often appears that the conflicts that led people to the courts were engineered for that purpose, to invoke judgement about larger issues of right and policy, 'to try the right'. I will offer two further instances: first, the case of *Arnold* v. *Mundy* (1821), which led to establishment of the public trust doctrine as law in America, and second, the oyster wars on Delaware Bay, in which fishermen tried, again, to make public trust a reality against attempts to privatize the commons.

Arnold v. *Mundy*: the first American construction of public trust

Arnold v. *Mundy* (1821) was a New Jersey Supreme Court case that considered access to oystering lands in the Raritan River. The contest concerned the rights of a property-owner, Robert Arnold, who gained title through the colonial proprietors, versus people who claimed common rights of fishing. The proprietors were a corporate body created in the seventeenth century to encourage European settlement and development of New Jersey. The 'commoners' were oystermen out of the township of Woodbridge. Arnold had a survey done and planted oysters on tidal land that he claimed was his through the proprietors; this he did to 'try the right', as there had been a history of trouble over similar attempts to claim private property in oysters on the river.

Benajah Mundy led a fleet of skiffs from Woodbridge across the river to the water off Arnold's farm, and took oysters from the planted bed. The lawyer for the Woodbridge men claimed that they took the oysters 'merely with a view of trying the plaintiff's pretended right, and not with a view of injuring the bed or taking the oysters further than was necessary for the purpose' (*Arnold* v. *Mundy* 1821: 2).

The Chief Justice, Andrew Kirkpatrick, held that Mundy and his friends from Woodbridge had the common right of fishing and thus the right to take oysters from the place off Arnold's farm. He ruled more broadly that the colonial proprietors had no business granting out property in tidal lands, below mean high-water mark, because, according to English common law, that property was special: it belonged to the sovereign, the king or queen in England and, in post-Revolutionary America, to the people, through their elected representatives. This came to be known as 'state ownership'. That ownership was really a prerogative exercised as a trusteeship for the common benefit of all the citizens, the idea of 'public trust': 'the property, indeed, strictly speaking, is vested in the sovereign, but it is vested in him not for his own use, but for the use of the citizen, that is, for his direct and immediate enjoyment' (*Arnold* v. *Mundy* 1821: 77). As such, the power of ownership could not be used to convert such lands to the private use of individuals. Common rights were inalienable.

A closely related oystering conflict, which took place in the same place but ten years later, eventually led to the US Supreme Court, where Chief Justice Roger Taney agreed with Kirkpatrick about the doctrines of state ownership and public trust for property washed by the tides (*Martin v. Waddell's Lessee* 1842). Thus was borne into federal law the public trust doctrine, which holds that states 'own' submerged soil and foreshore of all navigable and/or tidal bodies of water. It became firmly embedded in American constitutional law after *Martin v. Waddell's Lessee*, and its 'public trust' aspect was recognized as such in *Illinois Central Railroad v. The State of Illinois* (1892), where the highest court held that the Illinois state legislature did not have the right to give most of Chicago's waterfront property to a railroad.

On cultural invention and the law

Conflicts about rights to oysters and oystering grounds went quickly to court, and in the course of deciding them the judges 'Americanized' English common law (cf. Nelson 1975). Public trust/state ownership law is a particularly complex and interesting case of Americanization. The people involved did not seem to intend to create something different; they invoked English common law (and natural law) as their authority. But American public trust was new. In addition, the English common law used to legitimize it was itself a remarkable 'invention' based on specious authority from the past (Moore 1888, Anonymous 1970, Johnson and Johnson 1975, MacGrady 1975).

To summarize what must be a long exegesis about Roman, early English, Renaissance and later law is beyond the scope of this chapter. Two points about the construction of English common law can be briefly noted: first, English legal scholars reinterpreted Roman law to fit the English case, giving rise to the fiction that whatever was not owned by individuals must be owned by the monarch; and second, the notion that the monarch really owned foreshores and tidal waters appeared in the Elizabethan era as a money-making scheme; for some reason it was elevated by influential jurists into sacred principle much later without real support from common law.

The nineteenth-century American lawyers, judges and treatise writers who dealt with foreshore and tidewater cases relied on a few of the English sources, particularly Sir Matthew Hale, but constructed their own understanding of the law (MacGrady 1975). One part concerned equating navigability with tidality to determine the boundaries of the *jus publicum*, or public rights of navigation, fishing, etc. Ironically, by 1868 English judges were citing American jurists as authority for a ruling that merged bed rights with fishing rights and navigability with tidality, holding that an Irish river, where fishing rights were in dispute, was not 'technically' navigable if it was not tidal (MacGrady 1975: 586). The other important change concerned the nature of the sovereign's ownership. The English jurists (particularly Sir

Matthew Hale) recognized that the foreshore may be part of a manor or belong to a subject; ownership is only '*prima facie*' in the monarch, referring to an evidentiary presumption rather than a rule of substantive law as many of the American writers would have it. In other words, in English common law, ownership was considered a question of fact, of evidence, and from there it was assumed that the monarch was owner unless someone had evidence otherwise (through grant, 'presumption' or custom). But as the public trust doctrine developed in America, the state was owner of tidewater lands as a matter of principle, not just fact. Title from any source other than the state was contestable.

The oyster wars on Delaware Bay

Once invented in America and reinvented in Great Britain, the various aspects of the public trust doctrine underwent more confusion and re-construction than ever, particularly in the nineteenth century when riparian claims were important not only to fishermen but also, and most of all, to people working for industrial development. The oystermen and their problems continued to play an important role in bringing the attention of courts to bear on the critical question of the alienability of the public trust.

By 1850 in the Delaware Bay region of New Jersey, a major centre of oyster planting, the state had begun to sanction leases for oyster planting in a system run by an association of oystermen. In this system, certain oyster beds 'up the bay' were designated off limits to planting and leasing. The general and legal principle was and is that all natural oyster beds must remain common property, open to everyone with a licence, and may not be privatized through lease or sale. The oyster beds up the bay are the primary source of the young 'seed' oysters that are planted down the bay.

Between 1879 and 1893 a few enterprising oystermen got grants from the state Riparian Commission to about six miles of the bay shore that included some of the natural oyster beds (New Jersey Riparian Commissioners 1890, Hall 1894, New Jersey Bureau of Statistics of Labor and Industries 1897). This happened even though the law (a) did not allow grants of natural, i.e. productive, shellfish beds; and (b) specifically forbade the use of riparian grants for shellfish propagation. The Riparian Commission was always being accused of and investigated for corrupt activities, including overlooking the fine points of the law.

There were 'frequent collisions and arrests' between the riparian grantees and others in the oystering community who objected (New Jersey Bureau of Statistics of Labor and Industry 1897: 5). Some of the conflicts seem to have been orchestrated by lawyers. One in 1893–4 clearly was. In the spring of 1893, the lawyer for the local oystermen's association advised one of the members to take oysters from one of the disputed riparian grounds (Hall 1894: 519). He did, after giving notice to the owner, and was arrested.

Meanwhile the lawyer advised another test case, and at a meeting on 19 March 1894, members of the association decided to mount a collective assault on the riparian grantees by creating a test case that would, they hoped, defend the common property rights of everyone to the oystering lands 'up the bay'. They imposed a tonnage tax on all vessels to help pay the legal expenses and published their intent in the newspaper. A lawyer for the riparian grantees published a warning in the paper, not only that the proposed raid 'may, and in the ordinary course of human events, will, naturally lead to serious breaches of the peace, and perhaps even to graver results' (Anonymous 1894: 156), but also that the county would be held liable for damages. So the county sheriff obtained a steam vessel and organized a *posse comitatus*, warning a few boats off. All was quiet and the posse disbanded.

Sheriff and posse gone, the war began on 12 April 1894:

> in order that there might be a final settlement of the question in dispute and the rights of both parties defined, by advice of counsel various oystermen on a certain day in April, 1894, went upon these grounds and took oysters.
>
> (New Jersey Bureau of Statistics of Labor and Industries 1897: 6)

> Soon after [the sheriff's] departure many vessels appeared and began dredging. One of the riparian owners shot at the invaders for the purpose of frightening them off. Over thirty persons were subsequently arrested and held for court.
>
> (Hall 1894: 520)

Newspapers declared a major war and widespread social and economic disruption. Some cases went to court, where at least some of the riparian grants were seen as invalid. The legal cases that arose from this conflict and surfaced at higher and thus retrievable levels of New Jersey's court system are *Zebulon Polhemus* v. *The State of New Jersey* (1894) and *Polhemus* v. *Bateman* (1897). The deed given to Bateman, the riparian grantee, by the state riparian commissioners gave him the land under water adjacent to his 70 acres of shore property, plus 'the right, liberty, privilege and franchise' to build dikes to drain the lands, to fill the lands, to otherwise improve it, and 'to appropriate the lands above described to his exclusive private uses' (*Polhemus* v. *Bateman* 1897: 164). Since Bateman had used those underwater lands only to plant oysters or oyster shells (and perhaps take natural oysters), he did not qualify for the privilege of 'exclusive appropriation'. The privilege was contingent upon making improvements, which he had not pretended to do: 'The grant was only for the purpose of reclamation' (*Polhemus* v. *Bateman* 1897: 168). Thus Zebulon Polhemus and the other oystermen could take oysters there under common right.

The major consequence was that the state legislature created an investigating committee, appropriated money to buy out the riparian grantees, and articulated the public trust policy, as in this statement by the state shellfish bureau, discussing the oyster war:

> We sincerely trust that never again will there be a private ownership of the natural oyster beds in the bay . . . We are opposed to either selling or leasing any of the natural beds above the southwest line. These oyster beds are the natural heritage of all the people of the State, and should be forever preserved and kept sacred to the free public use of the inhabitants of the State, except in so far as their use may be reasonably regulated to prevent destruction.
>
> (New Jersey Bureau of Shellfisheries 1904: 40)

Just so the public trust was revived, through the actions of outraged oyster-men and the responses of government officials.

IMPLICATIONS AND EXPANSION OF PUBLIC TRUST IN AMERICA

The courts' interpretations of the public trust or state ownership nature of tidewater lands and resources extinguished some attempts to develop local institutions for managing marine resources. For example, in Cape May County, New Jersey, associations were formed in the early 1800s to manage 'the natural privileges', i.e. hunting, fishing, shellfishing and fowling in the county's wet-lands and inshore waters. Although evidence is unclear, it seems probable that the public trust rulings forced the associations to disband.

However, in shellfishing the pattern that emerged was what we would today call 'co-management': the state gave legitimacy and a little enforce-ment and fiscal support to locally run management groups. A true state bureaucracy devoted to fish and shellfish matters did not emerge until the mid-twentieth century, and even now it depends to some extent on local management, especially in the Delaware Bay region. The definition of 'public' and determinations of public interest can support such local-level or special-interest management even though other interpretations can challenge and undermine it.

On the national level, the ideology of public trust is sometimes brought up in connection with management of marine fisheries, particularly since 1977, when the federal government was forced to become very active because of the creation of a 200-mile zone of exclusive fisheries jurisdiction. In 1990 the first management plan to allocate private rights to fish resources went into effect, although government lawyers were careful to recast 'rights' into 'privileges'. The annual quotas for surf clams and ocean quahogs are divided into percentage shares that are allocated to owners of the 'privileges'. The shares can be freely bought, sold, leased or inherited. This way of managing marine fisheries is increasingly popular throughout the world because it deals directly with the social dilemma of open access. Does it alienate public trust and extinguish common property rights? The question is still an open one in the US as in Canada and Iceland, which have similar legal traditions and customary understandings.

Public trust doctrine has been generalized far beyond foreshores and tidewaters. A first, important, step was the inclusion of common rights for purposes of recreation, as well as serious fishing and navigation. This has made the doctrine central to coastal zone management. It was a long time coming. In 1821 an English court refused to expand the trust to include the right of bathing; apparently public bathing was too unseemly for some of the judges to agree that people should have the right to pass over sands owned by the lord of a manor on the Mersey river to engage in it (see discussion in Angell 1847: 28–35, Appendix, i–xl). However, since the 1970s at least, courts have recognized its expansion by upholding the public right to use the banks and foreshores of the ocean for recreational purposes.

An important New Jersey case was *Borough of Neptune City* v. *Borough of Avon-By-The-Sea* (1972, Jaffee 1974). There, Judge Hall, who explicitly resurrected the full public trust doctrine of *Arnold* v. *Mundy*, said:

> We have no difficulty in finding that, in this latter half of the twentieth century, the public rights in tidal lands are not limited to the ancient prerogatives of navigation and fishing, but extend as well to recreational uses, including bathing, swimming and other shore activities. The public trust doctrine, like all common law principles, should not be considered fixed or static, but should be molded and extended to meet changing conditions and needs of the public it was created to benefit.
>
> (Borough, quoted in Goldschore 1979)

The concept of public trust has become extremely important in the adjudication of cases concerning public rights of access to the beaches of New Jersey (*Matthews* v. *Bay Head Improvement Assoc., Inc.* 1984). The concept has also gained new strength as part of the environmental movement of the 1960s and 1970s. An article by Joseph Sax, 'The public trust doctrine in natural resource law: effective judicial intervention' (1970), provoked and guided a revival of legal scholarship into public trust law (Anonymous 1970, Jaffee 1971, Johnson and Johnson 1975, MacGrady 1975, Stevens 1980, and more). Sax and others helped incorporate (and revive) the doctrine of public trust into the rhetoric and practice of state and federal government agencies venturing into environmental protection and coastal zone management (Stevens 1980). Environmentalists are now challenging state, federal and regional agencies with mandates for marine resource and environmental management to improve their stewardship over the public trust.

CONCLUSION

As suggested in the cases reviewed and supported by a much larger study, the intended and unintended actions of oystermen and clammers contributed to debates about and construction of the meaning of public trust in America. Even when the public trust seemed little more than a misleading gloss for fee simple, alienable state property – like used office desks – oystermen, clammers and others dependent on common rights to marine resources continued to insist on those rights, particularly against attempts to create private property in oyster-planting grounds. Through their actions they helped keep the public trust a possibility and, from time to time, a reality, while in turn lawyers and judges played their parts in defining permissible and actionable reality.

The public trust in shellfish lands was maintained in state and federal court decisions and through policies established after conflicts and 'wars' like the ones that took place in response to riparian grants of shellfishing grounds. The policies remained the same over a long period of time, but this was no artifact of a distant historical event. Cultural persistence, as well as cultural change, was a product of the actions of people engaged in similar conflicts over time; the public trust requires constant vigilance and organized conflicts to keep it from changing.

REFERENCES

Angell, J. (1847) *A Treatise on the Right of Property in Tide Waters and in the Soil and Shores Thereof.*

Anonymous (1894) 'Oysters and the riparian grantees', *New Jersey Law Journal*, 17: 155–7.

—— (1970) 'The public trust in tidal areas: a sometimes submerged traditional doctrine', *Yale Law Review*, 79: 762–89.

Archer, J.E. (1990) *By a Flash and a Scare: Incendiarism, Animal Maiming, and Poaching in East Anglia 1815–1870*, Oxford: Clarendon Press.

Gabriel, R.H. (1921) *The Evolution of Long Island: A Story of Land and Sea*, Port Washington, New York: Ira J. Friedman.

Goldschore, L.P. (1979) *The New Jersey Riparian Rights Handbook* (2nd edition), prepared for the County and Municipal Government Commission, Trenton, New Jersey.

Hall, A. (1894) 'Notes on the oyster industry of New Jersey', in *Report of the Commission* (US Commission of Fish and Fisheries) for the year ending 30 June 1892: 463–528, Washington: Government Printing Office.

Jaffee, L.R. (1971) 'State citizen rights respecting great-water resource allocation: from Rome to New Jersey', *Rutgers Law Review*, 25 (4): 571–710.

—— (1974) 'The public trust doctrine is alive and kicking in New Jersey tidalwaters: Neptune City v. Avon-by-the-Sea – a case of happy atavism?', *Natural Resources Journal*, 14: 309–35.

Johnson, J.J. and Johnson, C.F. III (1975) 'The Mississippi public trust doctrine: public and private rights in the coastal zone', *Mississippi Law Journal*, 46 (1): 84–117.

Kennedy, V.S. and Breisch, L.L. (1983) 'Sixteen decades of political management of the oyster fishery in Maryland's Chesapeake Bay', *Journal of Environmental Management*, 16: 153–71.

MacGrady, G.J. (1975) 'The navigability concept in the civil and common law: historical development, current importance, and some doctrines that don't hold water', *Florida State University Law Review*, 3: 511–615.

McCay, B.J. (1981) 'Optimal foragers or political actors? Ecological analyses of a New Jersey fishery', *American Ethnologist*, 8: 356–82.
—— (1984) 'The pirates of Piscary: ethnohistory of illegal fishing in New Jersey', *Ethnohistory*, 31: 17–37.
McCay, B.J. and Acheson, J.M. (eds) (1987) *The Question of the Commons: The Culture and Ecology of Communal Resources*, Tucson: University of Arizona Press.
Merry, S.E. (1990) *Getting Justice and Getting Even: Legal Consciousness among Working-Class Americans*, Chicago: University of Chicago Press.
Moore, S.A. (1888) *A History of the Foreshore and the Law Relating Thereto: With a Hitherto Unpublished Treatise by Lord Hale, Lord Hale's 'De Jure Maris', and Hall's Essay on the Rights of the Crown in the Seashore* (3rd edition), London: Stevens and Haynes.
Nelson, W.E. (1975) *Americanization of the Common Law: The Impact of Legal Change on Massachusetts Society, 1760–1830*, Cambridge, Massachusetts: Harvard University Press.
New Jersey Bureau of Shellfisheries (1904) *Annual Report*, Trenton, NJ.
New Jersey Bureau of Statistics of Labor and Industries (1897) *Nineteenth Annual Report, for Year Ending October 31st, 1896*, Trenton, Part I, The Oyster Industry of New Jersey.
New Jersey Riparian Commissioners (1890) Annual Report of the Riparian Commissioners of the State of New Jersey 1889, *N.J. Legislative Documents* 1890, III.
Power, G. (1970) 'More about oysters than you wanted to know', *Maryland Law Review*, 30 (3): 199–225.
Reaney, B. (1970) *The Class Struggle in 19th Century Oxfordshire: The Social and Communal Background to the Otmoor Disturbances of 1830 to 1835*, History Workshop Pamphlet 3, Oxford: History Workshop, Ruskin College.
Rose, C. (1986) 'The comedy of the commons: custom, commerce, and inherently public property', *The University of Chicago Law Review*, 53 (3): 711–81.
Rosen, L. (1989) *The Anthropology of Justice: Law as Culture in Islamic Society*, Cambridge: Cambridge University Press.
Sax, J.L. (1970) 'The public trust doctrine in natural resource law: effective judicial intervention', *Michigan Law Review*, 68: 471–5.
—— (1980) 'Liberating the public trust doctrine from its historical shackles', *U.C. Davis Law Review*, 14 (2): 185–94.
Starr, J. (1989) 'The "invention" of early legal ideas: Sir Henry Maine and the perpetual tutelage of women', in J. Starr and J. Collier (eds) *History and Power in the Study of Law*, Ithaca, New York: Cornell University Press.
Stevens, J.S. (1980) 'The public trust: a sovereign's ancient prerogative becomes the people's environmental right', *U.C. Davis Law Review*, 14 (2): 195–232.
Territorial Sea (1982) 'Tangier Sound Waterman's Association v. Douglas: Chesapeake Bay blue crab restrictions held unconstitutional', *Territorial Sea*, 2 (2): 2–5, 10–12.
Thompson, E.P. (1975) *Whigs and Hunters: The Origins of the Black Act*, London: Allen Lane.
—— (1976) 'The grid of inheritance: a comment', in J. Goody, J. Thirsk and E.P. Thompson (eds) *Family and Inheritance: Rural Society in Western Europe, 1200–1800*, Cambridge: Cambridge University Press.

Court cases

Arnold v. *Mundy* (1821) 6 New Jersey Laws 1 (Sup. Ct. 1821).
Borough of Neptune City v. *Borough of Avon-By-The-Sea* (1972) 61 New Jersey Laws 296, 294 A.2d 47.

Illinois Central Railroad v. *The State of Illinois* (1892) 146 U.S. 387, 435 (1892).

Martin v. *Waddell's Lessee* (1842) 41 U.S. (16 Peters) 367.

Matthews v. *Bay Head Improvement Assoc., Inc.* (1984) 95 New Jersey Laws 306, 471 A.2d 355 (1987).

Polhemus v. *Bateman* (1897) 37 A. 1015, 60 New Jersey Laws 163.

Pollard's Lessee v. *Hagan* (1845) 44 U.S. (3 How.) 212.

Shepard v. *Leverson* (1808) 2 New Jersey Laws 391 (N.J. Sup.).

Zebulon Polhemus v. *The State of New Jersey* (1894) 57 New Jersey Laws 348–51.

Chapter 7

The precautionary principle

Use with caution!

Lynda M. Warren

Although, as is described below, environmental legislation is not a new branch of law, changes in political and social perceptions of the environment have led to subtle changes in approach. The environment now occupies a central place on the international political agenda, and policies for environmental protection are recognized as being worthy in their own right and not just as adjuncts to other policies. The elevation in importance of the environment has not, however, been matched by an increase in the understanding of the environment by those charged with making policies and laws to protect it. It is, in fact, very difficult for any one individual to gain a full, broad understanding.

The single most important characteristic of the environment is that it is multi-faceted. Depending on one's viewpoint, it is a concept that incorporates scientific facts (real or imagined) about physical surroundings and/or the social, and even political, framework through which this physical world impacts on people.

Unfortunately, it is the scientific dimension of the environment that comes to the forefront in the formulation of government policy and legislation. The need for environmental protection, especially the control of pollution, is defined in terms of the physical damage that will result. There is an implied assumption that the degree of risk can be quantified by measuring changes in concentrations of pollutants and computing the toxicity from laboratory experiments.

This is not to say that the social element of environmental protection is discounted but rather that it is taken for granted. The summary of the evolution of environmental law given below supports the idea that modern environmental law is different because it is about the environment and not just about the people living in that environment. The emphasis then is on moving away from a purely anthropocentric approach that views the environment in terms of its immediate impact on people to a recognition that the environment needs protection for itself. This, effectively, means that the human element is ignored. Instead scientific criteria are used to provide the basis for the new laws.

Newby (1991) has expressed concern at the failure of sociologists to contribute fully to the study of the environment and presents a strong case for the integration of scientific or technical approaches and sociological ones.[1] He does not, however, question the validity of the scientific part of the equation. Others have done just this.[2] It is not the purpose of this chapter to enter into this argument but rather to address an issue that is of relevance for any approach to environmental matters and of crucial importance to the formulation of environmental policy. This is the inability of specialists in different disciplines to understand and communicate with each other. The problem is exacerbated because, in many instances, the same terminology is used but in different senses. While the problem is general and widespread, it is addressed here with specific reference to environmental law and policy in Britain.

Leaving aside the question of the appropriate balance between the different disciplinary threads contributing to environmental policy, I think there is an urgent need to address the problem of disciplinary barriers that, at best, frustrate effective communication and, at worst, can be used deliberately to mislead. Ravetz (1990) likens scientific experts dealing with complex environmental problems to amateurs and mere contributors to a dialogue in which other disciplines participate. He goes on to say that the 'critical assessment of their information, in the context of its use, is a task for all participants, and not merely those with narrowly defined, technical expertise'.[3] Unfortunately, critical assessment can only be achieved through knowledge and understanding, and in contemporary British society it is all too easy to be blinded by science.

BACKGROUND TO ENVIRONMENTAL LAW IN BRITAIN

Statutory law affecting the environment has developed along three main lines: pollution law, planning law and conservation law. It is at least arguable that, in all three branches of environmental law, the primary motive has been to protect humankind rather than the environment as such. Thus, pollution law has its origins in public health measures introduced during the last century to combat serious disease epidemics brought about by the combined effects of industrialization and urbanization (for further details see Hughes 1992). The objective of pollution law may be summarized as the protection of human populations and their natural resources from damage. Similarly, planning law is geared towards achieving a suitable balance between development and aesthetics. Again, it developed from a desire to address the social problems caused by industrial sprawl into rural areas. Landscape conservation, which evolved alongside planning control, is also viewed from the human perspective with the emphasis on public enjoyment and access. Only in the case of wildlife conservation is the environment in a central position. Even here, however, the selection of species for protection is reflective of their popularity and proximity to humankind. Thus, the Wildlife and Countryside Act 1981 includes four schedules exclusively on birds but only one on plants, and even this is heavily biased towards flowering plants (for further details of the history of conservation law see Warren 1991).

The last few years have seen a major change in emphasis on the environment at government level. Ever since Margaret Thatcher (1988) made her speech to the Royal Society acknowledging the need to nurture the environment, environmental matters have played a prominent role in the political agenda. There is now an acceptance, in theory, that it is no longer enough just to protect the environment in those instances where its health impinges directly on our well-being. Real environmental protection thus means looking after the environment both for its own sake and because one can never tell how it may affect us in the future.

While this is a laudable objective, it is a very tall order to put into practice. The environment is all encompassing and environmental matters are of relevance to all sectors of government (as acknowledged by the appointment of ministers responsible for the environmental affairs of each government department). Above all there is a need to think big, i.e. to consider the consequences of any given action on all aspects of the environment and not just the direct effects (see, for example, the incorporation of BATNEEC[4] principles into pollution controls); to consider the long-term effects of action and not just the immediate effects (the problems of methane accumulation in landfill sites and the effects of CFCs – chlorofluorocarbons – on the ozone layer are just two examples); and to integrate environmental policies into management (for example, through environmental assessments and audits).

If this new-style environmental philosophy is to be put into practice, it requires people with the right qualifications and experience to carry it through at all levels within the legislature, the executive and the judiciary. Unfortunately, for the most part, these people do not exist. There is no requirement for academic qualifications in any particular discipline for entry into these professions. In law, the legal qualifications can all be obtained at postgraduate level and practical training is of great importance. The same is true of the administrative Civil Service, where even a non-graduate can progress through the system. Once qualified, lawyers will tend to concentrate on a particular area of law and become more specialized. Civil servants, on the other hand, are likely to be moved from job to job in order to broaden their experience and develop administrative skills.

Given the lack of preference for any particular academic speciality it might be expected that students of all disciplines would be equally attracted to the professions. This is not the case, of course, and all three branches tend to be arts-oriented, with relatively few people with advanced qualifications in science.

In recognition of the inability of administrators to deal, unaided, with all matters, there are well-established sources of advice. Legal advice, for example, may be obtained from the Treasury Solicitor or from in-house lawyers; scientific advice on conservation matters is available from the various nature conservancy agencies; policy ideas can be tested through consultation papers. Within Parliament, members rely heavily on non-governmental bodies for information; select committees can appoint specialist advisers knowledgeable in the topic under consideration.

Advice alone, however, is not enough. In order to make full use of it, the recipient must have a sound grasp of the basic principles involved. This is especially the case with the new approach to environmental policy, where the ramifications of one policy decision may potentially affect areas un-thought of and about which, therefore, no advice has been sought.

Scientific advice is needed in all three organs of state. Thus the senior civil servant will need advice in formulating ideas for legislation, and the parliamentary draftsman or draftswoman will need advice to translate these ideas into draft legislation. During the bill's passage through Parliament, members will rely on the lobby to advise them on amendments. Later, when the Act comes to be construed in court, scientific information may be heard in evidence. At local level, the administrator will need advice, in the form of government circulars, as to how to implement the legislation. The following section includes examples of situations in which a scientific understanding is needed.

THE NEED FOR SCIENTIFIC UNDERSTANDING IN LEGISLATION

Pollution

The legal definition of 'pollution' provides a good example of the confusion that can arise where scientific implications are not fully considered. There are several scientific definitions of pollution. The most comprehensive is probably that presented by Holdgate (1979: 17), which is based on the definition used by the United Nations Joint Group of Experts on the Scientific Aspects of Marine Pollution: 'The introduction by man into the environment of substances or energy liable to cause hazards to human health, harm to living resources and ecological systems, damage to structures or amenity or interferences with legitimate uses of the environment'. This definition incorporates an element of social acceptability that is more pronounced in the following one: 'The consequences of discharge into the environment of materials which, in the short or long term, are offensive and socially un-acceptable' (Select Committee on the European Communities 1983: ix).

The various definitions of pollution included in the Environmental Protection Act 1990 are closer to the first definition, but put the emphasis very much on the protection of the environment for its own sake. The definitions are expressed in scientifically definable terms. Section 1(3) defines pollution for the purposes of integrated pollution control as: 'Pollution of the environment due to the release (into any environmental medium) from any process of substances which are capable of causing harm to man or any other living organism supported by the environment'. Harm is defined in Section 1(4) as:

'Harm to the health of living organisms or other interference with the ecological systems of which they form a part and, in the case of man, includes offence caused to any of his senses or harm to his property'.

The references to interference with ecological systems and harm to the health of living organisms make the definition too broad. It totally ignores the social aspects of pollution which might, for example, allow that some harm is acceptable if it only targets organisms which there is no desire or need to protect. Similar problems arise in interpreting the meaning of 'pollution of the environment' in relation to waste management under Part IV of the Act. Adams (1992) questions whether the most important provision in this Part, which makes it an offence to treat, keep or dispose of waste in a manner likely to cause pollution of the environment, will be much used, because of the poorly drafted definition.

Genetically modified organisms

Under the Environmental Protection Act 1990, the Secretary of State is empowered to make regulations to control the release of genetically modified organisms so as to prevent pollution. As with other enabling statutes, the precise details of control are left to the regulations themselves. The Act itself creates three levels of control but does not define how these should be applied in relation to particular classes of organism. Indeed, so much is left to the subordinate legislation that it is difficult to assess the likely effect of the Act.

The reason for leaving so much to delegated legislation is to free Parliament from the task of drawing up detailed laws that may need to be changed in the near future. It is doubtful, however, whether most members of Parliament would have felt competent to contribute to the debate anyway. Draft regulations were issued for consultation in October 1991.[5] They show signs of multiple authorship. Thus, there are detailed requirements for recording each stage of the manipulative procedures that are couched in technical jargon. Where a deliberate release is proposed, a long list of environmental information must be amassed and reported. To a non-specialist, the list looks comprehensive, covering everything from an ecological survey of the release site to data on the known effects of the organism on target species. In practice, obtaining the information may prove prohibitively expensive and may not even be of use in risk assessment. The emphasis on the acquisition of data masks the fact that prediction is very difficult.

THE NEED FOR SCIENTIFIC UNDERSTANDING IN ADMINISTRATION

Several of the advances in environmental protection have come out of international or European initiatives. In negotiating the text of agreements at these levels, it is often preferable not to seek precise definitions of all the terms but to allow each party a degree of flexibility (for further details of approaches to international environmental regulation see Birnie 1992). Such imprecision is an anathema to the scientist and it is not surprising that when scientific terms are used in this way confusion results.

The precautionary principle

The best example is provided by the interpretation of the 'precautionary principle'. The UK government first endorsed the use of this term at the Second International Conference on the Protection of the North Sea, in London in November 1987, where it was agreed to apply it in relation to the release of certain polluting substances into the North Sea.

Under the name *Vorsorgeprinzip*, the principle had been worked up in Germany and formed part of the Federal Government's *Guidelines on Antici-patory Environmental Protection*. As expressed in this document, the principle is really nothing more than the 'legitimate embodiment of normal conservatism and common sense' (Bewers 1989: 15). The wording in the text of the North Sea Declaration echoes these sentiments. There was agreement to:

accept the principle of safeguarding the marine ecosystem of the North Sea by reducing polluting emissions of substances that are persistent, toxic and liable to bioaccumulate at source . . . This applies especially when there is reason to assume that certain damage or harmful effects on the living resources of the sea are likely to be caused by such substances, even when there is no scientific evidence to prove a causal link between emissions and effects.

(Department of the Environment 1988: 9)

The principle is thus an acknowledgement that the system is so complex that it may be impossible to obtain statistical proof of cause and effect, at any rate within a meaningful timescale. The principle has been adopted in a number of international agreements (see Freestone 1991).

Unfortunately, as Gray (1990) points out, the principle can be used to take the objectivity out of scientific judgement by giving undue weight to results that are not statistically significant if they show a trend in the right direction. Material distributed by Greenpeace at the Irish Sea Conference in 1990 seems to confirm these fears by stating that the principle involves 'eliminating and preventing pollution emissions where there is reason to believe that damage or harmful effects are likely to be caused, even where there is *inadequate* or inconclusive scientific evidence to prove a causal link between emissions and effects' (emphasis added). In practice, Greenpeace appear to go even further by contending that the principle means that no activity that might impact upon the environment shall be allowed to proceed unless it can be shown that it will, in fact, be harmless.

The government, on the other hand, has narrowed the principle. Although there is no definition of the phrase from a UK viewpoint, the White Paper on the Environment, *This Common Inheritance*, describes the government's approach to precautionary action as follows:

> Where there are significant risks of damage to the environment, the Government will be prepared to take precautionary action to limit the use of potentially dangerous materials or the spread of potentially dangerous pollutants, even where scientific knowledge is not conclusive, if the balance of likely costs and benefits justifies it.
>
> (HMSO 1990: 11)

This is not the place to discuss further what the term actually means. Suffice it to say that it appears to mean different things to different people (see, for example, Gray 1990, Earll 1992). The confusion would seem to result from the juxtaposition of scientific reasoning and administrative policy within a single principle.

Environmental assessment

Under regulations implementing the EEC directive on the assessment of the effects of certain public and private projects on the environment (85/337/EEC), local planning authorities and others are responsible firstly for deciding whether an assessment is necessary and then for making the assessment. Both functions require a level of scientific understanding that is not generally available in-house. In deciding whether to require an assessment the authority is assisted by various government circulars and guidelines (Department of the Environment 1991). It may also consult locally with interested parties such as the local county wildlife trust. Its actual assessment, should one be required, is based on the environmental statement made by the developer.

THE NEED FOR SCIENTIFIC UNDERSTANDING IN THE COURTS

Scientific evidence can play an extremely important part in court proceedings. As with any other evidence, the court must assess its validity. Because scientific reasoning is outside of the experience of most people, including the judiciary, the task may not always be easy. In many cases, scientific evidence is taken at face value because the means of questioning it are not part of the legal repertoire. Recent cases involving forensic evidence demonstrate the problems that can result.

Scientific values can also distort judgments. The case of *R. v. Azadehdel*[6] provides an illustration. The case was brought under regulations giving effect to the Convention on International Trade in Endangered Species (CITES). The defendant was found guilty of various offences consisting of dealing with specimens of rare orchids without a licence. He was well known to the authorities at the Royal Botanical Gardens at Kew (the body responsible for advising on plant licences under the Convention) as an expert on orchids and was party to scientific discussions with them. On inspection of his property, it was discovered that he had many protected orchids, of a total value exceeding £40,000, under illegal propagation. He was fined £10,000 and sentenced to twelve months' imprisonment, eight months of it suspended, and ordered to pay £10,000 prosecution costs. On appeal against sentence, the fine was reduced to £2,500 and the term of imprisonment shortened to six months suspended. The order for costs was remitted. The court used scientific values in reaching these decisions. It was held that, seen in the light of the full scope of the Convention, the offences did not merit such severe penalties. The Convention protects animals as well as plants and it was decided that trade in, for example, ivory, which necessitated the deaths of elephants, was more serious than the collection of entire plants from the wild which could then be propagated in cultivation. On face value, the logic seems sound enough, until it is realized that cultivated plants become inbred and can seldom be returned to the wild. In the case of very rare plants, such as the slipper orchids taken by Mr Azadehdel, collection can decrease the wild population to such low numbers that it is no longer viable.

In another case,[7] Mr Justice Schiemann upheld Poole Borough Council's decision to grant itself planning permission for the development of a Site of Special Scientific Interest (SSSI) of such international importance that it was a candidate Special Protection Area under the EEC Birds Directive (79/409/EEC), even though the authority had failed to consider whether or not an environmental assessment was necessary under the Town and Country Planning (Assessment of Environmental Effects) Regulations 1988. The judge held that the planning authority members had considered environmental factors in reaching their decision and that, as this was the whole purpose of a formal assessment anyway, the authority had not failed to take account of all material considerations. The judgement fails to consider the possibility that, had the planning authority properly directed its attention to the need for an environmental assessment, it would have looked at the issue in isolation rather than as part of the overall balancing act involved in any planning application. Had it then decided that an assessment was necessary, the information submitted might have led the authority to give greater weight to the environmental considerations.

SCIENTIFIC KNOWLEDGE

The above examples make it clear that, as long as environmental policy is founded in scientific reality, a basic understanding of scientific principles is essential if workable environmental policy is to be developed, implemented and enforced. Expert advice can fill in gaps in knowledge but the final decision must be made by the appropriate authority. Do the key personnel possess the necessary scientific skills to be able to evaluate the advice given and incorporate it into practical results? At the same time, do the advisers have sufficient grasp of the legal implications of policy to be able to decide what sort of advice is needed?

In order to obtain some insight into these problems, I have surveyed biologists, lawyers and administrators by means of a detailed questionnaire. Responses were canvassed from academics, students, professional lawyers, environmental consultants, government scientists and administrative civil servants. All responses were made in confidence and are presented anonymously. There was, as expected, a high percentage of non-returns, but only one government department actually stated that it would be improper to make a return. However, the response from administrators was much poorer than that from scientists and lawyers. The results are presented qualitatively and semi-quantitatively as percentages based on a response from fifty individuals. No attempt has been made to test the data statistically because the selection of potential participants was not random. Nevertheless, the results do suggest a profound lack of basic scientific understanding on the part of non-scientists and indicate a different approach to the more complex environmental issues. The questionnaire was divided into several sections, each of which is dealt with here.

Pollution

Over 95 per cent of participants recognized that pollution is something introduced by humankind that is capable of causing harm. About two-thirds preferred the following definition of pollution: 'The introduction by man into the environment of substances which are capable of causing harm to man or any other living organism *or of causing damage to structures or interference with legitimate uses of the environment*'. Slightly less than a third preferred a definition that omitted the purely social element emphasized above. There was no difference between individuals of different ages, qualifications or work experience.

Further probing into the understanding of 'pollution' revealed some contradictions. Thus the majority of biologists choosing the first definition thought that pollution was *always* damaging. When asked specifically whether pollution was introduced into the environment, less than 50 per cent of biologists answered affirmatively, compared with 70 per cent of lawyers. Only the first definition implies that pollution is socially unacceptable, yet a greater proportion of those choosing the other definition thought that pollution was always unacceptable.

In general terms biologists and lawyers agreed as to the main purpose of pollution law although they differed in detail, with biologists being more idealistic. They gave greatest weight to prevention whereas lawyers thought that minimizing and controlling pollution were the main aims. Both agreed that the law was not much concerned with punishing polluters or making them pay for clean-up measures.

The precautionary principle

Participants were asked to assess the validity of eighteen unaccredited statements on the precautionary principle, mostly taken directly, or with slight modification, from published material. The most obvious result was that, for most statements, opinions differed. Only in response to the following statement was there clear-cut support for the proposition made:

> The precautionary principle means that the burden of proof is changed. Instead of the environmentalist having to demonstrate that damage has occurred before any action to control pollution is taken, in future it will be up to the potential polluter to demonstrate that his activities will not cause environmental damage before he is allowed to proceed.

Over 80 per cent supported this statement, including all of the biologists. The differences between biologists and lawyers were less well marked than might have been expected, but a greater proportion of lawyers were unable to make an assessment.

Three-quarters of biologists recognized a need for a strong scientific basis and refused to accept that science played no part in the precautionary principle. As a group, lawyers were less sure. Only half of them were convinced that acceptance of the principle involved a scientific element and only 40 per cent believed that it was founded in science. The difference between the two groups perhaps reflects the dual nature of the principle as referred to above. On the other hand, neither group seemed clear as to whether 'the precautionary principle is a policy tool for bringing scientific reasoning into the decision making process'.

Participants were also invited to provide their own definitions of the precautionary principle. Of the thirty-one responses, six clearly equated it with prevention, seven defined it as meaning no action to be taken until the activity is proved harmless, and nine thought it meant considering the effects before taking action. The other responses were less easy to categorize.

Environmental assessment

Asked to decide whether environmental assessment is a scientific, administrative, political or legal process, 68 per cent of lawyers thought it was a scientific process and 26 per cent thought it was an administrative process. Among biologists, 48 per cent thought it was a scientific process, the remainder being equally divided between thinking of it as an administrative and as a political process.

Over half the biologists thought that environmental assessment was carried out by the developer, with most of the remainder seeing it as the role of environmental scientists. Lawyers, however, were equally divided between placing the responsibility on the developer and placing it on the administration.

If an environmental assessment fails to predict environmental damage, most lawyers thought that no one would be responsible for clean-up while 62 per cent of biologists thought that the developer would be responsible.

Over 60 per cent of biologists correctly distinguished between environmental assessment and environmental audits, but only 32 per cent of lawyers could do so.

Sustainable development

Participants were questioned indirectly about the difference between sustainable development and sustainable use. Over 20 per cent of lawyers were unable to decide whether statements were correct or not, three times as many as the biologists in the same position.

Fifty per cent of biologists thought that there could be no such thing as sustainable development, but only 39 per cent of lawyers held the same opinion. Surprisingly, biologists appeared to be slightly more optimistic about the future, and a greater proportion thought that future technology had a bearing on the concept. Over 80 per cent of both groups thought that sustainability required the conservation and enhancement of resources, but, while 71 per cent of biologists thought it required the conservation of genetic diversity, only 28 per cent of lawyers agreed. Of the remainder, 62 per cent did not know, suggesting, perhaps, that they did not understand the question.

Definitions

Participants were asked to say whether a number of statements about the terms 'animal', 'species' and 'organism' were correct. Ninety per cent of biologists were able to answer correctly (in scientific terms) questions about the nature of an animal. Lawyers also performed well, but there were predictable exclusions of insects, worms and, to a lesser extent, fish from the definition of animals. This is a prime example of the potential for communication problems. Biologists are trained from an early stage to make precise categorizations of living things according to strict criteria. The non-scientist, however, is more likely to restrict the use of the term 'animal' to those creatures that are most familiar to people, thus emphasizing a perceived difference between higher and lower creatures. Lawyers were also less able to identify species. For example, only 32 per cent of lawyers knew that blue tit and great tit are separate species, whereas only 4 per cent of biologists gave an incorrect answer.

Proof

Participants were asked to assess the validity of five statements about the nature of scientific proof. The overall response was the same for biologists and lawyers but, as a group, lawyers were less sure. For example, 76 per cent of biologists thought it was impossible to prove that an event cannot happen, compared with 53 per cent of lawyers. Similar percentages were obtained in support of the statement that 'scientific proof is based on a balance of probabilities as tested by statistical analysis'.

A surprisingly small number of both groups, and a minority of biologists, agreed with the Popperian theory that 'it is never possible to prove that a theory is correct, only that it is wrong'.

There was far less similarity between the groups when questioned about the nature of legal proof. Over 80 per cent of biologists failed to understand the nature of a criminal trial and felt that legal proof in such cases is based on a balance of probabilities as judged by the reasonable person.

Questions on the nature of strict liability generated almost complete unanimity of response among lawyers. The majority of biologists gave the same answers, but nearly 20 per cent felt unable to answer the questions.

THE RELATIONSHIP BETWEEN SCIENTIST AND POLICY-MAKER

The results of the questionnaire reveal some differences in thinking between biologists and lawyers, but also a lack of consensus within each group. Lawyers lacked knowledge of basic scientific definitions such as 'animal' and 'species' and were confused as to the difference between environmental assessment and audit. They did, however, have a reasonable grasp of the nature of scientific proof; far better than the biologists' understanding of legal proof. With the more complex questions covering aspects of 'pollution', 'the precautionary principle', 'sustainable development' and 'environmental assessment', contradictions and inconsistencies arose in both groups. In the case of pollution these intra-group differences were greater than those between biologists and lawyers. Both groups registered a considerable number of 'don't knows' when faced with questions outside of their disciplines. Within their own discipline, there was a tendency for each group to read more into a question and register a 'depends on the circumstances' response.

The results confirm that great care must be taken in using scientific information as part of environmental policy development. Clearly there is a need for expert advice, but the scientist needs to ask the following questions before preparing the brief:

Why is the advice wanted?
Is this the sort of advice that is actually needed in the circumstances?
Will the recipient understand all the terms used?
If detailed advice is given, will it be summarized by a non-scientist?
What are the scientific credentials of the recipient?

The policy-maker then has to assess the importance of the advice given. To do this, he or she must be able to:

assess the credibility of the advice;
assess the independence of the adviser;
identify any gaps in his or her knowledge;
apply the advice to the situation in question.

To do any of this requires a basic understanding of science and a familiarity with the scientific community. In practice, this does not exist. Policy-makers, administrators, judges and legislators are not scientists. And they do not have time to digest detailed information that might enable them to make sense of the scientific advice. In particular, they do not want a statistically reasoned analysis that encourages uncertainty. In the final analysis, all these people require clear-cut answers in black and white. As the then Netherlands Minister of Transport and Public Works said, 'doubts are a luxury' undermining political confidence. Speaking at the 3rd North Sea Seminar 1989 (for further details see Hallers-Tjabbes 1990), Mrs Smit-Kroes called on scientists to present their findings with a minimum of detail and advocated the use of diagrams to present complicated data. The problem with such an approach is that, without the scientist being available to expand and explain, it is unlikely that the full implication of the data can be appreciated. Presenting results diagrammatically is easy; explaining them in this manner may not be so practical.

Speaking at the same conference, Professor R.B. Clark expressed a belief that policy decisions direct science to certain ends and hence prejudge scientific issues. The question of blinkered science is beyond the scope of this chapter. It is clear, however, that government reliance on publicly employed scientists may not lead to the independent information needed to formulate sound environmental policy, if only because, as government scientists only carry out research under direction, they may not cover areas of importance on the topic in question.

CONCLUSIONS

To summarize, it can be seen that environmental law concepts are based on science as it is interpreted by the non-scientist. Because of the lack of scientific expertise, the policy-maker is likely to react to scientific information in one of two ways. At one extreme, the response will be super-critical, with questioning of the validity of the science as the basis for action. At the other extreme, the scientific data will be accepted without question. Because of the lack of sociological input into the environmental debate, the latter is the most likely scenario. In neither case will the quality of the scientific information be tested. At the same time, the policy-maker requires the science to be presented in simple, easily digested morsels and does not realize that over-simplification will weaken the basis for decision-making. When it comes to complex environmental principles such as the precautionary principle, where there is a mix of scientific and social factors to be considered, it is not surprising that no one can agree on what is meant.

The need for a more effective means of integrating science into policy has been addressed before. This chapter attempts to demonstrate the extent of the gap between the two areas and to explain why the advent of real environmental protection makes it imperative that a solution be found. The precautionary principle, whatever it may mean, was devised to deal with environmental problems. It would seem, however, that a similar principle could be formulated to cope with the interface between scientist and non-scientist. It might, perhaps, go as follows:

> In communications between scientists and non-scientists, the scientist should assume from the outset that the other party has no understanding of scientific principles and that all terms need to be explained. At the same time, the other party should assume that the scientist is narrow minded and, in particular, has no knowledge of other specialisms.

ACKNOWLEDGEMENTS

I am grateful to all those colleagues who took the time to complete the questionnaire. I should also like to thank the following people who gave me more detailed information on their ideas about the precautionary principle: Rick Boelens, Bob Earll, Paul Horsman, Chris Reid and Duncan Shaw.

NOTES

1 Michael Redclift, speaking at the 1992 ASA Conference, endorsed this viewpoint in his discussion of global environmental change. He concluded that closer relationships between natural and social sciences would be of benefit.
2 See, for example, Robin Grove-White in this volume.
3 I am grateful to Newby (1991) for drawing my attention to Ravetz's work.
4 BATNEEC: Best Available Techniques Not Entailing Excessive Cost (Environmental Protection Act 1991, Section 7).
5 Now published as The Genetically Modified Organisms (Contained Use) Regulations 1992 (SI 1992/3217) and The Genetically Modified Organisms (Deliberate Release) Regulations 1992 (SI 1992/3280).
6 *R.* v. *Azadehdel* (1990) 11 Cr App R (S) 377.
7 *R.* v. *Poole Borough Council* ex parte *Beebee* (1991) JPL 643.

REFERENCES

Adams, T. (1992) 'Legislation and practice – UK', *Environmental Law*, 6 (1): 17.
Bewers, J.M. (1989) 'Marine environmental protection initiatives in Europe: steps to emulate and steps to avoid', paper produced for the US/Canada Gulf of Maine Inquiry.

Birnie, P. (1992) 'International environmental law: its adequacy for present and future needs', in A. Hurrell and B. Kingsbury (eds) *The International Politics of the Environment*, Oxford: Clarendon Press.

Department of the Environment (1988) *Second International Conference on the Protection of the North Sea. Ministerial Declaration*, London: Department of the Environment.

—— (1991) *Environmental Assessment. A Guide to the Procedures*, London: HMSO.

Earll, R.C. (1992) 'Commonsense and the precautionary principle – an environmentalist's perspective', *Marine Pollution Bulletin*, 24 (4): 182–6.

Freestone, D. (1991) 'The precautionary principle', in R. Churchill and D. Freestone (eds) *International Law and Global Climate Change*, London: Graham and Trotman/Martinus Nijhoff.

Gray, J.S. (1990) 'Statistics and the precautionary principle', *Marine Pollution Bulletin*, 21 (4): 174–6.

Hallers-Tjabbes, C. ten (ed.) (1990) *Proceedings of the 3rd North Sea Seminar 1989*, Amsterdam: Werkgroep Noordsee.

HMSO (1990) *This Common Inheritance: Britain's Environmental Strategy*, Cm 1200, London: HMSO.

Holdgate, M.W. (1979) *A Perspective of Environmental Pollution*, Cambridge: Cambridge University Press.

Hughes, D. (1992) *Environmental Law*, (2nd edition), London: Butterworths.

Newby, H. (1991) 'One world, two cultures: sociology and the environment', a lecture given to mark the fortieth anniversary of the founding of the British Sociological Association, February 1991, reprinted as *Network* No. 50, May.

Ravetz, J. (1990) 'Knowledge in an uncertain world', *New Scientist*, 22 September: 18.

Select Committee on the European Communities (1983) *The Polluter Pays Principle*, Session 1982–3, 10th report, London: HMSO.

Thatcher, M. (1988) *Speech to the Royal Society*, London: Conservative Party.

Warren, L.M. (1991) 'Conservation – a secondary environmental consideration', in R. Churchill, J. Gibson and L.M. Warren (eds) *Law, Policy and the Environment*, Oxford: Blackwell.

Chapter 8

Tribal metaphorization of human–nature relatedness

A comparative analysis

Nurit Bird-David

This chapter is a pilot extension of an argument advanced in a number of earlier papers (Bird-David 1990, 1992a, 1992b). These examined how the Nayaka (a tribal group in South India) relate metaphorically to their natural environment, and how their metaphors link with economic behaviour, thought and organization. Among other things, it was argued that the intra-family caring relationship, especially the adult–child, constituted for the Nayaka a core metaphor,[1] in terms of which they thought about their related-ness to the natural environment.[2] Here, I further explore the broader claim[3] that the Nayaka illustrate a variation on a theme found globally, especially in cultures in which engagement with the natural environment by means of 'hunting and gathering' (shorthand for diverse ways of procuring what the environment gives; see Bird-David 1992b) is viewed as a significant part of the traditional way of life. Examples will include groups from among Australian Aborigines, North American Indians, Southern African Bushmen, Central African Pygmies and Asian Negrito. I argue that in all these cultures, human–nature relatedness is variously represented in terms of personal relatedness.[4] While the Nayaka, Mbuti and Batek draw extensively on 'adult–child caring relatedness' in representing their relatedness with the natural environment, the Canadian Cree draw extensively on 'sexual relatedness', Western Australian Aborigines on 'procreational relatedness', and the Bush-men on 'name-sake' relatedness.[5] Furthermore, I argue that some of the central cultural constructs of these cultural groups are systematic elabora-tions of their respective metaphorization of human–nature relatedness.

The chapter consists of four sub-arguments. The first three, concerning Cree, Australian and Bushmen examples, engage in three separate conver-sations[6] with the three regionally based discourses (the references and problematic of each are introduced *inter alia*). The fourth, concerning the Nayaka, Mbuti and Batek, sums up earlier work (Bird-David 1990, 1992a) and places it in the present broader framework. The method of analysis and presentation of data are influenced by the work of Lakoff, and especially Lakoff and Johnson's *Metaphors We Live By* (1980). These authors are con-cerned with metaphors as cognitive devices, and although their claim for certain universal metaphorical concepts is arguable (not least because it has as yet to be explored universally outside the – mostly white and middle-class – English-speaking world), their method of analysis is effective and yields a 'thick' kind of description (to borrow Geertz's phrase). It is to trace inferences of central metaphors in wide-linguistic expressions and expose the inner inferential logic (metaphoric systematicity) underlying them. Linguistic analysis has been long used in anthropology as a model for analysing culture, and their method, though primarily concerned with language, extends to culture generally. Let me turn, then, to the four cases to be compared.

THE FIRST CASE: 'SEXUAL RELATEDNESS'

The first case draws on Adrian Tanner's *Bringing Home Animals* (1979), which describes in great detail the hunting ideology and ritual of the Cree in the Mistassini area. In its broad outline, however, what Tanner describes in reference to this one area also applies to other Cree groups and, more generally, to subarctic boreal forest indigenous populations in North America and even in Eurasia (see the literature review in Ingold 1986: Ch. 10). Like many other ethnographers of Northern Indians, Tanner reports that the Cree describe hunting as an act of sexual intercourse and their mythic relationship with prey animals as one of marriage (Tanner 1979: 148). I want to argue, refining his excellent analysis, that these are just two aspects of a much wider area of metaphorical systematicity around a 'sexual' metaphor of human–nature relatedness. The supernatural side of the hunt from beginning to end is inferentially consistent with a sexual narrative (i.e. courtship/seduction/abduction; consummation; and procreation/reproduction). Moreover, central and characteristic concepts widely mentioned in Northern ethnography (e.g. Speck 1935, Paulson 1968, Martin 1978, Nelson 1982, Ingold 1986: Ch. 10; and see also Gudeman 1986: Ch. 8) – including 'showing respect to the carcass', 'avoiding waste', 'charming the prey to give itself in' and 'killing prey to ensure human and animal reproduction' – may also link inferentially with this metaphor. Consider the following cultural particulars (we follow the hunt from beginning to end).

The hunt usually starts with divination rites that include most commonly a dream appearance of a stranger, a woman (Tanner 1979: 125). The hunter, then, wears special garments, decoration and charms and goes to hunt (Tanner 1979: 140–3). The animal often voluntarily gives itself up to the hunter (see also Sharp 1988: 186). However, sometimes the prey is reluctant, so the hunter uses magic and songs to trick it to give itself up against its will (Tanner 1979: 136, 148–9).

In Tanner's view, these two modes stand at odds with each other (1979: 173). However, clearly, they logically complement each other in a hunter–prey reality metaphorized by sexual relationship. In this reality, a prey is courted – and seduced, when courting fails.

The killing itself then is metaphorized as sexual intercourse between hunter and prey. Hunters often talk about the killing in sexual terms, and about inter-human sexual intercourse in hunting terms (Tanner 1979: 178).[7] The hunter then returns to the camp and, in striking contrast to the other cases discussed below,[8] submits the carcass to the women's charge (Tanner 1979: 153). The women, like everybody else, take great care of each and every one of its parts, throwing nothing away – they have to 'show respect' and 'avoid waste' (see also Speck 1935: 92, Paulson 1968, Martin 1978: 18, Nelson 1982: 219).

While these actions are commonly interpreted as expressions of respect to the spirits – especially the Animal Masters (see Ingold 1986: Ch. 10) – and have sometimes been viewed in connection with what Nelson (1982) calls a 'conservation ethic', they clearly link inferentially with the 'sexual' metaphor. If killing 'is' an act of sexual intercourse, the corpse, its outcome, 'is' the joint offspring of hunter and prey, and it is important then that it is carefully looked after, mainly by women. Significantly, Tanner comments in passing (1979: 163) that the feast in which the game is distributed is similar to feasts that are held after the birth of a baby.

Like many other Cree groups, the Mistassini Cree believe that killing safeguards the reproduction of both human and animal populations. Indeed, if killing is 'seen' as sexual intercourse, then by 'sexual' logic it is self-evidently a prerequisite of procreation.

THE SECOND CASE: 'PROCREATION'

Western Desert Aborigines provide the second case. They have been the study-subjects of major ethnographic work, including Spencer and Gillen (1968 [1899]), Roheim (1945), Strehlow (1947), Stanner (1956, 1966), Meggitt (1972), Munn (1970) and Myers (1986). I shall focus in particular on two domains which figure prominently in the ethnography and which characterize Australian Aborigines more generally: kinship, and that immensely complex Aboriginal cosmological construct glossed as 'the Dreaming'. While the ethnography has provided a variety of illuminating perspectives on both issues, I want to highlight an additional metaphorical dimension made conspicuous in the comparative approach used here. I argue that a great many cultural details are inferentially linked to a 'procreational' metaphorization of human–nature relatedness.

It is well known that in addition to patrilines and matrilines, Western Desert Australian kinship[9] recognizes what might be termed 'country-lines'. The place of birth (in some cases place of conception) – not only the position of one's parents – influences one's kinship status, marriage possibilities and property rights, linking one by rights and obligations to other persons born (or conceived) in the same place. This is the case even when the birthplace is random, as, for example, when delivery occurs while the mother is travelling (see Spencer and Gillen 1968 [1899]: 124, Meggitt 1972: 78, Myers 1986: 14). The Aborigines sometimes recognize a resemblance of sorts between a person and their birthplace, and believe that birthmarks correspond with features of the country (Munn 1970: 146). The country, as Myers so eloquently shows in his book *Pintupi Country, Pintupi Self* (1986), is an organizing principle of the Aborigines' kinship system, and an integral part of their social organization.

In dealing with the Dreaming, I shall draw on Munn's seminal analysis based on the myths of Western Desert peoples, the Walbiri and the Pitjantjatjara (Munn 1970). I have selected Munn's analysis from many other insightful contributions (e.g. Spencer and Gillen 1968 [1899], Roheim 1945, Strehlow 1947, Stanner 1956, 1966, Meggitt 1972, Myers 1986) because in it she makes the important argument that the relationship she calls 'transformation' provides an interpretative framework for drawing together and making sense of a great deal of the Dreaming material. And I want to argue, reinterpreting her excellent interpretation, that the relationship in question is procreation.

Munn insightfully points out that the Dreaming is concerned, above all, with the binding relation between persons and things and the transformation of one into the other – epitomized in the relationships between the mythic Ancestors and the country, the mythic Ancestors and sacred things. Such relationships, she argues, are more common in Walbiri and Pitjantjatjara thought than relationships between people through things (glossed by Mauss as gift relations). She conceptualizes this type of relationship as 'transformation of subjects into objects', and defines it as follows:

> By 'transformations' I mean on the one hand various recurrent operations through which an ancestor – a sentient being – takes on or produces a material form, an object, consubstantial with himself, and on the other hand the products of these operations, the resultant objects.
>
> (Munn 1970: 141)

And further:

> we may say, then, that a transformation is constituted by a kind of 'double movement': on the one hand a process of separation from the originating subject; on the other hand a binding of the object to him in permanent, atemporal identification.
>
> (Munn 1970: 144)

Her definition is cumbersome, and I think the reason is that Munn clings to the Western experience of the material world and the country as inanimate entities. And she goes *against* what is so fundamental in the native experience – their view of the country and the material world as animate entities. If we take her general point but allow for an animated material world and nature, it is clear that what she describes is a mythic epoch of procreation: sentient beings procreating – not transformed into – parts of the world. Procreation involves 'separation' yet also 'continuity' – indeed 'a binding in permanent, atemporal identification'. It involves 'producing' and 'becoming' (in the sense of generation-replacement). It involves 'products' that stand for, are 'consubstantial with' and descend from the 'producers'. All of these, and much more besides (since metaphors are fertile sources of meaning), are implied by the metaphorical statement that the Ancestors procreated the country and the material world.

To read 'procreation' for 'transformation' (with respect to human–human, nature–nature *and* human–nature relatedness) is also to avoid Munn's 'native-as-child' proposition. Her elaborate analysis labours to stretch and bend the ill-suited 'transformation' to accord with her fine ethnographic observations. In the end, the object-orientation model leads her to reject the 'native-as-simpleton' argument, only to replace it with the 'native-as-child' one. She writes:

> How then shall we interpret the psychological grounds of this orientational model? An older Anthropology regarded orientations of this type as indicative of a 'confusion of categories' or a failure to distinguish the subjective from the objective, the self from the object world. On the contrary, it should be apparent from the present analysis that this orientation is grounded in the awareness of subject–object distinctions. Indeed, it seems obvious enough that it is merely a recasting in institutionalized form of certain general psychological processes of individual development: on the one hand, the separation of the self from external reality which is a necessary part of the maturation and socialization process; on the other hand, the symbolic reincorporation of the self into the external world which occurs through the infusion of this world with ego's subjective life experience.
>
> (Munn 1970: 158)

Far from being an institutionalization of childlike individuation and separation from the external world, there may be here an elaborated conceptual system framed within the 'procreation' metaphor – where metaphor is seen as a key device not unlike ones used by Western scientists (see Boyd 1979, Kuhn 1979) to accommodate language to the casual structure of the world (Boyd 1979: 317).

It would seem from the ethnography that the Aboriginal notion of 'creation' is itself organized by the 'procreation' metaphor. Where Westerners associate 'creation' with 'material production' (i.e. to make, to do), Aborigines associate it with 'procreation' (e.g. to deliver, to bring to life, to give life).[10] Illustrations abound in Walbiri and Pitjantjatjara myth, as cited by Munn. Creation concerns:

- Taking something out of the body: for example, in the important myth of the two kangaroos and the owl who travelled across the country together, the kangaroos are said to have pulled *guanidja* or 'many men' out of their chests (Munn 1970: 149). In another myth, the kangaroos made their 'tails' by pulling them out of their bodies (Munn 1970: 144). In yet a third myth they so created the sacred 'string cross' (Munn 1970: 151).

• Fecundity and replication: for example, the Sacred Ancestors have 'a kind of originating power' – the power 'to create one's own identity without limitations' (Munn 1970: 145). They are highly fecund – they constantly travel and leave everywhere emanations 'like progeny' (Munn 1970: 149, 154–6).

• A simultaneous bringing-into-being and naming; that is, the Ancestors name things as they physically create them; one tends to imply the other (Munn 1970: 143).

• Continuity in spite of death; the Sacred Ancestors died (disappeared, went into the ground) but did not die out: they left 'indefinite records of themselves' and 'images of permanency' (Munn 1970: 143). They did not 'become nothing', but 'became the country' (Munn 1970: 148).

THE THIRD CASE: 'NAME-SAKE'

The third case includes !Kung Bushmen, the study-subjects of the prolific and influential Harvard Kalahari research project (see Lee and DeVore 1976, Lee 1979), and other Bushmen groups studied in depth (e.g. the Nharo by Barnard, !ko by Heinz, G/wi by Silberbaur). Since work on their worldview and on ritual and myth remains fragmented – largely outside mainstream research, influenced by the ecological–evolutionary paradigm – it was found instructive to group them and use diverse work.[11]

I shall focus in particular on what Marshall glossed as the 'medicine complex', and Katz described as the 'primary expression of "religion"', "medicine" and "cosmology"' (Katz 1982: 36). The sources offer various perspectives on the performative aspects of the 'medicine complex' – the dance (Marshall 1969), the curing (Katz 1982), rock art (Lewis-Williams 1982, 1984, 1988) and folk-stories (Biesele 1976, 1978) – but there has been no attempt to look beyond them at the system at large. My argument is that as a whole this cultural complex illustrates an extensive metaphorical use of name-sake relatedness. This form of relatedness is common and important in (at least) !Kung social organization (Marshall 1957; see also Lee 1984), where it allows individuals with identical names to assume each other's kinship identity with all the rights and prohibitions this confers, and grants them access to the social and physical resources of name-sakes.[12]

From the outset, it is clear that the 'medicine complex' is essentially about pairing people, dances, songs and medicines with details of the natural environment such as eland, giraffe, mantis and rain. The eland, for example, links with the people of the eland, the eland-dance, the eland-song and the eland-medicine, while rain connects with the rain-people, the rain-dance, the rain-medicine and the rain-song. These, then, are name-sake ties, crossing between, and linking, nature on the one hand and society and culture on the other.

The sharing of names is associated with a certain kind of potency called *n/um* (in the !Kung vernacular) which all constituent parts in the system are believed to have. It is invisible, bestowed by the great god, creator and controller of all things (Marshall 1969: 351–3). As far as human beings are concerned, it resides throughout life in the pit of the stomach and the base of the spine, and has to be 'awakened' ('boiled') in order to be effective. This is done by various means, including rhythmic singing which, the !Kung say, also 'awakens their hearts' (Marshall 1969: 352). Leaving aside the many other graphic details provided by Marshall (1969) and Katz (1982), what do people do with it? Consistent (inferentially) with the name-sake metaphor, they use the *n/um* to gain access to resources of their (super)natural name-sakes, just as they do in the 'human–human' sphere. Once it is activated – barring the occasions when it is too strong, whereupon it is dangerous and can even cause death (Marshall 1969: 351–2) – people use the *n/um* to take on the form of their (super)natural name-sakes, put themselves in their position, get nearer to, even control, the (super)natural name-sakes' relatives, and, generally speaking, draw on the name-sakes' power and resources for various ends including, importantly, the curing of illnesses and other forms of malaise. Cultural expressions of this include the following:

- A /Xam man told Bleek that medicine-men of the eland could see what the eland saw and thus knew eland whereabouts (Bleek 1935: 16, Bleek 1866–77, L.V.25.6008-13, cited in Lewis-Williams 1988: 207). Significantly, Lewis-Williams himself reads it to imply 'an *identity* between a shaman and the animal, whose potency he harnessed'. Furthermore, 'He [the shaman] could as it were, *slip from one persona to the other*' (Lewis-Williams 1988: 208, emphasis added).
- A /Xam woman described how she put on a cap with antelope ears, and, followed by the antelopes, led them into an ambush (Bleek 1935: 46). An informant said that she sent her castrated springbok among the antelope to lead the herd to the hunters (Bleek 1935: 44–6).
- A !ko informant told Heinz that lion medicine-men could 'mix' with a pride of lions while in their feline form (Heinz 1975: 29) – the pride itself 'seen' metaphorically as kin of the lion.
- A !Kung man informed Biesele that as a giraffe medicine-man his power as a trancer and curer partook of the giraffe's power – 'Just yesterday, friend, the giraffe came and took me again' (Biesele 1976: 33). In the medicine dances themselves, held frequently, often weekly among !Kung, the trancers draw on their *n/um* 'to bring the protective powers of the universe to bear on the patient' (Katz 1982: 53). The dances 'are' also the battle-field for competing kinship claims over ill persons, between their living relatives on the one hand, and their dead, supernatural relatives on the other (Katz 1982: Ch. 4).

Commenting that !Kung explained *n/um* in terms of 'strength', thinking this was so evident and sufficient an explanation that nothing else could be added (1969: 351, 369), Marshall suggests we think about it as a kind of electricity (invisible, strong and, in controlled measure, beneficial in a variety of ways). Like Munn, she self-evidently draws on Western material imagery (though electrical, not just mechanical). But if we work *with*, and not against local imagery, it is preferable, in my view, to think about it in immaterial terms of sociality and personal relatedness, especially as in the 'name-sake' relatedness. The inferential field of meaning then includes a great deal of what the local people do with, and say about, the *n/um* (invisible, strong, usually beneficial, has to be 'awakened', whereupon 'it awakens the heart', etc.).

A whole range of other cultural particulars is connected inferentially with the 'name-sake' metaphor, especially with the dual identity it implies: separation yet sameness, not temporarily as in procreation, but contemporarily, as in alter-parts. Consider the following cultural expressions:

- The Bushmen's 'key creation myth' – the 'myth of double creation' – tells us how people were doubly created with animals. In the Old Days, the first human beings were animals, and the first animal beings were humans. Then a reversal occurred, the first human beings turned into animals, and the first animal beings became humans. But the reversal was not complete, and today people and animals still carry within themselves residual traces of their previous state (Guenther 1988: 193, Biesele 1976).
- Hunters are careful to control their own body and actions during and before the hunt because, they believe, much of what happens in the hunter's body and psyche also happens in his prey animal, and vice versa. Thus, nineteenth-century /Xam told Bleek and Lloyd that the hunter's body was astir with the 'antelope sensations' at places that correspond to those on the antelopes, such as ribs, back and eyes (Bleek and Lloyd 1911: 33–5). !Kung hunters avoid fat and certain other foods before setting out on a hunt, lest the poison in the prey passes through its urine, or sticks to the arrowhead instead of circulating in its blood (Marshall 1962: 55).
- Unlike his Cree counterpart, the Bushman hunter neither charms nor seduces his prey but, seeking cunning and stamina – the desired attributes here – he sets out to outsmart an opponent in an evenly matched, tricky duel, where prey and hunter are fused together and each internally sense what the other is up to. Bushmen characteristically mimic animal behaviour in ritual, recreational dances and children's games (see, for example, Barnard 1980: 36), and this may be another inferential expression of the name-sake relationship – slipping from the human to the animal persona in recreational activities also.
- Finally, Bushmen rock art abounds with anthropomorphic and therianthropic motifs, which, among other things, emphasize animal–human duality (see Lewis-Williams 1982, Guenther 1988).

THE FOURTH CASE: 'ADULT–CHILD CARING'

The Nayaka of South India (studied by Bird-David 1990, 1992a, 1992b), the Batek of Malaysia (studied by Endicott 1979) and the Mbuti of Zaire (studied by Turnbull 1961, 1965)[13] provide the fourth variation. Notwithstanding differences between them – the significance of which diminishes, however, when these groups are compared with others – they illustrate metaphorical systematicity around an 'adult–child caring' metaphor of nature–human relatedness. In ritual (as well as in everyday) discourse, these peoples frequently describe and address the forest as a parent, and thank it for affection, food and other provisions. They often say that the forest 'gives' them food and other necessities. This has been described in some detail in two earlier papers (Bird-David 1990, 1992a), and will be summarized briefly here within this broad comparative framework.

The focus on the 'adult–child caring' metaphor marks an important difference from the other cases treated above. For the Bushmen, major ritual is connected with activating the *n/um* and slipping into a supernatural persona; for the Cree, it is connected with the hunt, seen as a sexual act that reproduces hunter and prey; and for Australian Aborigines, it is connected with sacred rites, songs and designs, seen as embodiments of the Ancestors and as deeds for the inheritance (both inferentially related to procreation). For the Nayaka, Mbuti and Batek, however, major ritual involves getting together with the forest and other supernatural spirits. These spirits visit them in their hamlets, and they all share cooked food (normally done within the domestic unit), converse, sing and dance (the Nayaka even share cigarettes with the visiting spirits). For Nayaka, at least, this is an occasion where people and supernatural spirits voice their expectations and complaints – the Nayaka demand to be looked after and fed, and the spirits request them to follow in the ways of their parents.

A similar range of differences occurs in the subsistence pursuits of the four cases. The Cree hunter adorns himself before he sets out to seduce prey, the Australian invests his supernatural effort in securing deeds and rights over inheritance, and the Bushman hunter purifies and controls his body and psyche before he sets out to outsmart his prey counterpart. The Nayaka, Batek and Mbuti, however, do nothing at all. Rarely, if ever, do they use supernatural means to secure, or increase, success in subsistence pursuits. They do not try to foresee where they may encounter prey by means of divination (as do Cree and Bushmen). They trust that the forest-seen-as-parent will provide for them, unconditionally.

A final set of differences is provided in terms of the creation myth. The Bushmen creation myth tells how people were *doubly created* with animals, the Cree myth how people were *married* with animals and Aboriginal myth how people were *procreated* by bestial and human ancestors. In the fourth case (at least with respect to the Nayaka), however, the 'creation' myth (so presented) tells that right from the beginning, the Nayaka lived in the area, a pair in each location, hunting and gathering in the forest, cared for by the forest and other (super)natural beings. They insist that that is all, that there is nothing more to tell.

CONCLUDING REMARKS

I have argued here for the predominance of metaphorical frames in four clusters of cultures, a different metaphorical frame in each. The argument should not be taken as one of exclusivity, but as one of relative prominence (revealed by cultural comparison). Furthermore, it should not be taken as a totalizing argument – reducing complex, variable and changeable cultural complexes to elaborations within single metaphorical frames. Rather, it is a mapping of symbolic trails running through complex lands of cultures. As suits the large-scale comparison presented here, the mapping is on a large scale, using symbols that aggregate rather than finely differentiate phenomena. My intention was to provide this map to complement existing maps – all of which give diverse perspectives on varied scales – in the belief that the ethnographic atlas of culture should include them all.

What are the implications of the four tribal metaphorical frames that have been discussed here with respect to environmentalism? In the traditional Western view, nature and humankind have been 'seen' as detached and in opposition. Furthermore, they have been viewed within a 'subject–object' frame: nature 'seen' as a resource to be utilized, controlled, possessed, dominated, managed and (more recently) looked after by humankind. In the four tribal cases, however, nature and humankind are 'seen' within a 'subject–subject' frame as interrelated in various forms of personal relatedness. Since these tribal peoples share an intimate and time-proven knowledge of their respective natural environments, their representations cannot be dismissed outright in favour of the Western one. On the contrary, they press the need for a pluralistic view of the natural environment and human–nature relatedness.[14]

ACKNOWLEDGEMENTS

I am grateful to colleagues who participated in the 'culture' discussion group in the Sociology and Anthropology Department in Tel Aviv University for their helpful comments, and especially to Eva Iluz, Sasha Wietman, Haim Hazan and Avi Cordova, to Jose Bruner and Shai Shein for their help with literature on the metaphors, and to Steve Kaplan for editorial help.

NOTES

1 I use 'metaphor' in the sense first discussed by A.I. Richards (1936) and Max Black (1954–5), and since then developed in a wide range of works (see, for example, anthologies edited by Ortony 1979, and Johnson 1981). Briefly, it is

seen as a cognitive device, often used when literal language fails to accommodate and describe the casual structure of complex phenomena. It can generate insight into 'how things are'. It evokes 'associative commonplaces' which are 'active together' resulting in 'inter-illumination' – that is, the metaphor reorganizes users' views both of its 'source domain' and its 'topic domain' ('vehicle' and 'toner' in other terminologies).

2   The animation of the natural environment, and the idea that some of its constituents interrelate with human-like kinship relationships, is well known in the ethnography (and not just in reference to the 'Primitive'). The point of the papers was that contiguity – rather than just analogy – is at stake in these cases; the human and the natural world themselves are interrelated through personal relationships. The world as a whole (constitutive of human–human, human–nature and nature–nature relations) is seen as one cosmic system.

3   It was raised as an hypothesis in the conclusion to Bird-David 1990: 194.

4   Comparative work based on secondary sources necessarily draws on authors of various persuasions working under different historical conditions. While its inherent limitations should not be treated as negligible, neither should they be exaggerated. The analysis is offered as a moment in what Gudeman and Rivera (1990) aptly called 'conversation', inviting the engagement of specialists.

5   See Marshall (1957) and Lee (1984) on the 'name-sake' relationship.

6   I borrow the term from Gudeman and Rivera (1990).

7   Metaphorical 'interaction' – assumed but not fully discussed in this chapter for lack of space – is very clear here.

8   For similar Eskimo examples see Bodenhorn (1989) and Fienup-Riordan (1983).

9   Variations which exist between groups do not seem to be crucial for the purpose of this analysis.

10 Note, however, that in some contexts, Westerners also draw metaphorically on procreation, and delivery, as in describing an artist giving birth to an art-piece.

11 Studies used include Barnard (1980) on the Nharo; Biesele (1976, 1978), Katz (1982) and Marshall (1957, 1962, 1969) on the !Kung; Silberbaur (1981) on G/wi, Heinz (1975) on !ko; Guenther (1988) on Bushmen in general; Lewis-Williams (1982, 1984, 1988) on Southern Bushmen rock art, using nineteenth-century texts, especially the Bleek collection (1866–77) on the now-extinct Southern /Xam. This is not quite as 'Frazerian' as it seems since, as Lewis-Williams (1984) argues, there are strong cultural continuities between Bushmen groups.

12 The name relationship occurs in a formalized way among the !Kung (=Au//ei, Zu/'hoa, Kwankala and Sekele) and Nharo (who borrowed it from the !Kung) and some very small groups closely related to the Nharo (Ts'aukhoe and =Haba). It is not found among !Xo, G/Wi or /Xam, though these groups do have universal kinship, as far as we know. (I am grateful to Alan Barnard for this comment.)

13 Turnbull's work, it is now well known, suffers from rhetorical excess and a larger-than-usual dose of romanticism. However, in its broad outline his thesis on the Mbuti's close relationship with the forest has not been disproved, and while there is new culturally oriented work on Pygmy groups (e.g. Grinker 1990), it has not yet concerned itself with this issue.

14 See also Ingold (1991).

REFERENCES

Barnard, A. (1980) 'Kinship and social organization in Nharo cosmology', paper presented at the Second International Conference on Hunting and Gathering Peoples, Quebec.

Biesele, M. (1976) 'Aspects of !Kung folklore', in R.B. Lee and I. DeVore (eds) *Kalahari Hunter-Gatherers: Studies of the !Kung San and their Neighbours*, Cambridge, Massachusetts: Harvard University Press.

—— (1978) 'Sapience and scarce resources: communication systems of the !Kung and other foragers', *Social Science Information*, 17 (6): 921–47.

Bird-David, N. (1990) 'The giving environment: another perspective on the economic system of gatherer-hunters', *Current Anthropology*, 31 (2): 183–96.

—— (1992a) 'Beyond "The Original Affluent Society": a culturist formulation', *Current Anthropology*, 33 (1): 25–47.

—— (1992b) 'Beyond "the hunting and gathering mode of subsistence": observations on Nayaka and other modern hunter-gatherers', *Man*, 27 (1): 19–45.

Black, M. (1954–5) 'Metaphor', *Proceedings of the Aristotelian Society*, N.S. 55: 273–94, reprinted in *Models and Metaphors* (1962) Ithaca, New York: Cornell University Press.

Bleek, D. (1935) 'Beliefs and customs of the /Xam Bushmen', *Bantu Studies*, 9: 1–47.

Bleek, W.H.I. (1866–77) Unpublished manuscripts, J.W. Jagger Library, University of Cape Town.

Bleek, W. and Lloyd, L. (1911) *Specimens of Bushmen Folklore*, London: Allen and Unwin.

Bodenhorn, B. (1989) 'The animals come to me, they know I share': Niupaiq kinship, changing economic relations and enduring world views on Alaskan North Slopes', Ph.D. thesis, Cambridge University.

Boyd, R. (1979) 'Metaphor and theory change: What is "metaphor" a metaphor for?', in A. Ortony (ed.) *Metaphor and Thought*, Cambridge: Cambridge University Press.

Endicott, K. (1979) *Batek Negrito Religion: The World View and Rituals of a Hunting and Gathering People of Peninsular Malaysia*, Oxford: Clarendon Press.

Fienup-Riordan, A. (1983) *The Nelson Islands Eskimos: Social Structure and Ritual Distribution*, Anchorage: Alaska Pacific University Press.

Grinker, R.R. (1990) 'Images of denigration: structuring inequality between foragers and farmers in the Ituri forest, Zaire', *American Anthropologist*, 17 (1): 111–30.

Gudeman, S. (1986) *Economics as Culture: Models and Metaphors of Livelihood*, London: Routledge and Kegan Paul.

Gudeman, S. and Rivera, A. (1990) *Conversations in Colombia: The Domestic Economy in Life and Text*, Cambridge: Cambridge University Press.

Guenther, M. (1988) 'Animals in Bushmen thought, myth and art', in T. Ingold, D. Riches and J. Woodburn (eds) *Hunters and Gatherers 2: Property, Power and Ideology*, Oxford: Berg.

Heinz, H.J. (1975) 'Elements of !ko Bushmen religious beliefs', *Anthropos*, 70: 2–41.

Ingold, T. (1986) *The Appropriation of Nature: Essays on Human Ecology and Social Relations*, Iowa: University of Iowa Press.

—— (1991) 'From trust to domination: an alternative history of human–animal relations', paper presented at a conference on Animals and Society: Changing Perspectives, Royal Society of Edinburgh.

Johnson, M. (ed.) (1981) *Philosophical Perspectives on Metaphor*, Minneapolis: University of Minnesota Press.

Katz, R. (1982) *Boiling Energy: Community Healing among the Kalahari !Kung*, Cambridge, Massachusetts: Harvard University Press.

Kuhn, T. (1979) 'Metaphor in science', in A. Ortony (ed.) *Metaphor and Thought*, Cambridge: Cambridge University Press.

Lakoff, G. and Johnson, M. (1980) *Metaphors We Live By*, Chicago: University of Chicago Press.

Lee, R.B. (1979) *The !Kung San: Men, Women and Work in a Foraging Society*, New York: Cambridge University Press.
—— (1984) *The Dobe !Kung*, New York: Holt, Rinehart and Winston.
Lee, R.B. and DeVore, I. (1976) *Kalahari Hunter-Gatherers: Studies of !Kung San and their Neighbours*, Cambridge, Massachusetts: Harvard University Press.
Lewis-Williams, J.D. (1982) 'The economic and social context of Southern San rock art', *Current Anthropology*, 23: 429–49.
—— (1984) 'Ideological continuities in prehistoric southern Africa: the evidence of rock art', in C. Schrire (ed.) *Past and Present in Hunter-Gatherer Studies*, Orlando: Academic Press.
—— (1988) 'People of the eland: an archaeo-linguistic crux', in T. Ingold, D. Riches and J. Woodburn (eds) *Hunters and Gatherers 2: Property, Power and Ideology*, Oxford: Berg.
Marshall, L. (1957) 'The kin terminology system of the !Kung Bushmen', *Africa*, XXVII (1): 1–25.
—— (1962) '!Kung Bushmen religious beliefs', *Africa*, 32 (3): 221–5.
—— (1969) 'The medicine dance of the !Kung Bushmen', *Africa*, 39 (4): 347–81.
Martin, C. (1978) *Keepers of the Game*, Berkeley: University of California Press.
Meggitt, M.J. (1972) 'Understanding Australian aboriginal society: kinship systems or cultural categories?', in P. Reining (ed.) *Kinship Studies in the Morgan Centennial Year*, Washington: The Anthropological Society of Washington.
Munn, N.D. (1970) 'The transformation of subjects into objects in Walbiri and Pitjantjatjara myth', in R.M. Berndt (ed.) *Australian Aboriginal Anthropology: Modern Studies in the Social Anthropology of the Australian Aborigines*, Nedlands: University of Western Australia Press.
Myers, F. (1986) *Pintupi Country, Pintupi Self: Sentiment, Place, and Politics among Western Desert Aborigines*, Washington and London: Smithsonian Institution Press and Australian Institute of Aboriginal Studies.
Nelson, R.K. (1982) 'A conservation ethic and environment: the Koyukon of Alaska', in N. Williams and E. Hunn (eds) *Resource Managers: North American and Australian Hunter-Gatherers*, Boulder: Westview.
Ortony, A. (ed.) (1979) *Metaphor and Thought*, Cambridge: Cambridge University Press.
Paulson, I. (1968) 'The preservation of animal bones in the hunting rites of some North-Eurasian peoples', in V. Dioszegi (ed.) *Popular Beliefs and Folklore Tradition in Siberia*, Indiana University Uralic and Atlantic Series 57, The Hague: Mouton.
Richards, A.I. (1936) *The Philosophy of Rhetoric*, London: Oxford University Press.
Roheim, G. (1945) *The Eternals of the Dream*, New York: International Universities Press.
Sharp, H.S. (1988) 'Dry meat and gender: the absence of Chipewyan ritual for the regulation of hunting and animal numbers', in T. Ingold, D. Riches and J. Woodburn (eds) *Hunters and Gatherers 2: Property, Power and Ideology*, Oxford: Berg.
Silberbaur, G. (1981) *Hunters and Habitat in the Central Kalahari*, Cambridge: Cambridge University Press.
Speck, F.G. (1935) *Naskapi: The Savage Hunters of the Labrador Peninsula*, Norman: University of Oklahoma Press.
Spencer, B. and Gillen, F. (1968 [1899]) *The Native Tribes of Central Australia*, London: Macmillan.
Stanner, W.E.H. (1956) 'The Dreaming', in T.A.G. Hungerford (ed.) *Australian Signpost*, Melbourne: F.W. Cheshire.

—— (1966) *On Aboriginal Religion*, Oceania Monograph no. 11, Sydney: University of Sydney Press.

Strehlow, T.G.H. (1947) *Aranda Traditions*, Melbourne: University of Melbourne Press.

Tanner, A. (1979) *Bringing Home Animals: Religious Ideology and Mode of Production of the Mistassini Cree Hunters*, London: E. Hurst.

Turnbull, C.M. (1961) *The Forest People: A Study of the Pygmies of the Congo*, New York: Simon and Schuster.

—— (1965) *Wayward Servants: The Two Worlds of the African Pygmies*, Connecticut: Greenwood Press.

Chapter 9

Rhetoric, practice and incentive in the face of the changing times

A case study in Nuaulu attitudes to conservation and deforestation

Roy Ellen

Part of the mythology of late-twentieth-century environmentalism is that certain 'traditional' peoples are uniquely adapted in ways which ensure that their material and spiritual resources are held in balance. Such peoples are usually assumed to be in some vague sense – though by no means exclusively – gatherers and hunters, practitioners of animistic 'natural' religions, remote and resistant to change. This is recognizably only the latest of a long and ignoble pedigree of views which perpetuate a pernicious dichotomy, which, however much some have tried to disguise it, unmistakenly reproduces the notion of a primitive, exotic Other. It is a view which Edmund Leach described with characteristic forthrightness as 'sentimental rubbish' (Leach 1971: 166).

Such beliefs persist, in the minds of neo-pagans in Highgate, among ordinary thinking folk, in the academy as well as outside it. Why this should be the case is a question addressed in other contributions to this volume; and whether or not the protagonists themselves have such beliefs and whether those beliefs have regulatory consequences is now the subject of a burgeoning literature (e.g. Martin 1978, Callicot 1982, Hughes 1983, Brightman 1987, Hames 1987). In an earlier piece (Ellen 1986) I tried briefly to explain why it should be that the myth of primitive environmental wisdom should have such tenacity. I concluded that it does so because some peoples do have cosmologies which stress environmental harmony, because at times anthropologists and others have appeared to describe populations which have something approaching an ecologically self-sustaining economy, and because many find it attractive to use the concept of adaptation to explain why societies should have achieved such an apparently favourable accommodation. None of this makes sense, however, except in relation to the recognition that such an illusion serves an important ideological purpose in modern or post-modern society. It is also not to deny that many peoples, among them those ironically on the receiving end of Western expertise and aid, have an impressive accumulation of practical knowledge which is largely ignored by a development industry driven by macro-political goals.

In this chapter I examine Nuaulu attitudes to a rainforest environment as these are reflected in their use of it over a 25-year period, and especially in their reactions to commercial logging and changes wrought by Indonesian government transmigration policy in the 1980s. My main focus is on how the Nuaulu reconcile a new ecological and political order which works for the present to their advantage, or at least to the advantage of some of them, with a 'traditional' set of beliefs which are underpinned by an entirely different set of cultural assumptions. Existing shared knowledge of how nature *works*, of how in different contexts it interacts with and contrasts with that shared abstraction which we call 'culture', presently co-exists with views which challenge this consensus, views brought about and sustained by wholesale transformation of the rainforest and the apparent possibility that humans can extract from the environment at levels previously non-comprehendable. The *rhetoric* of which I speak in the title is in the form of public and semi-public utterances which address directly or indirectly the changes, adjustments and values implicit in Nuaulu representations and utilization of nature. The *practice* refers to both the routine daily patterns of subsistence and social interaction, and the *incentive* to those changes in their environment which they perceive – or are persuaded to believe – offer new opportunities.

I begin by stating briefly the history of Nuaulu settlement between 1850 and 1970, and summarizing the position on land tenure as it existed between 1970 and 1980. I go on to examine the consequences of logging, local spontaneous immigration, government-controlled transmigration and new patterns of Nuaulu extraction in the Ruatan valley to which these led. I conclude by noting the effects of recent changes on forest extraction, in the light of Nuaulu conceptualization of forest and in relation to theories of the degradation of the commons.

A BRIEF HISTORY OF NUAULU LAND TENURE, 1850–1980

The Nuaulu consisted in 1970 of a group of 12–13 semi-autonomous clans with an overall population of 496, located in Amahai sub-district on the island of Seram (Map 9.1). Seram is part of the *kabupaten* of Maluku Tengah (the Central Moluccas), with an administrative centre at Masohi, and with the capital of the modern Indonesian province of Maluku in Ambon. I mention these details now, not as mere background, but because they feature in significant ways in the narrative which subsequently unfolds.

In 1970 the Nuaulu inhabited four hamlets, grouped into three administrative units within the *desa* of Sepa. Subsistence, then as now, was obtained largely through the extraction of palm sago, swiddening, hunting and gathering. By 1981 the population had grown to 747, and by 1990 to about 1,256.

What presaged this increase in population by a factor of 2.5 over a period of just two decades, and what consequences followed from it, will be discussed later, but for the Nuaulu themselves the single most important accompanying development has been the rapid growth in cutting forest for agricultural land along the Nua–Ruatan watercourse and, even more

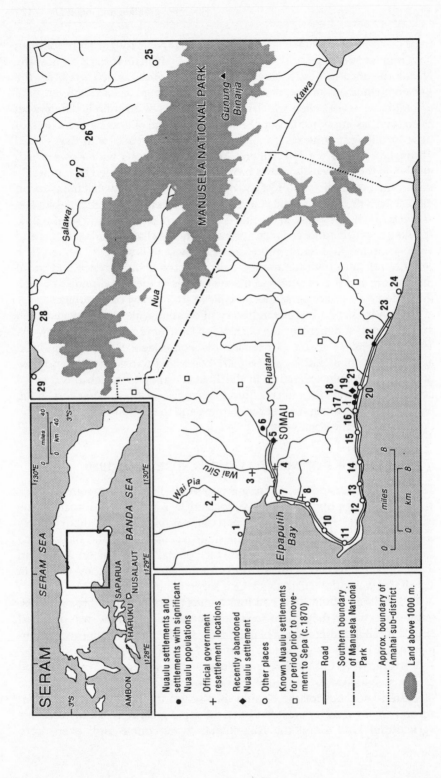

Map 9.1 The eastern part of the Amahai sub-district. The inset shows the location of the enlarged area in relation to Seram as a whole

Numbered settlements (Nuaulu settlements in italics):

1 Waraka
2 Wai Pia settlements
3 Wai Siru settlements
4 Wai Ruatan settlements (Kilo 5–Kilo 11)
5 *Simalouw* (Kilo 9)
6 *Tahena Ukuna* (Kilo 12)
7 Makariki
8 Haruru
9 Letwaru
10 Masohi
11 Amahai
12 Rutah
13 Hururu
14 Yainuelo
15 Hatuheno
16 Nuelitetu
17 *Bunara*
18 *Watane*
19 *Aihisuru*
20 Sepa
21 *Hahuwalan*
22 Rohua
23 Tamilouw
24 Yalahatan
25 Kanikeh
26 Roho
27 Huaulu
28 Rumah Olat
29 Sawai

potently symbolic, the re-establishment of settlements in this same area after a lapse of (in some cases) up to one hundred years, through migration from sites near Sepa (Map 9.1). Nuaulu speakers have inhabited the villages around Sepa, though not always permanently, for almost a hundred years, having moved from various clan homelands in the highlands along the southern watershed of the east–west spine of the island. The recent movement back to the Nua–Ruatan area is thus seen by many as a concrete manifestation of those assertions of belief, punctuating Nuaulu historical accounts (but occasionally extremely explicit), that the sojourn on the coast is no more than a temporary interlude. It would be incorrect to view this as some kind of fulfilment of prophecy, as in Nuaulu terms (and perhaps also in the terms of the peoples who surround them), it has always been taken for granted that there is an intrinsic connection between certain areas of origin and the very definition of Nuaulu ethnicity, and assumed by some to be wholly unremarkable that they would one day return. By contrast, their ethnographer has admittedly tended to view such assertions with patronizing scepticism, assuming that the Nuaulu would eventually adopt a modernist version of history in which progress, coastalization, villagization and development are all indicators of some inevitable trajectory towards a vaguely understood omega point. The same developments have also underlined the enduring importance of clan ritual and political autonomy, for when people began to recultivate and move back to the interior valleys it was not the decision of entire villages or of particular persons, but of individual clans.

Until the last two decades of the nineteenth century, the Nuaulu lived in highland settlements, though with a long history of intermittent relations with Sepa and other coastal domains (Ellen 1988: 118). Nuaulu society comprised geographically and politically autonomous patriclans, associated mythologically with a place of origin (see Ellen 1978: 14, Map 3). Swiddens, sago resources, groves of useful trees and hunting areas of the same clan were together, not separated by the resources of other clans, or even the land of other hamlets or cultural groups. In the short term land was identified with the living individuals and domestic groups who used it; and, simultaneously, in the longer term was deemed to belong to deceased predecessors and unborn descendants. In other words, it was conceptually atemporal. Within the last hundred years, however, the Nuaulu have been moving from the highlands and settling in the vicinity and under the putative authority of the Muslim polity of Sepa. The reasons for resettlement were various and not altogether clear. The movement began prior to full Dutch control of the area in the nineteenth century, but was intensified by colonial intervention. It had important implications for the social relations of land use which I have described elsewhere (Ellen 1977), a description which represents what we might regard as the 'traditional' and normative arrangements as they existed in 1970. But of course, and perhaps for as long as the Nuaulu had been resident on the coast, other changes had been taking place which were part of the reality of the early 1970s, and which have subsequently become even more important. These changes can be grouped under five headings: the creation of multi-clan settlements, cash-cropping, land scarcity, sale of land, and market individualism. Here I limit myself to a few remarks on the last two.

By the early 1970s, the sale of land, though still a rare event, was a well-established concept, as was the possibility of land becoming a truly exchangeable commodity. Alienation of land to non-Nuaulu obviously limits the amount of land available, and particularly threatens that which is more valuable. Land transferred within the sphere of inter-clan prestations is never entirely lost, as access to land may come through women marrying into the clan. Land sold to outsiders is lost forever from the pool of Nuaulu land resources; irrevocably transformed into a commodity. But sale of land is not merely a material loss, it is also a denial of the value of traditional exchanges; a complete negation of the continuity and context of social relationships.

Then there is market individualism. As the Nuaulu experience it, the market is all about deals transacted between individuals, though individuals may sometimes represent groups. When an individual sells land (which is usually held by a clan) it is to an individual who will be able to dispose of it as he wishes; when a Nuaulu buys land it is for that individual or his heirs, and is not absorbed into clan land. In this way an ideology of individual land-holding establishes itself, and although we presently find the simultaneous existence of *adat* (customary) rules and market rules, which privilege group and individual respectively, the ideology of individualism has come to impose itself on the customary sector, especially with respect to the growing of cash-crops by individuals, the value of which circulates not according to customary rules but according to supply and demand. Overall, individualism with respect to land is the cumulative ideological product of structural shifts resulting from resettlement, confrontation, and participation in a new political and economic order. In this sense, it is possible to identify contradictions between the 'rights' of individuals and those of the clan. But it is clear that similar attitudes antedate such changes, in the sense that although the land was ultimately clan land, the individual was responsible for day-to-day decisions regarding use. Here the community of interest of the clan and the individual are identical.

Thus, land tenure up until 1980 was a product of internal structural changes (the emergence of the principle of locality, and the fragmentation of clan land), and the partial assimilation of an external ideology of land relations already present on the coast. When I published my first account of Nuaulu land tenure in 1977 the interpretation assumed a modernist, 'progressivist' movement from mountain to coast, traditional to modern, resource to commodity. For outsiders, it was difficult to think of such shifts as anything but inevitable, permanent and ineluctable; perhaps in much the same way as many modelled post-war social democracy or the demise of capitalism. Few Western intellectuals could imagine a situation in which history might appear to 'unwind' or 'run in reverse'. But by the early 1980s the situation in south Seram, and Indonesian government policy at several levels, were providing the conditions by which this became possible. In particular, commercial forest extraction increased in the Amahai sub-district, there was an influx of migrants into the Sepa area, and the Nua–Ruatan valley was opened up to transmigrants. The consequences of all of this for the Nuaulu were, paradoxically, both to vindicate their enduring identity and rights with respect to a large geographical area and at the same time to undermine radically their conception of forest.

THE EFFECTS OF LOGGING AND IMMIGRATION

Commercial logging had been recommended by Dutch administrators for the Amahai sub-district as early as 1856, and some extraction took place during the colonial period (Ellen 1985: 584). After independence, logging was very limited until the 1970s. Apart from local uses, it was restricted to arrangements with Ambonese Chinese and other small businessmen to cut *meranti*, or requests from government bureaucrats or agencies for timber and rattan. In some cases administrators acted officially, in other cases their status was used as a means of obtaining personal access to resources which could then be sold privately at a profit. Such requests often involved the Nuaulu, who were hired as guides, porters and labourers, either commissioned directly to provide particular quantities of timber (for which they were paid in cash, or kind), or required to provide materials for government building works as a duty to the state. These latter requests continue to be much resented by the Nuaulu, and there have been occasions when there has been a shortfall in agreed payments, when payments have failed to materialize altogether and when local officials have financially benefited from Nuaulu labour given free in good faith to the state. This has not encouraged Nuaulu to participate further in such activities. Nuaulu have also served as guides for government surveys and in oil prospecting. I mention these things, not so much because they have had a significant physical effect on the forest, but because they mark the beginning of a new set of attitudes to forest. These arise from the recognition that there is a demand for forest resources on a scale far beyond the experience and comprehension of most Nuaulu, and that new means of transforming forest circumnavigate and thus deny the relevance of pre-existing conceptualizations of forest and those ways in which it is rendered socially useful through the mediation of clans and ancestors.

In recent years new technology, particularly the chain saw, has had a decisive impact on forest clearance. Large trees which were once left standing are now cut, while the efficiency of clearance has increased immeasurably. It has also brought with it logging for export on a quite unprecedented scale. Between 1969-70 and 1978–9 it expanded nine-fold (Ellen 1985), averaging around one million cubic metres a year for the Moluccas as a whole. All of this has brought only marginal benefits to the Nuaulu: a little short-term employment as labourers and guides and access to some new technology. The Nuaulu can now take advantage of discarded cut timber, the deserted buildings and rubbish of logging camps. Ironically, the driving of causeways through the forest has opened up new areas to hunters and foragers, while the gaps in the forest are used for driving game. As more open patches appeared, following timber extraction and its associated activities, or following the expansion of plantation crops, regrowth grasses and young saplings attracted deer, so improving short-term hunting prospects.

The long-term reality is that this itself threatens to destroy the fauna on which the Nuaulu depend. The damage done by mechanized logging is well documented elsewhere, and although Moluccan timber extraction is only 3-4 per cent of total Indonesian production, its ecological and sociological impact is disproportionate given the small size of the forest areas involved. Extensive logging, combined with increased clearance through swiddening, transmigration, government plantations and road-building, seems likely to destroy much of the lowland rainforest of Seram. In contrast to former patterns of timber extraction, typified by a gradual denudation of primary forest and the selective (but not exhaustive) extraction of a variety of species to cater for a wide range of essentially local uses, modern methods involve either the selective extraction of just a few species to exhaustion, or the total destruction of forest in a short period to cater for a narrow range of non-local uses. Additionally (and crucially), the control of the system is becoming increasingly remote. Decisions regarding the location and level of extraction are made by agencies of central government, and within them by individuals and committees in the highest echelons. None of this makes for sensitive responses to changing conditions on the ground.

We must now turn to immigration. The littoral of southern Seram between Elpaputih Bay and the eastern boundary of the Amahai sub-district is not new to incomers (Collins 1980, 1984). But apart from the movements of the Nuaulu themselves in the latter part of the nineteenth century, the population situation appears to have remained fairly stable between 1700 and 1960. From 1960 onwards there was a steady influx of Butonese from southeast Sulawesi, and with the extension of the road from Amahai, there was a dramatic increase in Butonese settlers in particular. There has been some intermarriage with Nuaulu, some conversion to Islam, but most importantly both Sepa and Nuaulu have sold considerable amounts of land to these incomers. This has put greater pressure on remaining Nuaulu land in the Sepa area.

THE TRANSMIGRATION PROGRAMME AND RESETTLEMENT ALONG THE NUA–RUATAN VALLEY

In the early 1980s the Indonesian government began to open up the valleys of the Ruatan and Nua rivers for resettlement (see Map 9.1). This was only part of a wider programme with implications for the island of Seram, but so far the national programme of transmigration has not directly involved the sub-district of Amahai. The south Seram developments have been organized by the provincial government with the principal intention of alleviating land shortage on the Ambonese islands and resettling victims of natural disasters, and as a means of relocating groups from the poorly connected and seismically unstable periphery to areas which are better connected and resourced.

By 1986 the government had improved access to the lower Ruatan valley by pushing through a semi-metalled road and by building bridges, and had provided some housing and schools. The Ruatan now comprises an ethnically diverse ribbon development as far as the Nua, settlements being indicated in terms of the number of kilometres distant from Masohi. Thus Kilo 5 is occupied by Selayor Bugis, while elsewhere there are Javanese, Bandanese, Saparuans; people from Sepa at Kilo 8, Kei-islanders and Tanimbarese at Kilo 9, and now Nuaulu at Kilo 9 and beyond.

From the government viewpoint, the movement of large numbers of people into the area required a clarification of the existing position on land rights. It is widely acknowledged by the inhabitants of the Amahai sub-district that the ownership of forest land over about 'five kilometres' from the coast rests with the Nuaulu by virtue of their prior historic occupation of this area, and that permission must first be sought from them if others wish to cut it. This is a recent convention, and really means five kilometres from the mouth of a particular river. I suspect that formerly no such clear-cut distinction existed between Nuaulu and coastal land, except the assertion that Nuaulu claims began in the headwaters of the smaller rivers emptying into the Banda Sea. The five-kilometre convention has, however, important practical consequences when much pressure exists on land. This is, naturally, something which the Nuaulu themselves assert, although until recently it has been a matter of little practical consequence. Nuaulu claim to 'own' all forest from Manusela in the east to the Tala river and the sacred mystical mountain of Nunusaku in the west, and across the spine of the island as far as the north coast, placing much emphasis on the distribution of sago reserves. Evidence for acknowledgement of the Nuaulu claim lies in oral histories, in claims to original clan territories, in the historical linguistic reconstructions which back this up (Collins 1980, 1984), in the evidence of very recent in-migration of non-Seramese and in the relocation of different groups within the sub-district. Whether the Nuaulu had exclusive use of this area before they moved to the coast is unclear, perhaps even doubtful, and in certain interpretations both Nuaulu and Sepa have joint rights at the

Ruatan–Nua confluence. But what is important is that it is now *assumed* to have been the case by Nuaulu and non-Nuaulu alike, and that this has resulted in Nuaulu being treated as if they had been granted legal title to what I conservatively estimate to be some 1,670˙square kilometres of land, with inland limits which are conveniently coterminous with the present boundaries of the Amahai sub-district. Thus, government policy has influenced Nuaulu constructions of their ethnic, social and land-holding status.

There is another sense in which government policy has worked to the advantage of contemporary Nuaulu. The Nuaulu, along with other interior Seramese peoples, have for many years been recognized by the government as *orang terasing*, the original inhabitants of a region. In practice, definitions of who was and who was not *terasing* have not always been obvious, but in the Nuaulu case their religion and the attitudes of those around them were clearly critical. Elsewhere, location in the mountains is what is important. But however the classification arose, it has had policy consequences. Generically, *orang terasing* are assumed to be undeveloped, often primitive, and therefore eligible for grants and projects emanating from the department of social affairs. Such assistance, of course, is not always in the real interest of those who are supposed to benefit, while often the material consequences are not worth the bureaucratic fiddle-faddle. But in the present case, being *terasing* has clearly affected the government's decision to recognize Nuaulu as the sole owners of the greater part of central South Seram.

From the time of first settlement at Sepa, Nuaulu retained an interest in the Nua–Ruatan basin, which they regarded as their own. It was an area regularly visited for hunting, containing long-deserted garden plots from which fruits could be regularly harvested, and providing ready access to the main source of sago, Somau. It was the location of many Nuaulu sacred sites and of the old hamlets themselves, of ancient and not so ancient clan spirits and ghosts, indeed of the spirits of individuals who are still remembered and who feature in genealogies of the living. More recently, Nuaulu interest has been exacerbated by shortages of accessible land in the Sepa area and by conflict with Sepa and Tamilouw over land.

In the early 1980s Nuaulu from the hamlets of Watane and Aihisuru began to travel to Somau by a new route, to cut sago, clear land for clove trees and protect their property (particularly sago palms) against incursions from newly arriving transmigrants. They were now able to take advantage of the easy though circuitous route via Amahai, Masohi and Makariki, upgraded to a metalled road with regular (though seasonally disturbed) transport. The old overland walking route to Somau took five hours, the more circuitous journey by truck (approximately 50 kilometres) takes half the time. Although many continue to commute backwards and forwards between the Sepa villages and the new settlements, in 1983 permanent settlers began to arrive. The site allocated to the Nuaulu was south of the track at Kilo 9, a settlement which has come to be known officially as Simalouw. By 1990 Simalouw comprised 100 households, government housing and a school. Of these, 56 were originally Nuaulu, the remainder consisting of Kei islanders and Tanimbarese. The Nuaulu inhabitants have their separate area, which now comprises 20 households, of people who once lived at Watane: the clans Sonawe-ainakahata, Penisa and Kamama. Only the *kapitane* Penisa currently remains in Watane, where he must stay until the *suane* (ritual house), the first post of which he planted, comes to the end of its natural life. As for individual clan ritual houses, those of Penisa and Kamama were rebuilt at Simalouw between 1985 and 1990. Inhabitants of Rohua and the other remaining villages around Sepa also maintain houses at Simalouw, but only occupy them from time to time.

The population of Aihisuru (Matoke-hanaie and Sonawe-ainakahata) had also first moved to Simalouw, but in 1985 moved to Tahena Ukuna at Kilo 12. The ostensible reason for this was to avoid the severe seasonal flooding which is a problem in lower parts of the Ruatan valley, such as Kilo 9, but it was also to maintain that isolation from non-Nuaulu which these clans feel their ritual requires, and which was effectively maintained at their previous hilltop site at Aihisuru. Moreover, the higher in the mountains they reside, the nearer they are to ancestral settlements – which is a matter of some importance.

Those Nuaulu who have relocated in the new settlements seem to derive considerable comfort from having achieved a kind of homecoming, and certainly this is reflected in the satisfaction it is said to have afforded the ancestors. But when all is said and done it has been the material benefits which have been critical: travel time to main sago forests has been dramatically cut, the festering problems over land with Sepa have been eliminated, there is as much easily accessible land at the new sites as they need for the foreseeable future, and hunting returns are greater. Although coconut palms and clove trees are still young, the important thing (as Merpati Sonawe explained to me) is to think about the grandchildren.

This brings us to the final (and perhaps most significant) consequence of the opening-up of the Ruatan valley for settlement, namely the sale of land by Nuaulu on a previously unprecedented scale. This has taken two forms: the granting of land to the government in exchange for houses and other facilities, and private sale to independent migrant settlers. In addition, the opening-up of land along the Ruatan for their own purposes has allowed Nuaulu to sell land in the more crowded vicinity of Sepa, most of which has gone to Sepa itself and to incoming Butonese. Although Nuaulu attitudes to land are being increasingly moulded by a market model, individual transactions involve a customary element. But the vagueness of the boundary between Nuaulu and non-Nuaulu land, especially along the lower Ruatan where the 'five-kilometre' rule seems to break-down, has resulted in litigation. One case involved Nuaulu reselling land to some people from Makariki which they had previously granted to the government. A second case involved land which Nuaulu had sold to settlers but which was claimed by Makariki. The case was settled in favour of the Nuaulu at the Masohi court, although in 1990 Makariki appealed against the decision and the case is still before a higher court. The legal difficulty here arises, at least in part, from the absence of any written and codified customary law which the courts can refer to.

THE EFFECTS OF RECENT CHANGES ON FOREST EXTRACTION

We are now in a position to examine the effects which the events of modern Nuaulu history have had on the lowland rainforest of Seram, and on Nuaulu conceptualizations of their relations with it. It is clear that the consequences of extraction for the Nuaulu in the decades 1970–80 and 1980–90 have been markedly different.

On the basis of detailed ecological and ethnobotanical data (Ellen 1978: 81–3, 212–19; 1985: 560–3, 568–77), we can make certain generalizations about the impact of Nuaulu subsistence practices for the period up to 1980. In terms of the geography of disturbance, most interaction during this period took place within a fairly short radius of each village, in secondary or denuded forest. Only during hunting, and on expeditions to collect rattan, resin and some other products, is it necessary to exceed the boundaries of the most distant gardens on a routine basis (Ellen 1975, 1985: 566–7). Swiddens were, and continue to be, usually cut from secondary forest (typically bamboo scrub) within a four-kilometre radius of the settlement, and although the percentage of garden land cut from primary forest is high by comparative southeast Asian standards, official estimates of forest destroyed due to traditional swiddening are grossly overstated. Low population densities have ensured that little land has succeeded to grassland climax, and fires seldom get out of hand to the extent that they cause obvious and non-recoverable environmental damage.

For the most part, timber cutting has been intermittent, patchy and economical; some wood is cut without killing trees, while the greatest volume of firewood continues to come from non-timber-producing trees. There are, of course, examples of what some might call waste: some trees are felled in order to obtain only their bark, or while engaged in hunting arboreal mammals, to create space for the performance of other activities, to provide clear-views for animal drives; living wood is preferred to fallen stands, large trunks are left to rot in swiddens, and a restricted technology means that certain methods of reducing logs are extravagant. Though not uniformly ecologically efficient, and while it is true that the effects of 'traditional' modes of rainforest extraction have sometimes been underestimated, a low population density, the forest vastness, and low rates of extraction have ensured that the techniques used minimize forest damage, including gratuitous destruction.

The historical movement of the Nuaulu to the coast (1870 onwards) had the twin effects of preserving patches of interior forest which might otherwise have been transformed, and of marginally intensifying the cutting of coastal forest, where they were in competition with pre-existing populations. However, Nuaulu have continued to extract from highland areas, even from old village sites, for a period in excess of a hundred years, frequently travelling as far as the Nua–Ruatan confluence. The opening-up of this area for settlement by the government, and the provision of various useful infrastructures, is therefore seen by many Nuaulu as no more than an opportunity to resume a higher rate of extraction in areas which have always been important, but which are now much more accessible.

Since 1980, forest has been transformed on a qualitatively different scale. The continuing growth in the Nuaulu population and the increase in cash-cropping have placed greater demands on resources, and this has been exacerbated by in-migration and uncontrolled commercial logging. With the opening-up of the Nua–Ruatan area, Nuaulu can afford to sell land in large quantities without it threatening – in their perception at least – their own subsistence base.

NUAULU CONCEPTUALIZATIONS OF FOREST

Changes in the pattern and intensity of extraction bear some relation to how the Nuaulu conceptualize forest, and on the face of it we might expect to be able to identify an emergent but fundamental shift in the way forest has been viewed over the last two decades. We can infer Nuaulu conceptualizations of forest and attitudes towards it from systematic ethnobiological data, subsistence practices, notions of land tenure, general statements about forest, rules relating to the extraction of resources and sanctions consequent upon their infringement, indirectly from myths, stories, taboos, and so on. From these we can distil four general characteristics which, taken together, embody the most important aspects of Nuaulu conceptual engagement with 'forest'.

Forest is a complex categorical construction

Although uncut forest is recognized as a single entity (*wesie*), it contrasts in different ways with other land types depending on context. It may contrast with *wasi* (owned land, which may sometimes display very mature forest growth), emphasizing a jural distinction; with *nisi* (garden land), emphasizing human physical interference; or with *niane* (village), emphasizing landforms: empty as opposed to well-timbered space, inhabited (dwelt) as opposed to uninhabited space, untamed as opposed to tamed space, all with various symbolic associations and practical consequences for Nuaulu consumers. Although there are no Nuaulu words for either 'nature' or 'culture', it is in the various and aggregated senses of *wesie* that the Nuaulu come closest to having such a term, and from which the existence of an abstract covert notion of 'nature' can reasonably be inferred (see e.g. Valeri 1990).

Forest is not homogeneous

Wesie is a complex category in another sense. Despite the generic label, it is anything but uniform or empty in the way the Nuaulu perceive, understand and respond to it. It is more like a mosaic of resources, and a dense network of particular places each having different material values. In this first sense it is much like the modern scientific modelling of rainforest as a continuous aggregation of different biotopes and patches, varying according to stages in growth cycles, underlying geology, altitude, geography and natural contingency: old village sites, sago swamp, *Agathis* patches, bamboo scrub, hills, river-beds, neglected swiddens, caves and so on. Seventy-eight per cent of the 272 forest trees named by Nuaulu have particular human uses, and it is through their uses that they are apprehended.

There is an inner connection between history, identity and forest

The values with which Nuaulu invest forest are multi-faceted and differential, simultaneously materially useful and culturally meaningful. And in the same way that the material uses to which forest is put must be understood in specific and local terms, so too the social implications. While our conception of environment is something which is 'opposed' to people, or some kind of medium in which we dwell, and which is therefore bounded, the Nuaulu conception of environment is not as a space in which they hang, but much more like a series of fixed points to which particular clans and individuals are connected. These points are objects in an unbounded landscape linked to their appearance in myths; use of land is at every turn inseparable from specific sacred knowledge, sometimes mutually contradictory and obscure, though never absent. But Nuaulu are moving from a model stressing age-old certainties and continuities to one which stresses discontinuity, transformation, linearity and inhabited, four-dimensional space, and which most importantly gives recognition to the extent to which humans can overcome previously uncontrollable natural forces. In the Nuaulu case this is largely being achieved through market mechanisms and the approaching of carrying capacity.

Forest is a moral construction

The undeniable effect of merging practical usefulness, mythic knowledge and identity in the construction of the category *wesie* is to give it a moral dimension. That is, there are right and wrong ways in which to engage with forest, which arise in part from the specific social histories of parts of it, but also from its intrinsic mystical properties. Forest is unpredictable, dangerous and untamed, and various attempts are made to control it. This is reflected in the inferential symbolic opposition between 'nature' and 'culture' evident in most ritual, in the specific rituals conducted prior to cultivating forest, in the charms which are used to protect travellers in the forest, in the prohibitions on certain behaviours and utterances while in the forest, and in the correct ritual disposal of its products.

It is in the context of this that we must understand the ritual restrictions on harvesting forest products at particular times. But none of this prevents gratuitous destruction of wayside saplings or the felling of entire trees in order to capture one arboreal marsupial, and is certainly insufficient to support elaborate feedback models of ritually controlled conservation (Ellen 1985: 563–6). It is palpable that if there is sufficient pecuniary motive, land and resources can be disposed of despite the existence of *sasi*, displeasure on the part of the 'Lord of the land', or the ancestors. The irregularity of such transactions is partly moderated by appropriate ritual payment, as we have seen for recent land transfers. It is understood that in the eyes of the ancestors this may be insufficient compensation, and that at a later date those who have engaged in the transaction may suffer because of it. But these sanctions are only partially effective, and many feel able to live with the vague threat for short-term gain, and take other appropriate piacular measures retrospectively, as they become necessary. There is no reason to believe that such attitudes in themselves are particularly new, but their invocation with respect to massive land alienation is.

OF COMMONS AND CONSERVATION

It is difficult to find any unambiguous Nuaulu ethic which might reinforce mechanisms for forest conservation. Garrett Hardin, in 'The tragedy of the commons', argues that resources owned collectively will eventually be destroyed as no one individual is motivated to take overall responsibility (Hardin 1968; see also McCay and Acheson 1987). But if the Hardin argument applies it does so in a qualified and somewhat modified sense. To begin with, although common land ownership and claims to territory have hitherto existed as a theoretical condition for the Nuaulu, in practice most of the land theoretically available has not been accessible, partly because low indigenous population levels have resulted in little general pressure on resources, partly because abstract assertions of general Nuaulu territoriality have been less important than the claims of individual clans, and partly because of uncertainty as to the actual boundaries between Nuaulu and non-Nuaulu land. If, however, we follow Brightman (1987: 134) and recast the situation 'as one of loss of boundaries and the inability to control incursions', it begins to make sense. The government encourage Nuaulu clearance, land sale and resettlement; indeed they have facilitated all this by redefining (or confirming) the boundaries of Nuaulu land in new ways which work to their advantage. Now that the Nuaulu have exclusive tenure and can use the apparatus of the market and the law to enforce such claims, they feel free to alienate in ways formerly impossible culturally. The opening-up of the Ruatan has brought in some thousands of transmigrants, presenting opportunities for Nuaulu land sale along the Ruatan itself, but also along the south coast as more Ruatan land is used by the Nuaulu themselves. Moreover, these areas are now very accessible. So, it is less – in Brightman's words – a 'tragedy of the commons' than a 'tragedy of invasion'. Apart from the very idea of land alienation to outsiders, there is nothing in Nuaulu beliefs which might have led them to anticipate the future and which might have placed a check on such developments; it is not a question of ignorance, of absence of knowledge of ecological process, so much as hard-headed pragmatism.

It is not short-termism which is replacing a conscious commitment to preserving longer-term cycles, but the emergence of a view in which long- and short-term mean something, combined with deliberate revision of the received version of Nuaulu–forest relations to accord with recent developments. The existence hitherto of a non-temporal, non-linear, space–time conception of environment, in which cycles are sensitively recognized and their local effects and causes noted sufficiently accurately to permit inferential reasoning with a range of practical benefits, does not necessarily provide the means or incentives to understand the consequences of long-term ecological change and its implications, or to see it as having any relevance to day-to-day decisions about hunting, gathering or cutting forest. Indeed, despite a recognition that resources in particular places can become scarce or even completely exhausted, it is barely conceivable that sago, pigs, timber and rainforest could become limited goods on Seram, or even in their small part of it, in any absolute or foreseeable sense. Recent Nuaulu experience of logging and deforestation following massive in-migration only serves to confirm this, and ironically permits the uneasy co-existence between traditional views of forest and emergent – exchange-based – views. This is a frequent response to the early stages of ecological change in pioneer zones throughout the tropical rainforest belt, but it is not one which has received much attention in the popular press, which is understandably more absorbed with the heroic and harrowing struggles of Yanomami and Penan against earth-moving equipment or immigrant ranchers, stories which lend credence to the primitive ecological wisdom model, and which so many in the post-industrial West wish to believe.

ACKNOWLEDGEMENTS

The fieldwork on which this chapter is based was conducted under the auspices of the Indonesian Academy of Sciences in 1969–71, 1973, 1975, 1981, 1986 and 1990; a period of twenty-four months all told working in the

Nuaulu area. Most information on matters related here was obtained in the Nuaulu settlements around Sepa, including many useful data on the situation in the new villages along the Ruatan. Additionally, in 1990, I benefited greatly from a short visit to Simalouw at Kilo 9, and from conversations with Merpati Sonawe, and with F.P. Resmol of the Kantor Pengadilan Negeri in Masohi. To both these particular thanks are due, without forgetting the unfailing kindness and cooperation of old friends in Rohua and Sepa. I am additionally grateful for advice received from Franz von Benda-Beckmann of Wageningen Agricultural University (the Netherlands), and from Kay Milton, while revising this chapter for publication.

REFERENCES

Brightman, R.A. (1987) 'Conservation and resource depletion: the case of the boreal forest Algonquians', in B.M. McCay and J.M. Acheson (eds) *The Question of the Commons: The Culture and Ecology of Communal Resources*, Tucson: University of Arizona Press.

Callicott, J.B. (1982) 'Traditional American Indian and Western European attitudes towards nature', *Environmental Ethics*, 4: 293–318.

Collins, J.T. (1980) 'The historical relationship of the languages of central Maluku, Indonesia', unpublished dissertation, University of Chicago.

—— (1984) 'Linguistic research in Maluku: a report on recent fieldwork', *Oceanic Linguistics*, 21 (1–2): 73–146.

Ellen, R.F. (1975) 'Non-domesticated resources in Nuaulu ecological relations', *Social Science Information*, 14 (5): 51–61.

—— (1977) 'Resource and commodity: problems in the analysis of the social relations of Nuaulu land use', *Journal of Anthropological Research*, 33: 50–72.

—— (1978) *Nuaulu Settlement and Ecology: An Approach to the Environmental Relations of an Eastern Indonesian Community*, Verhandelingen van het Koninklijk Instituut voor Taal-, Land- en Volkenkunde 83, The Hague: Martinus Nijhoff.

—— (1985) 'Patterns of indigenous timber extraction from Moluccan rain forest fringes', *Journal of Biogeography*, 12: 559–87.

—— (1986) 'What Black Elk left unsaid: on the illusory images of Green primitivism', *Anthropology Today*, 2 (6): 8–12.

—— (1988) 'Ritual, identity and the management of interethnic relations on Seram', in D.S. Moyer and H.J.M. Claessen (eds) *Time Past, Time Present, Time Future: Essays in Honour of P.E. de Josselin de Jong*, Verhandelingen van het Koninklijk Instituut voor Taal-, Land- en Volkenkunde 131: 117–35, Dordrecht-Providence: Foris Publications.

Hames, R. (1987) 'Game conservation or efficient hunting?', in B.M. McCay and J.M. Acheson (eds) *The Question of the Commons: The Culture and Ecology of Communal Resources*, Tucson: University of Arizona Press.

Hardin, G. (1968) 'The tragedy of the commons', *Science*, 162: 1243–8.

Hughes, D.J. (1983) *American Indian Ecology*, University of Texas: Texas Western Press.

Leach, E. (1971) 'New science: Theodore Roszak or Giambattista Vico?', *Humanist*, 86 (6): 166–7.

Martin, C. (1978) *Keepers of the Game*, London: University of California Press.

McCay, B.M. and Acheson, J.M. (eds) (1987) *The Question of the Commons: The Culture and Ecology of Communal Resources*, Tucson: University of Arizona Press.

Valeri, V. (1990) 'Both nature and culture: reflections on menstrual and parturitional taboos in Huaulu (Seram)', in J.M. Atkinson and S. Errington (eds) *Power and Difference: Gender in Island Southeast Asia*, Stanford, California: Stanford University Press.

Chapter 10

Natural symbols and natural history

Chimpanzees, elephants and experiments in Mende thought

Paul Richards

This chapter asks questions about natural history among the Mende people of rural eastern and southern Sierra Leone. The analysis focuses on two endangered forest mammals – chimpanzee and elephant. There are, to my mind, two main reasons for pursuing this type of enquiry. First, local natural history is often 'good science'; that is, it makes a worthwhile contribution to the global stock of knowledge concerning plants and animals (Richards 1985, 1991). Second, 'natural history' interacts with 'natural symbols' in ways that are complex and not always easy to anticipate. The intention is to contribute to discussion of the problem of empiricism and objectivity in (supposedly) pre- or non-scientific cultures in Africa. A long-running debate on this issue (Evans-Pritchard 1937, Horton 1967, Jackson 1989) is of importance to the fields of wildlife conservation and science education as well as to the anthropology of the environment.

ANIMALS AS ANIMALS AND IN SOCIAL THOUGHT

To the Lele of Kasai the curious pangolin is important as a 'cultural category'. As Mary Douglas (1975) has shown, there is a near perfect homology between the nature of this animal and the uses to which it is put in Lele social thought. But when an animal like the pangolin is subject to cultural construction – once it has been locked in place as a 'calculus' for the solution of certain classes of moral dilemma – what scope and incentive remain for further biological empiricism? Symbolically salient animals are often treated (by anthropologists, and perhaps by their informants as well) as if they were closer to (mythic) unicorns than to (real) lions. But it is far from clear that it is appropriate to allow the social tail to wag the biological dog in all cases. Lions have a nature that it is possible for humans to come to know; unicorns do not. Whether, and when, people might choose to exercise their options in the first case is the burden of my text.

Mende hunters are, in my experience, as clear in their minds as zoologists concerning the distinction between entities that are empirically knowable and those that are not, and for the same sort of reasons (learning about animals is work-in-progress, minds closed by social logic are apt to get jumped on by leopards when least expected). I once suggested to a hunter who had helped a colleague identify a research site for the study of the rare and furtive forest bird *Picathartes gymnocephalus* that he could help me locate a similar site to study the equally rare and furtive forest dwarves of Mende folk tradition – the *temuisia*. He laughed, and then simply commented that the birds were there, but the dwarves appeared only to (good) people when they – the dwarves – chose. He drew a firm distinction between observations and appearances: biological empiricism and morality were not to be conflated.

The burden of my argument is that Mende ideas about the way in which their world works depend significantly upon biological empiricism – and that, in particular, ideas about animals, even if cultural constructions, up to a point, are also shaped by systematic scrutiny of the *behavioural* similarities and differences between humans and other animals. The contention is that, in the Mende case, part of what it means to be human *derives* from careful reflection upon a solidly grounded natural history. This is in contrast to those cases documented by Douglas (1964, 1966), Tambiah (1969) and others, where the cultural construction of natural symbols serves to *demonstrate* what it means to be human. I explore the notion that there is a strand of debate, within the Mende experience of the world, that seems closer to sociobiology than to Durkheim.

The chapter concludes with a brief speculation on how and why this biological empiricism has emerged as an important focus for attention within Mende rural communities. Some consideration is given to the extent to which local defences of biological empiricism are effective in the face of political (and other socially constructed) claims to authority.

PETS AND PRIMATES

David Hume, spotting a continuity between animal and human consciousness, declared that 'reason is nothing but a wonderful and unintelligible instinct in our souls' (Hume 1739 [1984]: 228). Seeking to reserve a space for the symbolic, Schopenhauer divided the domain of consciousness into 'will' and 'idea', the former – 'the will to live, which constitutes the inmost kernel of every living thing' – being characteristic of humans and other animals. He saw that 'in man . . . the presence of reason means the existence of circumspection, which straightway throws a veil over the will' but that the will 'appears most unconcealedly in the higher, that is to say the cleverest animals' where 'its nature may in them be consequently observed most plainly'. For this reason, he declared, we take 'our pleasure in dogs, monkeys, cats, etc. . . . it is the perfect *naïveté* of all their actions which so delights us'. Failure to appreciate these continuities in consciousness between humans and animals he blamed on Christianity, for having in an unnatural fashion sundered mankind from the *animal world* to which it essentially belongs and now considers mankind alone as of any account, regarding the animals as no more than *things*. This error is a consequence of creation out of nothing, after which the Creator, in the first and second chapters of Genesis . . . hands them over to man for man to *rule*, that is to do with them what he likes.

(emphasis in the original)

He is blunt about the consequent tendency to privilege 'natural symbol' over 'natural history':

the Creator goes on to appoint [Adam] the first professor of zoology by commissioning him to give the animals the names they shall henceforth bear, which is once more *only a symbol* of their total dependence on him, i.e. their *total lack of rights*.

(my emphasis, all quotations from Schopenhauer 1970)

Schopenhauer's point of view encapsulates an approach to consciousness in humans and animals with which many of my Mende informants would find themselves in general agreement. Animals and humans share a 'will to live', even if at times it brings them into conflict. To have this will in abundance is a virtue: mothers conjure and coax it by all possible means in their sickly infants.

Pets are appreciated for the clarity with which they express this simple truth. A pet monkey, for example, will be appreciated for its incorrigible high spirits and inquisitiveness. A monkey is sometimes considered an especially suitable companion for a child under the age of 5 because it is so playful and mischievous a creature. By exhibiting the delightful 'perfect *naïveté*' of which Schopenhauer speaks it may stimulate a sickly toddler to overcome the will-sapping ravages of malaria.

The house where I live in Bo once had a pet monkey. Named 'Conservation' (I was working on a plan to 'save' the Gola Forest when it first arrived), it was forever poking its nose into matters not its concern. It was considered to be 'under training', as if it were a *makelo* – a child fostered out for instruction. Banter among the young people in the house regularly played off the monkey's abundant irrepressible wilfulness with the fact that it had not the slightest idea of how to behave in polite company. Its abiding antipathy towards me (perhaps reflecting my mixed feelings towards forest conservation?) was an occasion for much heart-searching. This antipathy was generally rationalized as lack of familiarity on the part of a bush creature with the (supposedly urbane) manners of a *puumoi* (white person). Nevertheless, the monkey's demise (stoned to death by a visiting schoolboy) was a cause of genuine distress: months later the fun and life it had brought into the house were still sorely missed.

Another primate – the chimpanzee – is a much less congenial creature as far as Mendes are concerned. Their ambivalent feelings reflect its strength, intelligence and evident hostility towards humans. Migeod, an Englishman fluent in Mende, reviewed the evidence for chimpanzee aggression towards humans in a section ('Man killing apes': 162–73) of a book published in 1926. He had personally examined a 12-year-old boy in Pujehun hospital 'who had been badly torn by a chimpanzee'. 'This species of ape,' he records, 'runs to a large size in Sierra Leone' and 'noted for its ferocity . . . will without hesitation when it gets the chance attack children and run off with them with the intent to kill them' (Migeod 1926: 162). Migeod discusses the evidence, compiled by colonial officers in Sierra Leone (cf. Stanley 1919) relating to several similar attacks. He quotes the post-mortem testimony of the father of a 4-year-old girl killed by a large female on a farm at Faama, Nomo Chiefdom, Gola Forest in September 1920. The animal did not run away after the attack, but gathering up its infant 'went up a tree and viewed the rest of the proceedings culminating in its own death [it was shot by a hunter] with complete mental detachment'. It is interesting to note that 'the young ape was tended for a fortnight [by the villagers], but died of a cold' (Migeod 1926: 167).

The chimpanzee is the subject of a complex set of Mende beliefs concerning witchcraft and lycanthropy (shape-shifting). It is also the object of much empirical enquiry by Mende hunters, and thus is of considerable interest in the study of the interplay of natural symbol and natural history.

KOLI-HINDA (LEOPARD BUSINESS)

Some Mende believe that certain humans practise a species of witchcraft to obtain ingredients from the bodies of human victims for the manufacture of *hale* ('medicine'), principally *bofima*, 'the all-efficacious charm that was believed to bring wealth, power, respect and untold advantage to its possessor' (Abraham 1975: 126). Migeod (1926) derives the word from *boro* ('bag') and *fing*, the Mandigo word for indigo. The rise of interest in this charm may be associated with the politically destabilizing impact of the spread of 'Mandingo' long-distance trading networks through the forests of southern Sierra Leone in the nineteenth century.

Those conspiring to make *bofima* attack (or are said to attack) their victims as leopards, crocodiles or chimpanzees (the three classes of man/woman-eating animals known to the Mende). One generic name for this activity is *koli-hinda* (leopard business). Fear of *koli-hinda* peaks in periods of great social, political or economic tension. The Sierra Leonean historian Arthur Abraham (1975) suggests that 'people resort to leopardism to get the protection of powerful medicines when they feel insecure' though it is clear that in many cases it is 'an important method of eliminating rivals' by means of false accusations. *Koli-hinda* was particularly marked in many parts of the Mende hinterland during the colonial take-over, as confidence in indigenous political structures crumbled. Today it is a feature of rural communities suffering power struggles among chiefs. Occasionally, it is a charge used to unseat national political figures.

The Mende are divided concerning the ontological status of leopards, crocodiles and chimpanzees. Some consider that the victims of *koli-hinda* are killed by witches with lycanthropic powers (the capacity to transmute into one or other of these deadly animals). Others take the view that all so-called 'human leopards', 'human chimpanzees' and 'human crocodiles' are nothing more than that – humans who seek to disguise their crime by dressing up in animal-skin costume and simulating the damage caused by a wild-animal attack.

The argument of the lycanthropists is ethological. Other animals – snakes, elephant, bongo and buffalo – kill humans, but in evident self-defence. Attacks by leopards, crocodiles and chimpanzees are considered in a different light. All three species attack their victims for food. The West African forest-zone races of chimpanzee are markedly carnivorous and fierce hunters. The Mende, who have known this longer than primatologists, are struck by the details of the damage caused. When a chimpanzee seizes a child it frequently tears off its victim's limbs, digits and ears, or lacerates the face and genitals. These are precisely the parts sought by the 'human chimpanzees' for their charms.

The opposing viewpoint (that 'human chimpanzees' are costumed killers rather than shape-shifters) comes to a different assessment of the character of the animal in question. Migeod records that, faced with the facts of chimpanzee killings, many informants found it hard 'to conceive that such wickedness existed in the ape', preferring to conclude that 'it must be a human being disguised as an ape' (1926: 168). The collection of documents concerning *koli-hinda* in Sierra Leone compiled by Kalous (1974) includes evidence from witnesses who describe the knives used to fake animal attack (whether by leopards or chimpanzees), or who claim to have surprised murderers in the act of donning their animal-skin disguises.

This debate addresses a genuine ambiguity. Not all leopards eat people. A rogue animal that menaces villagers is acting unusually (e.g. it is old or wounded and has lost the capacity to stalk more normal prey). Mende hunters know that chimpanzees have exceptionally acute hearing, sight and smell and are hard to approach. An animal that seeks out humans, by venturing into a farm to steal a baby, or attacking a child on a bush path, is acting out of character. There is thus a certain force to the argument that all such actions are unnatural. In this light, the conviction that these attacks are carried out by humans acting in disguise is not unreasonable.

A cynic might suppose that this ontological clash of opinion arises from the fact that Mende villagers (more especially those committed to the shape-shifting option) are under-informed and confused, peopling the world with absurd imaginary entities in the absence of hard biological facts. The classic anthropological defence against such a charge (taking its cue from Evans-Pritchard's [1937] account of Azande witchcraft beliefs) would be to point out that local thought is not at this point attempting to encompass zoological realities; the inner logic of the debate should be sought in the social and moral domain. But this is to draw an unhelpfully firm line between the spheres of social and biological explanation, at least in regard to chimpanzees.

The persistence, for Mende villagers, of ontological dispute about chimpanzees, I argue, arises not from misinformation, nor from pursuit of a social and moral debate drawing upon animal symbolism independent of the biological facts, but from the very close zoological and behavioural scrutiny to which the animal has been subjected over many years. The more people learn about the animal the more mysterious it seems. Belief in shape-shifting clearly has a sociological dimension (it relates systematically to witchcraft concerns occasioned by perceived threats to the moral order within the community, cf. Gittins 1987). But arguments about shape-shifting are also occasioned by Mende knowledge that they are dealing with a profound biological puzzle. For the Mende, as for primatologists, the chimpanzee is the animal that approaches most closely the presumed boundary between animal and human forms of life.

MENDE PRIMATOLOGY

Local empiricism thrives on this species-boundary issue. Mende hunters are fascinated by the evidence that the chimpanzee is a tool-user, and that these tools are used for social purposes. No opportunity is missed to seek observational confirmation.

Some hunters describe scenes in which a male chimpanzee throws down forest 'walnuts' (*ndokei, Coula edulis*) while the rest of the group shell the nuts with stones and pile up the kernels in a heap. Sessions are said to break down in chaos if any of the younger animals attempt to eat out of turn (i.e. before the cracking session is complete). The controlled distribution of food is considered one of the essential features of human sociality.

Chimpanzees are reputed to build fishing weirs, another characteristically 'human' project (cf. Ingold [1986] on the human significance of the difference between 'hunting' and 'predation'). In Sherbro country Migeod was told by hunters that they had observed chimpanzees catching fish by laying down sticks horizontally in shallow water and then embanking the sticks with mud.

The essence of Mende medical practice is knowledge of 'leaf' (i.e. use of forest herbs for curative or magical purposes). Hunters claim that chimpanzees also use 'leaf'. In Gola Forest, and heavily afflicted with scabies resistant to treatments in the medical kit, I was one day given a potential new remedy by one of the forestry department line cutters, who told me he had recently learnt the recipe from watching a chimpanzee in the forest chew up a certain leaf and spit it on to a craw-craw infested patch of skin. He had later found the leaf effective for human skin irritations. An English traveller in Liberia in the 1920s reports an almost identical case in which an old woman observed a female chimpanzee treat a skin complaint 'with some large, flat leaves, which, after crushing and pounding them between her fingers' were applied to her baby's affected parts. The old woman tried them out for herself and found them 'to be curative' (Mills 1926: 140–1).

Perhaps the most intriguing area of chimpanzee behaviour, for the majority of hunters – and one under keenest local observational scrutiny – concerns the notion that these animals somehow engage in cultural activities such as drumming and dancing (Power [1991] refers to these moots as 'carnivals'!). Some hunters think that chimpanzee groups actually carry a small drum about with them in the forest, similar to the Mende slit drum (*kelei*). Others assert that the sounds they hear from time to time when large parties of chimpanzees are gathered in the forest are caused by a leader of the group drumming on tree buttresses or on its chest.

Hampered by the difficulty of approaching close enough to observe without disturbing the activity in question (a frequent complaint among Mende hunters as it is among primatologists), one informant told me he had tried to resolve the issue by 'laboratory' methods – rubbing chalk on the palms of a tame chimpanzee owned by a Lebanese trader to see whether chalk marks would be found on the animal's chest or the legs of a nearby table (a particularly striking example of the local commitment to empiricism). There is a general consensus among hunters that, whatever the true nature of this performance, its purpose is 'for display' (to establish status).

Several of these observational claims (which at one time might have seemed extraordinary or far-fetched) are now confirmed by recent work in primatology, e.g. reports of chimpanzee tool-use, nut-cracking sessions, and self-medication (Sugiyama and Koman 1979, Boesch and Boesch 1981, Huffman and Seifu 1989). Research in the Tai forest in Côte d'Ivoire confirms rainforest chimpanzees as the fearsome, well-organized hunters of Mende belief (Boesch and Boesch 1989). Most striking of all is the evidence that, indeed, under some circumstances, chimpanzees turn to cannibalism. Suzuki (1971) describes one incident in which an adult male tore flesh from the thigh and groin area of a still living and faintly crying infant. Whatever it is that motivates the animal to kill its own kind, it is probably not for food. Norikoshi (1982) reports that a carcass taken from a top-ranking male after 24 hours was missing only the ears, arms, one leg and genitals.

Not surprisingly, the Mende, knowing these facts of chimpanzee behaviour, find the animal not so much a classificatory anomaly (spelling danger when juuged against some sociologically determined scheme separating the clean and unclean, or good from evil) as a creature that is *by nature dangerous* owing to the combination of its near-human cunning, great strength, and violent disposition towards human 'rivals' and members of its own group. Some Mende informants articulate a local 'evolutionary' theory to account for this aggressive closeness between chimpanzees and humans. This envisages that both classes of being belong to an original category of forest-dwelling primates (*huan nasia ta lo a ngoo fele* – 'the animals that go on two legs'). The chimpanzees are those that remained in the forest (*numu gbahamisia* – literally 'different persons', glossed by my research assistant Samuel Mokuwa as 'those animals that look like, but have failed to develop as, humans') when humans were first discovering civility. This theory sustains, in regard to the close kinship between the two species, an opposite conclusion to that espoused by conservationists. Conservationists tend to think that because humans and chimpanzees are so closely related this strengthens the case for chimpanzee protection. Mende villagers agree about the closeness, but (perhaps more pessimistic than conservationists in their assessment of both human and chimpanzee nature) think that any increase in chimpanzee numbers might increase the risk of human degradation. Their fear is that humans might revert to, or be tempted to copy, the barbaric ways of the excessively strong, violent and cannibalistic chimpanzee. That this fear is not entirely misplaced is suggested by evidence in Hayes (1951) that a human infant reared from birth with a chimpanzee acquired anti-social characteristics from imitating its animal peer. Some primatologists, by contrast, argue that chimpanzee violence is an adaptation to 'the stress . . . of being watched and followed by humans' (Power 1991: 103).

ELEPHANTS, RICE AND IVORY TRUMPETS

If Mende villagers' evaluations of the chimpanzee are largely negative, their attitude to elephants is much more ambivalent. Elephants are in a way as admirable as they are dangerous.

Chimpanzees and humans, coming from the same forest stock (as it were), are too close for comfort: everything hunters know about chimpanzees suggests that they are a standing incitement to humans to revert to a barbaric, violent, cunning individualism. It would probably not surprise Mende hunters to know that some primatologists think chimpanzees are capable of learning human sign language (though they would probably be appalled by the idea), since chimpanzees are seen to be currently evolving deep within the forest a perverted parallel to human forms of community life. Elephants, by contrast, are not contemporaneous rivals to humans, but ancestral voices. These great animals were quietly in control of the forest long before any 'creatures that go on two legs' began their drive for dominance. To secure a space for human occupance, Mende hunters had first to drive off the elephants. But since it was the elephants that put in much of the hard work that has gone into opening up the forest to habitation, they deserve respect as well as fear.

To a forest-edge, rice-farming people, with a strictly limited capacity to clear the high trees of the upland rain forest, elephants are the avatars of economic development. In the first place, elephants – in Kortlandt's (1984) graphic phrase, 'bulldozer herbivores' – make 'farms' by wallowing in the grassy swamp basins they favour as dry-season refuges. These grassy vents (perhaps first opened up by elephants) must have been among the most favourable sites for early experiments in rice agriculture. Even today it is these sites that Mende farmers seek out when establishing a pioneer settlement in high forest.

Elephants also 'plant' rice in their 'farms'. At times herds travel long distances through the forest, and having grazed in some remote farm, yield up to the observant farmer interesting new types of planting material in their droppings. Mende farmers group together any rice so acquired under the category label *helekpoi* – 'elephant dung'. Elephant droppings are said to contain large amounts of undigested grain. Informants claim this seed was once used as a famine food in times of dearth.

Other elephant 'projects' of benefit to the successor community of human inhabitants in the forest included 'road-building' and 'planting' of trees. Elephant tracks are a major asset to hunters penetrating thick forest (Martin 1991). These tracks, heading in the direction of dry-season fruit trees (e.g. *Irvingia gabonensis* and *Parinari excelsa*) grazed by humans as well as elephants, are at times marked by tree species adapted to germinate only after the seeds have passed through an elephant's gut (e.g. the forest-emergent timber species *Tieghemella heckelii* – *ngoofele* in Mende).

Elephants, in short, are the pioneers of rural settlement. But their farms, trees and roads cannot be taken over without hunters first driving the original owners away. To kill an elephant, therefore, is seen as a key to the establishment of human communities in the forest. According to Hill (1984) it is a cliché of Mende historiography to claim the establishment of the settlement on a site where a great hunter killed an elephant. At times a temporary camp formed to house those who came to butcher and smoke the meat might evolve into a more permanent settlement. A hunter with the vision to engage elephant 'society' in a struggle for habitable terrain was likely to have what it takes to mould a human community and overcome its powerful anti-social tendencies. Fittingly, such a leader would claim the tusks, and have carved from them ivory trumpets to symbolize the transfer of power from elephant to human domain.

THE ONTOLOGY AND NATURAL HISTORY OF THE ELEPHANT

Enmity between elephants and humans is a matter for comment among Mende hunters. An elephant nursing an old wound is credited with the ability to single out a former assailant from within a large hunting party by smell. No hunter returns to finish off an elephant he has wounded. Another hunter must do the job for him. People in Bo still tell the story, over twenty years after the event, of a Lebanese hunter who failed to heed this advice, and perished when ambushed by his quarry.

As with chimpanzees, uncanny cognitive abilities of this sort cause Mende villagers to reflect deeply on both the ontology and the natural history of the animal in question. When a hunter is attacked by a vengeful elephant, doubts arise about whether the assailant is an animal or a witch with shape-shifting powers (cf. Jackson 1989). The experience is often described in terms of an unexpected encounter between the hunter and a stranger deep in the forest. If threatened by an elephant shortly after such an encounter, the hunter presumes he has met the stranger's shape-shifted *alter ego*. But Mende villagers do not believe in the existence of 'secret societies' of humans–elephants. Elephants do not come within the scope of *koli-hinda*.

There are two ways to explain this. Those who doubt lycanthropy can opt for a purely practical argument. Murderous charades in chimpanzee or leopard-skin costume might be frighteningly realistic: by contrast, evil men lumbering around in elephant-hide costume would have as little chance of terrifying onlookers as a pantomime horse. But practical considerations of stage-craft are unlikely to carry much weight with those observers who countenance the possibility of shape-shifting by magical means. Elephants normally shun human presence. But people are killed by elephants from time to time. Other explanations must be sought when an elephant acts out of character in this way. Why is *koli-hinda* not invoked in such cases by believers in shape-shifting?

Chimpanzees (and leopards and crocodiles), whether real, shape-shifted or humans in disguise, direct unprovoked attack against the most vulnerable of individuals (especially children and young women) for reasons of profit or malice. Elephants attack because they have been attacked – by hunters, who are among the strongest and most autonomous figures in Mende society. An elephant (whether real or shape-shifted) kills only to seek redress, or to protect herd and offspring – elephant 'society' (as it were) pitted against human society in the course of attempts by the latter to consolidate control over the species-rich secondary successions in forest gaps. In effect, to account satisfactorily for the distinction between the two classes of beast requires *both* ethological data and 'social facts'.

Chimpanzees 'habituate' to human presence (indeed, this can pose problems for primatologists attempting 'participant observation'), and Mende observers sense in this the unwelcome threat of an all-too-contemporary rival 'lifestyle' when chimpanzees 'invade' human living space. The case for assuming that elephants have 'society' and the rudiments of 'culture' is almost as strong as for chimpanzees. Scientific accounts of elephant behaviour stress strongly the social character of the herd, within which loyalties stretch (apparently) as far as the performance of collective 'mortuary rites'. Mende hunters well versed in the ways of elephants are quite willing to credit them with a strong sense of 'social' responsibility, e.g. in defence of offspring. But this does not cause Mende hunters the same sense of unease that they feel with chimpanzees.

Elephant 'society' is a community in retreat. By and large, leaving aside the occasional 'misunderstanding', the elephants have handed over to the human generation and quit. Elephants are in consequence respected as ancestors. In one village in Kpa-Mende country, at the time I did fieldwork there, the acknowledged oldest descent group within the community was no longer considered very influential in local politics, despite the fact that everyone in the chiefdom deferred to this group as being the most ancient lineage. In fact so ancient (and apolitical) was the lineage that it was said that all its elders were descended from elephants, and would become elephants again when they died. Evidence of elephants is only now seen in the deepest recesses of the forest. Chimpanzees, by contrast, still invade the present human space from time to time (they readily raid fruit trees around villages) and noisily proclaim their own (repellent) alternative vision of social (dis)order. Far from acquiring ancestral status, chimpanzees occupy an ontological niche reserved for hooligans, robbers and power-crazed cannibals.

MAKING SPACE FOR EMPIRICISM

In a striking phrase, Robin Horton (1967) accounts for the alleged conservatism of African modes of thought by asking 'who is going to jump from the cosmic palm-tree when there is no hope of another perch to swing to?'. His argument seems to be that people must first have experience of a number of different kinds of explanation that work well in changing circumstances before they can develop confidence in the value of scepticism and 'open' thinking. 'Traditional' life in African villages sets up too few opportunities to develop confidence that contradiction and difference can be socially productive. The merit of this argument is that it directs attention to an empirical issue – what lessons does village life teach? If there are valid parallels between the natural history of Mende hunters and farmers and the methods and values of biological science, we should enquire into the circumstances that have brought this about.

My suggested answer to any such enquiry is that a strong feeling for discovery has arisen (for the Mende) in the context of rice agriculture on the edge of the West African forest. Two circumstances (in combination) seem to me crucial. The first is the very great diversity of changing environments that shifting cultivators have to cope with when pioneering in a forested environment. The second derives from the nature of the rice plant itself. Rice is a self-pollinating crop, and assiduous selection and separation of distinct phenotypes at harvest tends to lead to the stabilization of classes of planting material adapted to specific agro-ecological conditions. Farmers are encouraged to experiment because no two environments are the same. When they do so, they get coherent results. Because results add up they gain confidence that they can cope with further changes by further experimentation. Mende rice farmers have come to value experimentation over any given set of results. They have learnt (to draw upon Horton again) to enjoy the exhilaration of skating upon thin ice.

Mende rice farmers do not shape land for irrigation (they lack the labour) but match a range of rice types to different soil moisture conditions. It is widely known that panicle selection at harvest is the key to this adaptability. Mende communities, accordingly, tenaciously defend the most 'primitive' method of harvesting – reaping each head separately with a small knife. Smeathman (1783) found that farmers in Sherbro country in the eighteenth century refused to adopt his recommendation, the sickle, for fear of incurring witchcraft charges (which would have been well merited had they muddled up local planting lines as a result of the introduction of this labour-saving tool). Harvesting by head rather than by bunch remains the norm in Mende agriculture, despite the enormous effort involved.

The value of probing off-types rogued during harvest is well understood. Some rogues are the product of spontaneous crosses between rices of neighbouring stands (rice is subject to about 1 per cent natural out-crossing). Entirely new types can sometimes be coaxed out of edge-reaped materials. Such rices are known by the category name *mbeimbeihun* ('rice in rice').

Rogues of this sort are tried out in small experimental plots close to the farm hut (Richards 1992). Any such experiment will be described as *hugo* – to test, in the sense of 'to probe' or 'to look inside' something. The word *mawali*, by contrast, is used for 'test' or 'trial' when the sense is 'to doubt', or 'to contest the veracity of a statement'. A court case rather than a farm plot is the context for the latter kind of trial. Both kinds of investigation are seen in probabilistic terms – bets against nature, and bets against the person. Until the British stopped the practice, Mende litigants would sometimes place side bets on the outcome of contests in court, as a token of their degree of belief in the rightness of their cause. This distinction seems to imply an underlying recognition that within the social sphere (notably in court) there are few if any forensic tools capable of penetrating the performer's mask. When Shakespeare in *Macbeth* remarks 'there is no art to find the mind's construction in the face', his phrase matches a Mende sentiment about court hearings and social life exactly. Farm life is different. Here, interrogation of nature leads to real discoveries.

A rationale for the degree of tolerance of experimentation afforded by the wider society is apparent in the following Kpa-Mende account of a stranger made good (Richards 1986). A poor outsider is welcomed to a village and offered the chance to make a farm on land remote from the settlement. Steering clear of controversy and village political competition to concentrate instead upon the requirements of a new and unfamiliar environment, the visitor reaps an abundant harvest. Some of this harvest is used to bail out his *hota kee* (patron, literally 'stranger father'), fallen on hard times as a result of ill-judged litigation. Favoured for his loyalty, the incomer is accepted into the community as a big man in his own right. But turning away from rice farming in favour of politics, the man subsequently meets the same litigious downfall as his *hota kee*. This puts exactly the dialectical tension in Mende thought between outsiders who observe and insiders with the power to shape appearances. But both sorts are necessary to make a healthy society.

Ian Hacking's (1975) account of the history of the modern scientific theory of probability directs attention to the importance of the differentiation between the two distinct conceptions of hazard alluded to in the story above – *aleatoric* hazard (randomness in nature) and *epistemic* hazard (degrees of belief in the probability of various outcomes). Conceptual disaggregation of these two ways of thinking about hazard allowed, for the first time, a degree of creative interplay between them that Hacking shows was of seminal significance in the emergence of modern scientific method. The same conceptual differentiation seems to underlie the segregation of probabilities associated with nature and politics in a Mende village, and with the same progressive consequences for the absorption of innovation. The story of the poor stranger is based on a clear distinction between the variability that lies within nature itself and fluctuations of fortune within a political process sustained by reputation, confidence and degrees of belief. Authority claims emanating from centres of political influence, doubtless, are at times a threat to experimental freedom at the margins of settled society. The point of the story, however, is that such experimentation is tolerated, allowed or even encouraged, since the subsistence base of Mende society would be threatened without it.

CONCLUSION

Evans-Pritchard (1937) records that the Azande never pressed their oracular 'experimental' method to the point where it shook their confidence in witchcraft beliefs. A witch is detectable from a post-mortem examination of the spleen, and witchcraft is inherited in the male line. In principle, therefore, a sceptic could assemble sufficient post-mortem evidence to check whether or not the supposed mechanism of inheritance did indeed work, and thus confirm or refute the entire theory. No Azande seemed interested in any such analysis. Most commentators share Evans-Pritchard's view that it would be wrong to impute the aims and objectives of science to the Azande at this point (cf. Winch 1970). Lack of interest in decisive tests for the existence of hypothetical spirit beings is a reflection of the fact that the purpose of these beliefs is to sustain a social and moral order. Azande belief in witches is not 'bad science', it is 'non-science'.

Most contributors to the debate triggered by Evans-Pritchard's study seem not unduly worried by a notion of intellectual apartheid implicit in this distinction – that rural Africans carry out everyday tasks with a transparent practicality and restrict their capacity for abstract speculation to the social and religious domains. Horton (1967) is one of the few who have examined, in a serious and sustained way, the possibility of overlap or convergence between 'science' and 'African religion', but without being able to rid himself of the suspicion that African cosmology is undermined by a mismatch between the complexity of its hypotheses and the paucity of the means to test them decisively.

In this chapter I have begun the task of documenting, in a very provisional way, some cases where it seems to me this mismatch is not a problem, and where a progressive understanding of natural history is in the making. Mende farmers adopt a straightforwardly empirical approach to the improvement of rice agriculture, because rice germ plasm responds in predictable ways to farmer selective pressure. Everyday contingencies (e.g. discovery of high weed tolerance or disease resistance among rices as a consequence of unintended neglect) offer up valid experimental designs. In other cases sharp-eyed cultivators organize consciously adaptive experiments in response to new or changed environmental circumstances (cf. de Schlippe [1956], on Azande agricultural experimentation).

Mende ideas about animals present a more complex set of interpretative challenges. Since some animals are thought to be witches, there is a strong temptation to begin to shift the analysis away from the nature of the animals themselves and towards the sociological uses to which ideas about animals are put. But this is not necessarily in accordance with local usage. My hunter friend who conceded that *Picathartes* is hard to see because it is rare, but that dwarves are hard to see because good people are few and far between, seems quite capable of retaining a morally useful imagined entity without it damaging his capacity for objective natural history. Potential confusion between sociological and biological categories is more likely, however, in the case of the forest animals most hostile to humans. Even here – I have tried to show – Mende hunters are committed to improving their understanding through observation. Where ontological confusion arises, behavioural peculiarities of the animal itself are at times to blame.

I do not wish to overstate the case. Biological empiricism is perhaps a rare and delicate plant in many parts of rural Africa. But this is no reason to ignore it. A capacity for objective natural history is important to the environmental adaptive strategies of poor rural people in Africa today. Similar observational capacities may also have been significant in earlier phases of human evolution. Is there a grain of truth in the Mende notion that people became (and remain) human through living alongside and comparing themselves with their rivals, the apes?

REFERENCES

Abraham, A. (1975) 'Cannibalism and African historiography', in A. Abraham (ed.) *Topics in Sierra Leone History: A Counter-Colonial Interpretation*, Freetown: Leone.

Boesch, C. and Boesch, H. (1981) 'Sex differences in the use of natural hammers by wild chimpanzees: a preliminary report', *Journal of Human Evolution*, 10: 583–93.

—— (1989) 'Hunting behavior of wild chimpanzees in the Tai National Park', *American Journal of Physical Anthropology*, 78: 547–74.

de Schlippe, P. (1956) *Shifting Cultivation in Africa: The Zande System of Agriculture*, London: Routledge and Kegan Paul.

Douglas, M. (1964) *The Lele of Kasai*, London: Oxford University Press for the International African Institute.

—— (1966) *Purity and Danger: An Analysis of Concepts of Pollution and Taboo*, London: Routledge and Kegan Paul.

—— (1975) 'Social and religious symbolism of the Lele' and 'Animals in Lele religious symbolism', in M. Douglas, *Implicit Meanings: Essays in Anthropology*, London: Routledge and Kegan Paul.

Evans-Pritchard, E. (1937) *Witchcraft, Oracles and Magic among the Azande*, Oxford: Clarendon.

Gittins, A.J. (1987) *Mende Religion: Aspects of Belief and Thought in Sierra Leone*, Studia Instituti Anthropos 41, Nettetal, Germany: Steyler Verlag.

Hacking, I. (1975) *The Emergence of Probability*, Cambridge: Cambridge University Press.

Hayes, C.H. (1951) *The Ape in Our House*, New York: Harper and Row.

Hill, M.H. (1984) 'Where to begin? The place of the hunter founder in Mende histories', *Anthropos*, 79: 653–6.

Horton, R. (1967) 'African traditional thought and Western science', *Africa*, 37 (1 and 2): 50–71, 155–87.

Huffman, M.A. and Seifu, M. (1989) 'Observations on the illness of, and consumption of a possibly medicinal plant, *Vernonia amygdalina* (Del.), by a wild chimpanzee in the Mahale Mountains National Park, Tanzania', *Primates*, 30: 51–63.

Hume, D. (1739 [1984]) *A Treatise of Human Nature*, ed. E.C. Mosner, Harmondsworth: Penguin.

Ingold, T. (1986) *The Appropriation of Nature: Essays on Human Ecology and Social Relations*, Manchester: Manchester University Press.

Jackson, M. (1989) *Paths Towards a Clearing: Radical Empiricism and Ethnographic Enquiry*, Bloomington: Indiana University Press.

Kalous, M. (1974) *Cannibals and Tongo Players of Sierra Leone*, Auckland: Privately published.

Kortlandt, A. (1984) 'Vegetation research and the "bulldozer" herbivores of tropical Africa', in A.C. Chadwick and S.L. Sutton (eds) *Tropical Rain Forest*, Leeds: Special Publication of the Leeds Philosophical and Literary Society.

Martin, C. (1991) *The Rainforests of West Africa: Ecology, Threats, Conservation*, Basel, Berlin and Boston: Birkhauser Verlag.

Migeod, F.W.H. (1926) *A View of Sierra Leone*, London: Kegan Paul, Trench, Trubner.

Mills, Lady Dorothy (1926) *Through Liberia*, London: Duckworth.

Norikoshi, I. (1982) 'One observed case of cannibalism among wild chimpanzees of the Mahale Mountains', *Primates*, 23: 66–74.

Power, M. (1991) *The Egalitarians, Human and Chimpanzee: An Anthropological View of Social Organization*, Cambridge: Cambridge University Press.

Richards, P. (1985) *Indigenous Agricultural Revolution: Ecology and Food Production in West Africa*, London: Hutchinson.

—— (1986) *Coping with Hunger: Hazard and Experiment in an African Rice-Farming System*, London: Allen and Unwin.

—— (1991) 'Mende names for rice: cultural analysis of an agricultural knowledge system', in H.J. Tillmann (ed.) *Proceedings, Workshop on Agricultural Knowledge Systems and the Role of Extension*, Stuttgart: Institut für Agrarsoziologie, Universität Hohenheim.

—— (1992) 'Rural development and local knowledge: the case of rice in central Sierra Leone', *Entwicklungsethnologie*, 1: 33–42.

Schopenhauer, A. (1970) *Essays and Aphorisms*, selected and trans. R.J. Hollingdale, Harmondsworth: Penguin.

Smeathman, H. (1783) Appendix to C.B. Wadstrom (1794) *An Essay on Colonization*, London.

Stanley, W.B. (1919) 'Carnivorous apes in Sierra Leone', *Sierra Leone Studies* (old series), March 1919.

Sugiyama, Y. and Koman, J. (1979) 'Tool-using and -making behavior in wild chimpanzees, *Pan troglodytes*', *Animal Behavior*, 39: 798–901.

Suzuki, A. (1971) 'Carnivority and cannibalism observed among forest-living chimpanzees', *Journal of the Anthropological Society of Nippon*, 79: 30–48.

Tambiah, S.J. (1969) 'Animals are good to think and good to prohibit', *Ethnology*, 8 (4): 425–59.

Winch, P. (1970) 'Understanding a primitive society', in B.R. Wilson (ed.) *Rationality*, Oxford: Blackwell.

Chapter 11

Local awareness of the soil environment in the Papua New Guinea highlands

Paul Sillitoe

Soil, as everyone knows, is essential to plant growth, yet the Wola people of the Papua New Guinea highlands, who are highly skilful shifting cultivators, maintain that assessment of it does not feature in their selection of garden sites. Their apparently off-hand attitude to soil on potential cultivation sites is unexpected. According to them, an inspection of the soil before clearing it for cultivation is not among the considerations that constrain and influence their choice of site, which include issues like cultivation rights as stipulated by their kin-founded land-tenure system, site aspect and ease of enclosure, location relative to house and other gardens, and so on.

It is possible to 'explain' away their apparently nonchalant attitude to soil on the grounds that its validity is difficult to assess. The people know their local regions so intimately that they have no need deliberately to look closely at the soil at any place before deciding to cultivate it. They already know its status on those territories where they have rights of access to garden land by virtue of living there, constantly walking over them in the course of their daily lives. But my Wola friends insist that even if they found themselves in an entirely unknown part of their region (e.g. by virtue of affinal connections) they still would not closely inspect the soil before cultivating it.

On another tack, we may try to account for their assertions by arguing that while they think that they do not look closely at the soil before establishing a garden, this is only their perception, and that they are unconscious of their assessment of their soil resources (e.g. walking around barefoot, they are tactually aware of texture and structure). Furthermore, we might suggest that the vegetation growing on a site may give an indication of the soil's worth, by its health and the prolificness of its growth, even the presence of certain species above others. But again the Wola deny that this is so, and field observations support their assertions; no vegetational features were seen to be associated with their soil assessments.

The casual attitude that the Wola evince towards soil assessment reflects their off-hand attitude towards environmentalist issues. Unable to foresee soil agricultural potential, they acknowledge little control over or responsibility for their soil environment. The soil is there to be exploited, to the full, and they push it to its fertility limits, until costs oblige them to relent. The idea of environmentalism is alien to the Wola. According to their traditional perspective they are not in danger of destroying or using up their region's natural resources. The rainforest, for example, is so vast that its destruction is unimaginable, it taking days to walk through in some directions before reaching other human settlements. They think their environment has an infinite buffer capacity.

The Wola follow their shifting agricultural strategy and abandon garden sites to natural vegetation and regeneration, not, in their minds, to protect the environment, but because crop yields decline beyond a tolerable point where the labour put into their cultivation is inadequately repaid. This is not to suggest that they invite environmental degradation, for example topsoil erosion, if they can avoid it, although again not because of the environmental costs, but because of the wasted labour. No one likes to work to establish a new garden to see their efforts swept away, although the steep slopes they are obliged to cultivate leave them vulnerable at certain times, and intense rainfall can threaten serious erosion losses.

SOIL SURVEY

In an attempt to assess the status of Wola disclaimers about soil appraisal, and evaluate generally the standing of local soil knowledge, I conducted a soil survey in their region. The area surveyed comprised, by and large, the local territories of two neighbouring *semonda*, bilaterally constituted, patrifilially based communities, sub-divisions of which structure rights to, and tenure of, garden land (Sillitoe 1979). The survey was conducted following the *Soil Survey Field Handbook* procedure (Hodgson 1976). The survey sites, eighty-five in total, were not selected randomly, but with two aims in mind, related to the gardeners' disclaimers about soil appraisal: firstly, to describe and classify the soils of the area according to a framework sympathetic to local perceptions and judgements, and secondly, to investigate and assess the effects of local land use and agriculture on the soils (Clarke and Street 1967, Wood 1979).

The data were subjected to multivariate analysis using the SPSS-X statistical package. Different classes of soil were distinguished according to all the data collected, suggesting correlations that might help assess the effects both of soil status on local land use and of subsequent agricultural practices on the soils. These findings were compared with indigenous soil judgements and perceptions, to assess the validity of assertions that the soil does not significantly influence cultivation decisions.

The 'unearthing' of correlations between land use and soils, and local assessments of the cultivation potential of different soils, demanded the classification of the soils surveyed by profile and site, to produce a typology of entire soils, as comprising sequences of defined horizons occurring in specified site locations. This soil resource classification was then compared with land use and local assessments of soil-worth in an attempt to trace connections between cultivation practices and soil status.

The five *profile classes* distinguished were as follows:

(a) coherent, more clayey topsoil with aggregated less porous structure, over a slightly stony and moist, faintly mottled, firm, aerobic, orange clay subsoil: the most abundant profile in the region;

(b) looser, more silty topsoil with crumbly porous structure, over a slightly stony and moist, faintly mottled, firm, aerobic, orange clay subsoil: the second most abundant profile;

(c) coherent, more clayey topsoil with aggregated less porous structure, over a wet and distinctly mottled, very sticky, anaerobic, greenish-grey subsoil, a waterlogged and gleyed profile, uncommon in the region;

(d) coherent, more clayey topsoil with aggregated less porous structure, extending to considerable depths (50cm), a recent alluvial profile, uncommon in the region;

(e) thin organic horizon 1, over a slightly stony and moist, faintly mottled, firm aerobic, orange clay subsoil, an uncommon profile.

The *site classification* was as follows:

(i) higher altitude (2,015m), east-northeast-facing, steeply sloping, normally drained interfluve site on limestone, possibly supporting secondary regrowth;

(ii) mid-altitude (1,815m), east-northeast-facing, steeply sloping, normally drained lower valley side site on limestone, probably supporting grass or crops;

(iii) higher altitude (1,983m), northwest-facing, steeply sloping, shedding interfluve site on limestone, possibly supporting secondary regrowth;

(iv) mid-altitude (1,770m), west-northwest-facing, variably moderately steeply sloping, receiving (with some run-off), lower valley-side site on limestone, possibly supporting secondary regrowth;

(v) low altitude (1,230m), variably north- through west- to south-facing, level to steeply sloping, receiving (with some run-off), plane valley-floor or bench site on volcanics or alluvium, supporting secondary regrowth or crops.

When they are combined, fourteen of the possible soil profile and site class combinations are represented. Some of these *soil resource classes* are considerably more common than others (Table 11.1).

SOIL RESOURCE CLASSIFICATION AND LOCAL SOIL ASSESSMENT

We are now in a position to assess the status of Wola assertions regarding their non-inspection of soil before gardening it, by comparing the

Table 11.1 The distribution of sites surveyed between soil resource classes

	Site classes				
Soil profile classes	*(i)*	*(ii)*	*(iii)*	*(iv)*	*(v)*
(a)	16	21	11	8	2
(b)	7	8	3	1	1
(c)		1		2	
(d)					2
(e)			2		

computer-generated soil resource classes with local assessments of the cultivation value of the soils surveyed, and the use to which they actually put the land (Table 11.2). A cross-tabulation of local assessments of soils against the soil resource classes revealed no apparent relationship. It appears that none of the soil resource classes painstakingly distinguished correlates with any local assessment class, according to which the very best and worst soils are likely to occur in almost all the soil resource classes. We cannot say that any of the classes which the majority of soils surveyed fall into represent better or indifferent arable soils. The exceptions have too few sites to allow us to draw reliable conclusions. But there are some trends noticeable upon inspection (see Table 11.2).

The soil profile class (a), coherent topsoil over orange clay, predominates over the entire spectrum of assessment classes, except for (6), waterlogged soils. But the ratio to class (b), loose topsoil over orange clay, changes as assessment falls. In other words, any soil resource class featuring loose topsoil is more likely to be judged an agriculturally poor soil, looseness here frequently equating with over-dryness as opposed to granularity.

The predominant sites in all local assessment classes, except for (6), waterlogged soils, are (i) high-altitude, east-northeast-facing, up-slope sites, and (ii) mid-altitude, east-northeast-facing, down-slope sites. The feature they have in common is aspect, and this complies with Wola assertions that the best arable land faces the sun to the northeast. But aspect alone is not sufficient to give a soil agricultural promise, and sites facing in a north-easterly direction cover the entire range of assessment from good to poor. The distribution of site class (iii), high-altitude, northwest-facing, up-slope sites, between good and poor assessment classes further illustrates the importance of aspect, for these sites are twice as likely to occur in the poor classes (4) and (5) as they are in the good classes (1) and (2).

The low-altitude sites (v) occur without exception in the first assessment class. Although the sample is too small to allow firm conclusions to be drawn, the assessment reflects Wola assertions that soils occurring at lower

Table 11.2 The distribution of local assessment and land use classes between the soil profile and site components of the soil resource classes distinguished in this chapter

| | Soil resource classes | | | | | | | | | |
| | Soil profiles | | | | | Sites | | | | |
	(a)	(b)	(c)	(d)	(e)	(i)	(ii)	(iii)	(iv)	(v)
Local assessment class:										
1 Very good	10	2		2		2	5		2	5
2 Good	15	3				7	5	3	3	
3 Middling	6	2				1	6	1		
4 Poor	12	6				4	8	5	1	
5 Very poor	14	6			2	9	5	7	1	
6 Waterlogged	1	1	3				1		4	
Land use classes:										
1 Never cultivated	12	2	2		1	5	2	5	4	1
2 Long-abandoned garden	20	4				8	9	3	3	1
3 Recently abandoned garden	10	6		1		5	6	4	1	1
4 Sweet-potato garden (including fallow)	14	8				5	13	2	1	1
5 Taro garden	1		1	1					2	1
6 Mixed garden	1				1		2			

altitudes are better, that crops grow more quickly there. They say that they avoid them because they fear sickness (notably malaria) and also because they are adjacent to the region of the Foi people, whom they fear as sorcerers. It is difficult to say how important the warmer climate is to the perceived increased agricultural productivity of lower-altitude soils, and how important are the soils themselves. A considerable part of this lower region has recent alluvial soils, and soils surveyed in this profile class (d) fall into the best local assessment class (1).

The soil profile class (e), thin organic layer over mineral horizon, predictably falls into the worst assessment class (5), and profile class (c), gleyed soils, predominates in local assessment class (6), waterlogged soils suitable for taro. All the soils occurring in this assessment class fall, as expected, in the down-slope locations of site classes (ii) and (iv), where drainage is more likely to be poor.

It is the uncommonly occurring alluvial, gleyed and skeletal soils that display a certain predictability regarding their local assessment; the majority of soils show scant pattern. Furthermore, it seems dubious to build an argument on the basis of local assessments of soil potential, when the people themselves deny that they inspect the soil before they decide whether or not to cultivate it, and it is suggested that they are possibly unaware of any pedological judgements they make. We can overcome this objection to some extent by comparing the soil resource classes against land use.

The use people make of land is equivalent to their assessment of its worth in practice, although this approach has shortcomings too, for we cannot simply equate cultivation of land with good soil, because the condition of the soil may have deteriorated under cultivation; nor can we equate recently abandoned plots with poor soil, because factors other than soil-related ones can prompt abandonment. Again, the initial impression of a cross-tabulation was that no land use predominates in any of the soil resource classes, which suggests that none of them is indicative of good or poor arable soils. But there are, once more, some trends worthy of comment.

The soil profile class (a), coherent topsoil over orange clay, again predominates over the entire spectrum of land uses. There is no indication that a larger proportion of the soils in this class is likely to be under cultivation than under secondary regrowth or primary forest; they are fairly evenly spread. The profile class (b), loose topsoil over orange clay, is not so evenly distributed, the figures suggesting that it is more likely to be cultivated. This contradicts the trend of the local soil assessment comparison, where any class featuring the loose topsoil is more likely to be assessed as poor. This may be explained, at least in part, by the larger proportion of (b) profile class soils occurring in recently abandoned gardens. This suggests that more of them in any sample would be judged as agriculturally tired soils, occurring where cultivation has been abandoned to allow regeneration. It is also likely that some of the soils under cultivation were showing signs of tiredness, and with a larger proportion of soil profile class (b) soils under cultivation, there is an increased chance of them showing signs of becoming productively poor.

There is perhaps a weak trend for down-slope sites to be preferred over up-slope sites for cultivation. The aspect preference is again evident, with a greater proportion of northeast-facing sites under cultivation and northwest-facing ones under natural vegetation. The uncultivated land under primary forest covers the whole range of soil site classes, indicating that none of the soil resource classes identified is either the product of cultivation, or is so preferred above others as to occur less commonly under virgin forest. It also suggests an adequate supply of those soils adjudged adequate for cultivation by the Wola. The low-altitude soils also show an even spread over the land-use range, and the position with wet soils and sites under taro is not so clear cut as might be anticipated.

The conclusion of this comparison of local assessment and land use with a computer-generated soil resource classification is that, where we might have expected some correlation, we have found surprisingly little. We cannot tell the local Wola people, using the soil resource classification painstakingly built up by analysing data on their soils, what they might be looking for in selecting a site for cultivation. The analysis has striven to identify a series of soil and site types, to uncover some hidden pattern underlying them that might relate to soil potential and cultivation use, and it has largely failed, for the vast majority of soils, to reveal anything other than a few trends, some of which are fairly weak.

In some regards this may be deemed a negative result, but only if one believes in the omnipotence of Western environmental science, and that it should produce a more insightful and informed interpretation of soil resources than the people who, for generations, have successfully derived their livelihood from them. If one believes that the knowledge of local people is valid and informed, the study is a success; the efforts to generate an objective, scientifically grounded appraisal of soil resources has failed to go beyond what the local people know.

INDIGENOUS APPRAISAL: VARIABLE SOIL PROPERTIES

The soil survey analysis has vindicated Wola assertions that they have no need to inspect soil closely before cultivating it, not because they already know its status but because of the strikingly uniform nature, on the whole, of the soil resources available to them. There is not a great deal to choose between the majority of soils of their region by readily observed properties (i.e. those not involving laboratory analysis). While the foregoing analysis has distinguished between some of the grossly different soils (such as recent alluvial, gleyed and skeletal profiles), these cover only a small part of their region. The larger part of it comprises the dark topsoil/clayey subsoil types which the analysis consistently grouped together. When it divided up the horizons comprising these soils, it made some very fine distinctions, which neither local people nor soil scientists would consider significant. We can see that the Wola cultivate the majority of their crops (except for taro) on very similar soils, which cover far and away the larger part of their country. In the light of this evidence their assertions no longer seem so remarkable, the soils of their region being, by and large, so similar that close inspection would be pointless.

None the less not all soils are the same when it comes to cultivation. The Wola do assess soils, if not before gardening, then certainly when they are under cultivation. In this event, how do they judge the worth of any soil, and why is this a post-cultivation process? The Wola assess the agricultural potential of their soils according to a few properties which they take to be critical to their productivity. They relate to topsoil only, focusing understandably on the horizon in which crops largely root and grow.

The properties central to the appraisal of a soil's productive status include its depth, strength, stoniness, *iyba* 'grease' content, and water state, as follows.

The *depth* of topsoil, which may be assessed as *onduwp* (much) or *g^enk* (little) or qualified versions of these words, is important as the medium in which crops are recognized to grow well. Although there is really no lower limit to the thickness of topsoil acceptable in a garden, the thicker it is the better, and if the subsoil shows through in places the site is likely to be abandoned.

The *strength* of the soil and its assessment relates in part to concerns over its depth, because the clayey subsoils are judged too strong for good crop growth. By strength the Wola are referring to the consistence and friability of the soil. They talk of soil as *buriy* (strong) or *tomiy* (weak) or as a qualified version of these terms, and assess it as a handling characteristic. If a soil is *buriy* its agricultural usefulness is low because they say roots and tubers have trouble penetrating it; the mechanical resistance to growth results in stunted development and poor yields.

The *stoniness* of a soil only becomes critical when it exceeds a certain percentage, hindering cultivation and acting to increase soil strength, impeding adequate root development. Some stones are judged beneficial to a soil. They act to warm it up, the Wola say, heating in the sun and retaining the absorbed heat longer than soil alone, so promoting the growth of crops which prefer a warm soil to a cool one. Stones also promote porosity, creating cavities and points of weakness in the soil which roots can exploit, and so off-set soil compaction. And some stones, especially *araytol* chert, promote the development of *iyba* 'grease'.

The *iyba* ('blood' or 'sap') or *hobor* ('fat' or 'grease') content of a soil derives from rotting plant matter. It is assessed by the soapy, silty feel that organic matter imparts to soil – the greasier the better. It dries out under cultivation, little rotting plant material being returned to the soil, until the soil becomes exhausted, *iyba na wiy* (literally, *iyba*-'grease' not resides). Interestingly, a weak, sick person is also *iyba na wiy*; that is, without blood. The growing crops exhaust the *iyba* until little remains. The only crop that can continue to yield on a considerably *iyba*-depleted soil is the staple sweet potato. When the garden is abandoned, the rotting of vegetation deposited by the regrowth will replenish the *iyba* levels of the topsoil.

The *water state* of a soil, its *iyb* content, is critical for the healthy growth of crops. The majority require a moist, aerobic soil; the staple sweet potato cannot tolerate conditions too wet. The exception is taro which thrives in a waterlogged soil. While the distinction of waterlogged *pa* sites from others is straightforward, differentiating between moister and drier better-drained soils is not easy. When under natural vegetation soils tend to be wetter, and the extent to which they will dry out and improve when cleared and exposed to the sun is difficult to assess.

The element of chance features in all of these appraised properties, which relates to Wola assertions that they do not inspect soils before cultivating them. They are all subject to change once under cultivation. The depth of topsoil is liable to diminish due to erosion, notably in newly planted gardens where the soil is exposed. The considerable slopes on which the majority of gardens are sited, and the intensity of the region's rainfall, exacerbate this problem, and loss of fine soil particles, leaving the larger stones behind, can increase stoniness beyond the point where it imparts beneficial qualities to the soil, hindering cultivation and crop growth. The soil's strength is thus likely to increase and diminish yield potential, especially if subsoil is exposed with erosion and subsequently mixed with the topsoil during cultivation.

It is not only the incorporation of clayey subsoil that increases *buriy* strength; some topsoils, when exposed to the sun for a considerable period of time in a garden, can become excessively dry and hard, which, if they have a non-granular structure, can render them unsuitable for further cultivation. The change in soil water content under cultivation is difficult to judge, but it usually falls. Until the sun has 'looked on' the soil, as the Wola put it, they cannot be sure of its water state under cultivation; it is possible that the soil might rapidly become too dry and strong. Furthermore the water state can be adversely affected during cultivation. When establishing a garden, people are careful to keep off the site after prolonged heavy rain for fear of puddling it, degrading the soil's structure and rendering it unsuitable for cultivation.

The organic-matter-related *iyba* content is certain to decline under cultivation, a fall in carbon content being long associated with fertility decline and site abandonment under shifting cultivation (Nye and Greenland 1960, Zinke *et al.* 1973, Brams 1971, Sanchez 1976). Again, rate of depletion is not easy to estimate. Although some locations are customarily recognized as more likely to retain respectable *iyba* levels than others (such as folds and down-slope locations), these may be too shaded for optimum crop growth (sufficient to reduce water content, warm the soil, and give crops maximum exposure to the sun's energy).

AGRICULTURAL POTENTIAL OF SOIL: DEVELOPMENTAL SOIL STATES

While the Wola have no series of appraisal class terms that they can apply to a soil before cultivation to label its agricultural potential, they have a clear idea of what comprises a good, bad or indifferent soil. But using these criteria, they talk only in generalities, not specific predictions. A good topsoil, for example, should extend to a fair depth, ideally with an abundant store of *iyba* organic matter, have a not too moist water content, and perhaps a modicum of stones. Structure features too in any soil assessment, the Wola having a keen sense of soil structure, referring to aggregates of any size as *suw ombo*. A good soil has a loosely packed, non-coherent, porous crumb structure. A commonly heard phrase for such a granular soil is *dowhuwniy nonbiy* ('sweepings like'), the Wola likening it to the crumbs of rubbish, grit and dirt periodically swept from houses. We can perhaps sense, in part, what they are looking for in the survey distinction between loosely packed soils of low density, poor coherence and highly porous crumb structure, and more packed soils of higher density and coherence, and a less porous, more aggregated blocky structure (although the parallel is not exact, some of the loose soils being unfavourably over-dry and *iyba*-grease poor).

These criteria, by which the local people assess the agricultural potential of a soil, cut across their soil classification classes (Sillitoe 1991), although they may be used to qualify a class, by referring, for example, to *pombray buriy*, 'strong topsoil', or *pombray iyba wiy*, 'topsoil with *iyba* grease'. These criteria relate more to a series of soil states distinguished by the Wola than to soil classification. They serve to demonstrate further how appraisal of soil potential is largely a relative issue for them, closely associated with time and use. It is an ongoing rather than a predictive process, based on observed soil performance under cultivation, and occurs during and after land use rather than before. While the soil state classes relate to soil assessment, they do so post-cultivation only. Indeed they refer to both use assessment and a broad developmental sequence soils may follow under cultivation. They are as follows:

1 *Suw ka* ('soil raw') is either soil under long-standing natural vegetation or newly cleared soil that has not been cropped. It has a good *iyba* content but its final water state and strength are difficult to judge.
2 *Suw hemem* is the best soil state, and few soils achieve it. It occurs where a considerable depth of vegetation waste accumulates, notably at the foot of slopes and on small flat areas. It is often human-made as a result of the build-up of decaying vegetation and topsoil along a fence line at the bottom of a slope. It rots down to produce a thick layer of soft, black, *iyba*-rich topsoil in which crops flourish. It is common, as a consequence, to see a variety of crops growing at the foot of the slope in an established garden adjacent to the fence where *suw hemem* accumulates, the remainder of the site being given over almost exclusively to sweet potato.
3 *Suw huwniy* is a soil state achieved in some gardens following exposure to the sun. It is a good soil for sweet potato. It is not as soft as *suw hemem*, comprising coarser crumbs, and it is relatively deficient in *iyba* 'grease'. But it is porous and *tomiy* weak, so tubers can penetrate and grow well in it. It only occurs following the break-up of the topsoil, when women have heaped it up into mounds for sweet potato, and the more times it is cultivated the better the granular *huwniy* structure may become for sweet-potato cultivation. If a soil develops into the *huwniy* state, the time that it remains cultivatable is related to the depth of the topsoil. If it is considerable, and the garden slope so gentle that erosion losses are small, then it can remain in this state indefinitely and support a sweet-potato garden for decades. A common strategy with these gardens is to work in a rotational manner around them, leaving an area to rest for some months

under *bol* grass (*Ischaemum polystachyum*) to replenish its *iyba* levels, a practice called *suw hombshor* ('soil share-out', i.e. share out its use, to conserve a modest organic matter content).

4 *Suw taebowgiy* is the worst soil state. The soil is *buriy* strong, hard and cloddy. Sweet potato tubers find it hard to penetrate, and weeds can compete effectively with the crop. It is entirely deficient in *iyba*. Any tubers that grow are small and stringy, and may be so poor as to become what the Wola call *hokay haeriy*, that is, bitter tasting with a flesh that turns an unpalatable grey colour when exposed. When a garden soil becomes *taebowgiy* it is time to abandon the plot. The time that soils take to reach this condition varies, from one or two years under cultivation onwards.

5 *Suw pa* is waterlogged soil. It is unsuitable for any crops other than taro and skirt sedge, although a range of other crops may be planted on any higher ground, notably around the base of trees where transpiration has somewhat dried out the topsoil and bound it together. Waterlogged soil does not follow the above development sequence but remains *pa*. Nevertheless, it quickly becomes tired under cultivation. Taro is a heavy user of *iyba* supplies, and these soils are cropped once only and then allowed to regenerate their natural vegetation cover and *iyba* fertility.

The foregoing gives further credence to Wola assertions about feeling no compulsion to investigate soil before cultivating it. They can hardly assess the favourability or otherwise of any soil beforehand, if its character only becomes evident under cultivation. It is necessary to clear a site and allow the soil to dry out somewhat in the sun to appreciate better its potential. This also becomes more apparent following its break-up and mounding, when the extent to which it may develop the favourable, porous, granular *huwniy* structure becomes clear. The extent to which its *iyba* reserves might be conserved is also largely unknown, although certain localities are more favourable to this than others, such as down-slope and in folds where the best *hemem* soils are likely to form.

The locations where favourable soils are likely to develop are limited on any site. It would be pointless to assess an entire garden from one of these favoured locations alone, when they make up only a small part of its area. Similarly, assessment of topsoil depth, the criterion that might be thought readily determinable, is not feasible because it can vary greatly over short distances within a garden. There is little point in checking it in one or two places when it will probably differ elsewhere. The same applies to the assessment of stoniness. The gardeners themselves exploit these site microvariations as they become apparent when they plant their crops, siting taro on particularly wet spots such as seepages, and a variety of crops such as greens, pulses and cucurbits along the bottom of slopes and in folds, where the topsoil is likely to be deeper and more *iyba* organic rich.

SOILS UNDER CULTIVATION AND LOCAL ENVIRONMENTAL KNOWLEDGE

The soils of the Wola region not only display a considerable homogeneity overall, being similar in a broad classificatory sense, as the survey analysis demonstrated, but also, in the variations they do manifest, vary in a largely unpredictable and continuous manner, both in the way some of their properties respond to cultivation and spatially as distributed across gardens. Where soils are generally so similar, and crucial variations between them not readily perceived, even canny and experienced farmers are hard put to make reliably informed comments about their possible potential. They cannot be at all sure about their behaviour. After all, some soils, they maintain, progressively improve the longer they are under cultivation, and the only way to find out is to garden them. This is the exact reverse of the current image of soils under shifting cultivation regimes, as being rapidly run down and forcing a change of site.

The understanding that we have of tropical subsistence agriculture derives in considerable part from work in regions of old soils, like Africa and South America, and there is a tendency to generalize from it to the equatorial tropics as a whole, whereas we should not expect people living throughout this region necessarily to follow similar practices. The shifting cultivation practices of these New Guinea highlanders appears to contradict accepted wisdom. Regarding soil inspection, their disinterest when selecting a garden site contrasts with the behaviour of people elsewhere who look at vegetation and soil, and even reportedly subject it to tests like tasting it (Gourou 1962: 25, Conklin 1957: 36–7, Allan 1967: 94, Ruthenberg 1976: 37). The evidence suggests that we should not lump the subsistence cultivators of New Guinea, nor those elsewhere cultivating on relatively young soils (e.g. on other Pacific islands and parts of southeast Asia), with shifting cultivators living on ancient land surfaces. The uniformity of the soils that occur across the Wola region, which has been central to the extrapolation of local pedological lore, can be attributed in part to their young age. Soils of the Inceptisol order show relatively little variation compared to older orders because they have not existed long enough to bear the imprint of local environmental variations. The geologically recent volcanic rejuvenation of the region's soils has further contributed to their uniformity and youth (Pain and Blong 1979, Blong 1982).

We have a long way to go before we understand the dynamics of these tropical agricultural systems. Clearly, those who have lived by them for millennia can only help further our knowledge (Chambers 1983, Richards 1986). No matter how technically unsophisticated people may appear, or lacking in environmentalist concerns, we should not allow this to lull us into assuming that their understanding of their environment is somehow deficient. If this study has achieved nothing beyond demonstrating that a scientific survey and computer analysis cannot better local lore, so lending support to the tenets of participatory development now gaining ground, then it was worthwhile. It is high time that we anthropologists convinced experts that they must respect local knowledge and consult it closely, before they try to improve on it (Thomasson 1981, Chambers *et al.* 1989, Skoog *et al.* 1990).

Nevertheless it would be erroneous to depict the Wola as innate conservationists, as culturally conditioned environmentalists who can be relied upon to use new technologies and innovations in a naturally sound way. They evidence little interest in environmentalism in their use of their soil resources, neither displaying apparent cultural recognition of responsibility for the natural world nor acting as if they have a duty to conserve it. It will look after itself under their farming regime. If a soil develops favourable agricultural attributes under cultivation they are likely to crop it to exhaustion, adopting cultivation strategies, like short-term grass fallow and green composting, to extend its useful life. There is no notion here of protecting the natural environment from the potentially harmful effects of human activities, only of exploiting it to its maximum.

Wola ideas on the environment differ from those of the environmentalist; the Wola hold not only that they can take from it with impunity whatever they require, but also that human use might improve its natural endowment. This notion is evident in their use of soils and has parallels elsewhere in the world. In opposition to the contemporary 'green' view that whenever humans interfere with the environment they destroy it is the belief that intervention improves upon nature. The creed of gardeners, whether Western, Oriental or Islamic, is that by bringing nature under control they can direct its productivity to their benefit.

The Wola have plentiful soil resources and can move to new sites as they exhaust old ones; with abundant land available, they are not exploiting their resources near to the margins, given their current technology. The abandoned sites in turn recover under natural vegetation. This is an inevitable natural process, not one dependent on human agency. It is their agricultural technology, coupled with a modest population density, rather than their cultural ideology, that protects the Wola environment in the long term.

ACKNOWLEDGEMENTS

I thank my Wola friends in the Southern Highlands Province for their assistance and hospitality while investigating the soils of their region, particularly Maenget Pes, who helped me throughout, and Ind Kuwliy, Wenja Muwiy, Mayka Yaeliyp, Huwlael Kombap, Mayka Waeriysha and Ind Haendaep, who carried equipment for me on my journeys throughout their region; also Dr R. Shiel of the Department of Agricultural and Environmental Science at the University of Newcastle-upon-Tyne for his good-humoured assistance with the study, notably with the computer analysis, which proved more awkward than we anticipated because of the large volume of data; and the British Academy for a grant to pursue the fieldwork and conduct the soil survey.

REFERENCES

Allan, W. (1967) *The African Husbandman*, London: Oliver and Boyd.
Blong, R.J. (1982) *The Time of Darkness: Local Legends and Volcanic Reality in Papua New Guinea*, Canberra: ANU Press.
Brams, E.A. (1971) 'Continuous cultivation of West African soils: organic matter diminution and effects of applied lime and phosphorus', *Plant and Soil*, 35: 401–14.
Chambers, R. (1983) *Rural Development: Putting the Last First*, London: Longman.
Chambers, R., Pacey, A. and Thrupp, L.A. (eds) (1989) *Farmer First: Farmer Innovation and Agricultural Research*, London: Intermediate Technology Publications.
Clarke, W.C. and Street, J.M. (1967) 'Soil fertility and cultivation practices in New Guinea', *Journal of Tropical Geography*, 24: 7–11.
Conklin, H.C. (1957) *Hanunoo Agriculture: A Report on an Integral System of Shifting Cultivation in the Philippines*, Rome: FAO.
Gourou, P. (1962) *The Tropical World*, London: Longman.
Hodgson, J.M. (ed.) (1976) *Soil Survey Field Handbook: Describing and Sampling Soil Profiles*, Harpenden: Soil Survey.
Nye, P.H. and Greenland, D.J. (1960) *The Soil under Shifting Cultivation*, Commonwealth Agricultural Bureau Technical Communication 51, Harpenden: Commonwealth Agricultural Bureau.
Pain, C.F. and Blong, R.J. (1979) 'The distribution of tephras in the Papua New Guinea Highlands', *Search*, 10: 228–30.
Radcliffe, D.J. (1986) *The Land Resources of Upper Mendi* (2 vols), Dept. Primary Industry Bulletin No. 37, Konedobu.
Richards, P. (1986) *Indigenous Agricultural Revolution*, London: Hutchinson.
Ruthenberg, H. (1976) *Farming Systems in the Tropics*, Oxford: Clarendon Press.
Sanchez, P.A. (1976) *Properties and Management of Soils in the Tropics*, New York: Wiley.
Sillitoe, P. (1979) *Give and Take: Exchange in Wola Society*, Canberra: ANU Press.
—— (1991) 'Worms that bite and other aspects of Wola soil lore', in A. Pawley (ed.) *Man and a Half: Essays in Pacific Anthropology and Ethnobiology in Honour of Ralph Bulmer*, Polynesian Society Memoir No. 48, Auckland: Auckland University.
Skoog, D. *et al.* (1990) 'Partnerships for sustainability', *International Institute for Environment and Development, Annual Report 1989-90*: 16–18.
Thomasson, G.C. (1981) 'Maximising participative planning: cultural and psychological aspects of user-centred soil resource inventory planning data preparation and presentation', in *Soil Resource Inventories and Development Planning*, United States Department of Agriculture (USDA) Soil Conservation Service Technical Monograph No. 1, Washington, DC: USDA.
Wood, A.W. (1979) 'The effects of shifting cultivation on soil properties: an example from the Kirimui and Borrai Plateaux, Simbu Province, Papua New Guinea', *Papua New Guinea Agricultural Journal*, 30: 1–9.
Zinke, P.J., Sabhasri, S. and Kunstadter, P. (1973) 'Soil fertility aspects of the Lua forest fallow system of shifting cultivation', in P. Kunstadter, E.C. Chapman and S. Sabhasu (eds) *Farmers in the Forest*, Honolulu: East West Centre.

Chapter 12

Political decision-making

Environmentalism, ethics and popular participation in Italy

Giuliana B. Prato

What is dangerous is not technology. There is no demonry of technology, but rather there is the mystery of its essence. The essence of technology, as a destining of revealing, is the danger.

(Heidegger 1977: 28)

Observers of Western society have long enquired into the human desire to control the external world. According to some, such a desire is essentially a 'will to more power' by which, in the era of modern technology, humankind becomes the object of its own domination (Heidegger 1977). Max Weber's observation on industrial capitalism (1949) has exposed the tendency to establish a 'technically rational control' not only over nature but also over social and political processes.

This chapter draws on participant observation and case material from Brindisi, on the southeast coast of Apulia, to examine the policies and discourses of 'professional politicians' and environmental protest groups, in relation to the construction of a power station in the 1980s.[1] I examine the formation and political significance of the protest, taking into account the relationship between structure, political action and the values and ideals related to such action (Leach 1964). Not only have the protest groups questioned capitalistic values; they have also brought to a head a widespread dissatisfaction with decision-makers riding roughshod over local affairs, raising moral and political issues about the Italian political system and its form of representation.

According to the 'anthropological philosophy' of Voegelin (1952), the study of representation should not be limited to its 'elemental' aspect; that is, the so-called 'representative' institutions and management of government. An analysis that leaves unaccounted for the 'substance' of representation, Voegelin says, obscures the structure of reality (1952: 50). In contemporary democracy, this 'substance' is constituted by the 'will of the people', as a fundamental part of a symmetrical relationship of obligation in which the 'rulers' are supposed to act in accordance with, and on behalf of, the *intencio populi*. This, Voegelin says, means that a government must be representative in the constitutional (i.e. 'elemental') sense, *and* in the 'existential' sense. It must embody, through the actions of its members, the 'idea' of the institution; in our case, the idea of democracy based on people's sovereignty.

Both these issues, and Voegelin's argument that human society should be understood by penetrating the meaning individuals give to it, are of particular concern to social anthropologists. Leach (1964), in his analysis of 'real society' as a 'process in time', shows that the 'overall process of structural change' can be understood through the individuals' inventive manipulations, and their choices between alternative forms of action. In broad agreement with Abrams' structuration theory (1982), Pardo (1993) has addressed the problem of representation and value in Naples, arguing that our analysis benefits from the diachronic study of the relationship between the actors and the social system; the study, that is, of both action and structure, and the changes brought about by such action (see also Harris 1988). Above all, Pardo suggests that the nature and processes of individual action in the system are better understood in a perspective that accounts for what he calls a 'continuous positive feedback' between practical/material aspects and moral/spiritual aspects (1992: 252 and 270ff., 1993).

In accordance with this line of analysis, I have become increasingly convinced not only that it would be misleading to separate the instrumental aspect of political action (in the sense of Bailey 1970) from the moral one, but also that 'moral' themes should not be seen simply as a 'normative disguise' for instrumental motives.

ITALIAN ENVIRONMENTALISM AND POLITICAL REPRESENTATION

Although the formation of the Italian 'Green lists' is based on environmental issues *stricto sensu*, the initiative has been widely taken by social and political activists of the 1970s, who are particularly concerned with moral/ethical issues, and who reject the party structure and the traditional left/right opposition. Environmental demands have also been expressed by the Radical Party, the Marxist-Leninists of *Democrazia Proletaria* (Proletarian Democracy) and the FGCI (Youth Communist Federation). The Radicals, in particular, have contextualized these demands in the wider issue of representation, opposing the role played by the traditional parties in favour of the more direct participation of citizens, through referenda, in political decision-making.

The subordination of every aspect of government to the interests of the political parties, it is argued, has changed the representative system to a system of *partitocrazia* (party-ocracy), in which the parties' power is morally condemned as an autocratic aspect of *sottogoverno* (sub-government). Kertzer (1980), referring to the USA model of the distribution of goodies, has described *sottogoverno* as a system of bestowal of spoils on the party's loyalists. Apart from the interplay of industrial, financial and political interests on which *sottogoverno* is based, the Italian situation is complicated by proportional representation (now under parliamentary revision). According to Bobbio (1983), Italy represents an extreme case of a syndrome that affects all advanced capitalistic countries, as a consequence of the proliferation of various centres of organized power. This situation of decentred power reminds us of Weber's analysis of the bureaucratization of the modern parties (1970), according to which the compromise between different interest groups has become the rule, and each group is likely to obtain benefits. Under such circumstances the 'elemental' aspect of politics and the related process of decision-making often take place at a *sottogoverno* level, in strong association with the 'wheeling and dealing' aspect of the 'political game' (Bailey 1970). As this occurs at the expense of the 'existential' representation, ordinary people increasingly distrust the traditional parties and their values (Pardo 1993). Thus, room is made for alternative discourses and forms of representation (Voegelin 1952: 49).

The processes regarding the construction of the power station in Brindisi exemplify the way in which environmental themes are used to construct such political alternatives.

THE ETHICS OF CAPITALISTIC RATIONALITY: LOCAL IDENTITY AND DEVELOPMENT POLICIES

During the 1960s, Brindisi became involved in the state's programme of industrialization of the south. The petrochemical plant built in 1961 and the thermoelectric power station built in 1966 by ENEL (the State Electricity Board) are particularly significant in our analysis. In the early 1980s, ENEL obtained government permission to convert the power station from combustible oil to coal, and to build two more power stations in Apulia. As the regional council was not consulted, the Radicals argued that such a process of decision-making jeopardized the democratic principle of administrative decentralization, based on the assumption that the devolution of authority to regional bodies should limit the power at the centre and facilitate the citizens' participation in the government of the *res publica*.

Not only did the regional council ratify the government's decision, it also failed to consult Brindisi's town council when, in 1981, it reached an agreement with ENEL and central government, choosing the city as the site for the construction of a new coal power station. Also in this case the local administration, in the form of a purposely passive town council, did not oppose a decision taken over its head.

The construction of the power station met the interests of various Brindisini, who formed what is locally described as a 'cross-parties Party for Coal'. The local enterprises interested in the project mobilized old and new political allies, particularly Christian Democrats and Socialists. Some town councillors also had a direct economic interest in the construction of the power station. In a way that is reminiscent of the political climate of the early

1960s (Apruzzi 1979), many local politicians and trade unionists now, in the early 1980s, mounted a campaign in support of the new power station. Given the situation of economic down-turn provoked by the crisis of Brindisi's main industrial asset (the petrochemical plant), they argued that the new power station would provide good opportunities for local enterprises and the local labour market. Symptomatically, the Christian Democrats warned that, should the town council oppose the project, central government would withdraw its financial backing from local initiatives. Similarly, as the Communist Party was still promoting the industrialization of the south, many local Communists regarded the power station as an opportunity for unemployed industrial workers, particularly those from the petrochemical plant. This policy was opposed by the FGCI and by some leading activists, who left the party.

Although this safeguarding of local economic interests was used instrumentally by many politicians, their 'local patriotism' was, in many cases, nowhere near the 'amoral nationalism' expressed by some modern leaders of advanced capitalist countries.[2] The observation of 'behind-the-scenes' processes and in-depth case material has highlighted a more sophisticated aspect of the actions and choices of the actors involved.

One of the strongest moral imperatives was the urge to implement policies which would improve the lagging southern economy. This attitude is exemplified by the action of Guadalupi, a Republican town councillor and industrialist who opposes *partitocrazia* because, he says, 'it is economy that should colonize politics'; which, I note, is why he joined the Republican Party. Throughout his career, Guadalupi's political choices have been aimed at reversing the negative economic trend of the late 1970s and making Italy, particularly the south, competitive in Europe. From such a perspective he criticized Italy's dependence on foreign energy supply, arguing that home-produced energy would be cheaper and would make industrial production more competitive. The whole province of Brindisi, he stressed, would benefit from the new power station. In line with this policy, Guadalupi has also invested in the local agro-industry, for he finds it paradoxical that southern production should be excluded from the major national and international markets, while supplying primary products to northern industries. In spite of Apulia's uneven development, Guadalupi feels encouraged by its recognized role as a driving force for the economic and technological development of the south (Drudi and Filippucci 1988).

These themes acquire particular significance when we relate them to the government's economic policy since the 1950s. This policy, it is argued, has been one of 'assistance' based on a mixture of neo-classical and Keynesian theories (Gribaudi 1980). The funds devolved to the south have been used to create a market for the production of northern industries, failing to bring structural benefits, and encouraging, instead, clientelism and corruption (Pardo 1993). Moreover, according to the ISPE (Institute for Economic Planning), government expenditure in the south (including 'special aids' and 'ordinary funds') has generally been kept below the 'ordinary funds' devolved to centre-north regions.

Guadalupi's political action belongs to an 'identity choice' that, in a way reminiscent of Leach's argument on the Kachin (1964), is also a choice in the pursuit of power. This is a complex issue. For it should also be noted that Guadalupi could have profitably invested his capital in the north, where he had good business relations with prominent industries. But, as he says, he would have felt a 'privileged' emigrant; he has chosen, instead, to remain in Brindisi knowing that other people feel like him. Significantly, not everyone who shares Guadalupi's sense of local identity has taken the same political stance – on the same grounds, the environmentalists constructed their ethical/moral opposition to the power station (see below).

Differences apart, the action of politicians like Guadalupi and of the protest groups exemplifies the difficulty of opposing 'rational' interest to identity choice. This also suggests that, in agreement with a point made from slightly different perspectives by Parry and Bloch (1989) and Pardo (1992), 'capitalistic rationality' (instrumentally oriented or not) is only apparently more rational than the strictly 'moral rationality' expressed by the environmentalists. I suggest that it is, rather, a question of balance, and that the issue may well be where to draw the line between immediate or relatively short-term interests and long-term, cosmic interests.

Moreover, capitalist rationality appears to be as utopian (though present-oriented), with its 'dream' of unlimited economic growth and wealth creation, as is the environmental one with its rigid 'green' vision. It might be argued that in this 'capitalistic dream', materialist values have become the symbols of the political reality of contemporary society. In Brindisi, after a decade of struggles and bargaining at various levels, this symbolism remains significant, though many politicians recognize that the power station has produced less positive results than expected, especially regarding employment and the encouragement of local enterprise. The unemployed who found jobs during its construction have been made redundant on its completion.[3] As for local enterprises, it is true that the financial investments related to the power station have encouraged development; but it is also true that the local firms never gained access to the main contracts. Instead, as has often happened in the south (Pardo 1993), they were forced to sub-contract from, and often pay considerable sweeteners to, the northern firms that had been privileged in the process.

THE ETHICS OF ENVIRONMENTAL RATIONALITY: MORAL DUTY AND CONSTITUTIONAL RIGHTS

The opposition to the power station has often been described by the media, and by most politicians, as evidence of the 'social and cultural backwardness of the local population'. Many in Brindisi believe, however, that the politicians' tardy environmental concern has been determined precisely by the action of the protest groups; especially as most of them became organized in the CLC list (*Cattolici e Laici per il Cambiamento*: Catholic and Lay People for Change).

As early as summer 1981, people from all over Italy participated in a 'camping protest' organized by the *Centro Sociale*[4] in Cerano – the site, that is, where the new power station was to be built. The protest broadened local awareness of the energy programme, and of its effects on the local economy and environment. Apart from being a most beautiful spot in an otherwise unimpressive stretch of coast, as the protest groups stressed, Cerano is an agricultural area. It was, therefore, the local peasants who were most directly affected by the new situation. Some were small land-owners who mainly cultivated artichokes; the majority were vineyard sharecroppers. Following the camping protest, a large number of peasants organized an 'anti-coal committee' with the initial aim of opposing the compulsory sale of their land. They realized that, as the Italian Constitution states that private property can be 'expropriated, after compensation, for reasons of public interest' (Article 42), they would have to sell on behalf of a 'public interest' which scientific reports, made available by the *Lega Ambiente*,[5] gave them reason to distrust. Their protest soon took the form of a land occupation, which ended in 1985, when ENEL produced evidence that the claim to occupancy of some sharecroppers was legally weak. Above all, despite the protests, in 1984 Brindisi's town council had signed an agreement with ENEL. The question, however, was far from settled.

Apart from strictly environmental and local issues, the *Centro Sociale* opposed the project on 'ethical-political' grounds because, following a government decision, the coal for the new power station would be imported from South Africa. At the micro-level, the *Centro* acted through the 'Committee Against Capitalistic Power', obtaining the support of many industrial workers. This was made possible particularly by the actions of Bruno, a petrochemical worker and a leading member of the Committee. The Committee, Bruno said, was especially concerned with local culture and tradition, but they were not 'anti-progressionists', as their opponents argued. In a sense, it could be said that their protest challenged the faith in the constant 'driving forward of technology' (Heidegger 1977). They were concerned with the industrial future of the area, certainly, but they feared that the new power station would 'deprive local people of important fields of life and work' and would 'contribute to the further deterioration of the relationship between man and nature'.

Generally speaking, the power station has been opposed by very diverse people, who were driven by their sense of 'moral duty' to intervene actively in society. These people were critical, like Guadalupi, of the policy of 'assistance', which they believe has condemned the south to increasing economic and environmental degradation. Above all, in a fashion that reminds us of Muller-Rommel's analysis of European green movements (1982), they opposed the capitalistic development and values which, in their view, have motivated both the 'irrational' exploitation of natural resources, in the interest of a few individuals or corporations, and the town council's acceptance of the power station.

The environmentalists of the *Lega Ambiente* and the Catholic group PD (*Presenza Democratica* – Democratic Presence) have campaigned most actively on these themes, separately and as members of CLC (see below). In particular, PD's members contextualize the environmental protest in a wider political strategy which includes the development of 'economic democracy' – the only way, in their view, towards an egalitarian society and the end of *partitocrazia*. The *Lega* also promotes the direct participation of ordinary people and of environmental associations in the process of decision-making. It focused on the legal/juridical aspects of the 'coal question', arguing for a greater respect for the constitutional rights that guarantee the 'citizens' sovereignty, local autonomy, *and* the protection of the environment and of public health'. Thus, as has happened elsewhere in Europe (Cotgrove and Duff 1981), the environmentalists and the trade unionists found common ground in their emphasis on participation, while their visions of society remained far, and conflictually, apart.

The protest was supported by some Apulian bishops who, following PD's pressure, intervened on the 'moral' aspect of the project. They appealed to the political authorities, while encouraging ordinary people to express their opposition to the power station; for, they argued, non-participation is a 'sin of omission'. Although such intervention cannot be regarded as the official position of the Church on environmental issues, it is significant that the 1987 annual conference of Italian bishops stressed the Church's 'ethical-political' duty to enquire into the relationship between the development of new technologies and the 'mastery of man over the world'.

The protest groups did not always campaign separately. Close inter-personal relations were established between members of the *Lega Ambiente*, PD, the 'Committee Against Capitalistic Power', *Democrazia Proletaria*, and people who individually opposed the power station. This network provided the basis for the formation, in 1982, of a 'Committee Against Power Stations'. This attempt to organize the protest more efficiently became institutionalized in 1985, when Suma, a leading member of the *Lega*, proposed the formation of the CLC list, in view of the forthcoming local election. CLC obtained two of the forty council seats; but, despite their promising start, they were dissolved in 1990.

CATTOLICI E LAICI PER IL CAMBIAMENTO: PARTICIPATORY DEMOCRACY AND 'ECOLOGICAL POLITICS'

CLC can be described as an 'unorthodox' political formation made up of three groups with apparently incompatible political and ideological stances; that is, *Democrazia Proletaria*, *Presenza Democratica*, and the *Lega*

Ambiente.[6] These three groups found common ground in their opposition to capitalism, and to the 'degradation of administrative and political life'. They adopted the motto 'for an ecology of politics'.

CLC's manifesto stated that the construction of the coal power station was an expression of the 'political, moral, economic, and environmental crisis of Brindisi'. In line with the themes expressed by the *Centro Sociale*, CLC stressed the danger posed by the power station to the city's identity and historical heritage. Since Roman times, Brindisi's economy and fortune have been linked to the city's geographic position and, therefore, to the port's activities. The construction of the new power station, CLC argued, would jeopardize not only these activities but also the most significant symbol of the city's tradition and identity; that is, the Roman columns facing the entrance of the port.

Conflict about the way in which CLC's programme should be put into practice was one of the main issues that crippled this partnership. A major disagreement emerged in 1987, when, under the autocratic leadership of Suma, CLC town councillors supported a ruling coalition formed by Republicans, Christian Democrats and Communists, in defiance of the fact that most members wanted to remain in opposition. While most dissidents tolerated this move, *Democrazia Proletaria* withdrew its partnership. The uneasiness of *Democrazia Proletaria*'s activists had started months earlier, when the *Lega* supported Green candidates at the 1987 general election, whose politics they regarded as dubious. They, like PD, also argued that the Greens' political programme focused too narrowly on the environmental question, failing to propose a 'global' policy. Nevertheless, CLC as a group did manage to express a new rule of ethics that transcends mere concern with the environment. They promoted an 'anthropocentric' ethic which would not deny the intrinsic value of nature, arguing that human happiness and well-being do not necessarily imply the domination and exploitation of the external world.

It was on moral grounds that little more than two years later CLC was dissolved, following PD's uncompromising questioning of the rectitude of some CLC candidates proposed by the *Lega* for the 1990 local election. It is important to recognize, however, that for some years CLC succeeded in mobilizing a large number of citizens, with the aim of reaffirming what they described as the 'true meaning of politics'. Accordingly, the emphasis in their programme was on the actors' ethical discernment between good and evil; the evil being largely identified with capitalism and *partitocrazia*. On these lines, CLC could stress successfully that each citizen has the *moral* duty to participate actively in the process of decision-making.

In January 1988 CLC capitalized on the battle carried out by the 'Committee Against Power Stations' to promote a 'consultation of the people' in the province of Brindisi – the large majority of the electors opposed the coal power station. In Apulia, the Radicals had tried to promote a similar consultation in 1981. They appealed to the Statute of the *Regione* Apulia, which guarantees the 'wider democratic participation of the citizens . . . in the assessment of regional policy'. They stressed that such a 'consultation', unlike a referendum, is not 'an exception to the representative principle, but rather an integration of the representative relationship' (De Pinto 1982: 32). According to them, a consultation expresses the citizens' views in a way that is not juridically binding. The regional council opposed this initiative, fearing that the consultation would be followed by a referendum. Nevertheless, the controversy led to further protest and, eventually, to various consultations in Apulia and elsewhere in Italy. In 1987, Italians registered a 'no' vote in the national referendum on nuclear power.

The result of the 1988 consultation was described by CLC as evidence of the successful activity of their town councillors. CLC claim that they also succeeded in singling out central government as the direct interlocutor in the 'power station affair', beyond the intermediate position of the regional council. It was, however, in the town council that their role was particularly effective.

TRADITIONAL POLITICS AND INSTITUTIONALIZED PROTEST IN LOCAL ADMINISTRATION

Throughout the 1980s the activity of Brindisi town council focused mainly on issues related to the power station. In 1986 Galiano, the Socialist mayor of Brindisi, ordered ENEL to stop the construction work. This was the first of several interruptions. Apart from the 'green conscience' which Galiano is said to have opportunely developed,[7] his intervention is mainly explained by the pressure put by CLC councillors on the ruling coalition. Not only did they bring up juridical and legal issues, denouncing the way in which decisions had been taken by the regional and local administrations, but their opposition in the town council also forced several ruling coalitions to resign – the first 'victim' being that led by Galiano.[8]

In spring 1987 CLC supported a centre-left coalition (see above) because, they say, they hoped to find an ally in D'Antonio, a highly esteemed middle-aged professional elected as an independent in the Communist list, who was appointed as mayor. However, D'Antonio's goodwill and desire to solve the complex problem of the power station[9] did not add up to a policy that met CLC's expectations. D'Antonio acted on two levels. He put pressure on central government, threatening to close down the old power station, should an agreement on the new one not be reached. At the same time, he worked out a new agreement with ENEL that, in his view, would reverse the negative impact of the plant at the local level.[10] D'Antonio's policy was generally not welcomed by CLC, who also resented his statements that, as mayor, he had to represent the interests of *all* citizens, including the workers who had lost their wages when construction work had been stopped. With the trade unions' help, D'Antonio tried to negotiate their retrospective payment, in a situation in which ENEL claimed compensation for the financial losses caused by these interruptions.

Soon CLC began to express publicly their disappointment with the coalition led by D'Antonio. As they stepped up their opposition, they became, I was told, proportionally radical and dramatic in their behaviour, staging colourful demonstrations from the public gallery in the council hall. Many informants described how the political situation in the city became 'unbearable, destructive and inconclusive', leading quickly to the resignation of this ruling coalition also and, ironically, to the formation, in 1989, of a more traditional one led by a Christian Democrat. This new coalition pursued toothless policies, surviving with much difficulty but little impact for approximately a year, i.e. until the end of the legislature.

While CLC opposed the power station on legal-juridical bases, the town council continued to adopt different, sometimes conflicting, policies. Several meetings were held with representatives of the central government and of ENEL, which were attended by local politicians, industrialists, trade unionists and Green MPs. The only observable effect of these meetings was that the construction of the power station was repeatedly interrupted, but never definitely stopped.

With time, CLC's opposition began to fade, especially at the institutional level. To the dismay of many members, who expressed their disappointment in the relatively private surroundings of the town hall's cafeteria, CLC councillors failed to mount an effective opposition even during the town council meetings that were regarded as crucial for the settlement of the coal question.

The impact of the environmental argument lost power after the dissolution of CLC. However, both PD and the *Lega Ambiente* continued to play a role in local politics. PD formed a new list, called *Insieme per la Città* (Together for the City), with the Communists and a group of leftist independents.[11] Things were more problematic for the *Lega*. Many joined the Green list, but on conflicting positions. Suma and other leading members were accused by their comrades of using the *Lega* to support their own candidacy in the Green list, and of implementing a policy at the local level which contradicted the principles of the association. For instance, many activists, who were now also Green candidates, dissociated themselves from the local branch of the *Lega*, while retaining their national membership, because they resented the close identification of the *Lega* with the Green list (cf. note 5), which also had the effect of excluding other environmentalist groups from the list. Their attitude is exemplified by Stasi,[12] who appealed to the *Lega's* general secretary and to the Greens' national coordination, denouncing this 'improper identification', the machinations of Suma and his friends, and the subsequent hierarchization in the Green list as unacceptable transgressions of the Greens' (and CLC's) idea of the 'ecology of politics' and the symbolism of representation. As this conflict compounded with an electoral campaign based on character assassination, the Greens quickly lost credibility and support. Suma was the only candidate elected.

In such a situation, two events finally settled the 'energy question'. Firstly, in May 1990, the Minister for Industry issued two legislative decrees that ratified the planned output of the new power station. However, meeting at least in part the result of the 1988 consultation, these decrees stated that the power station should never work at its full potential, and allowed the use of different fuels for its functioning. Secondly, a new agreement with ENEL was approved in December 1991 by most of the town councillors, with the telling abstention of the only Green councillor. This agreement, which was publicized as a 'crucial move to solve the long stalemate on the issue', included, unashamedly, many proposals that had been made by D'Antonio during his mayoralty four years earlier. Paradoxically, it was now left to D'Antonio, who had resigned his councillorship in protest, to point out to his 'green friends' that those who would benefit most from this agreement were precisely the politicians involved in the 'cross-parties Party for Coal' which they claimed to oppose. The power station became operative in 1992.

REPRESENTATION AND THE CONFLICT OF TRUTHS

The case of Brindisi highlights the complex issues of representation that characterize the gap between the expectations and actions of ordinary people and the political programme, ideology and policy of local administrations, and of institutionalized politics generally (Pardo 1993). The fact that both those who supported the power station and those who opposed it justified their action by referring to their loyalty to, and pride in, the local tradition and identity, did not bridge this gap. On the contrary, the traditional politicians have basically failed in a fundamental aspect of representation, for they have disregarded the opposition expressed by the protest groups and later, quite unambiguously, by most of Brindisi's citizens through the consultation. As for CLC, the situation is more complex.

CLC's electoral success in 1985 might be seen, in agreement with Voegelin's theory, as evidence of ordinary people's dissatisfaction with politicians who are representatives only in the 'elemental' sense. Considering that, in Italy, the 'elemental' aspect of politics is usually associated with the most instrumental aspects of *sottogoverno*, it is significant that CLC succeeded despite their limited control over those resources which, according to Bailey (1970), are necessary for one to enter the political arena. Their ethical/moral position did not exclude, however, a concern with the material welfare of the society. They, in their task of defeating the 'corrupt politicians', wrestled with both moral and more immediate practical issues to construct a programme essentially based on participatory democracy and the 'ecology of politics'. The ability of CLC's different components to negotiate an alliance on common moral positions, despite their heterogeneity, made the group even more appealing to the electorate, for they apparently formed a unitary political actor able to express different positions.

We should, therefore, ask ourselves why was CLC short-lived, despite their successful challenge to a symbol of political reality (i.e. *partitocrazia*) in which most citizens did not recognize themselves? It would be simplistic to explain this by CLC's internal disagreements. A more articulated explanation lies, perhaps, in the 'conflict of truths' between the symbolism expressed by the 'politicians of capitalism' and the new symbolism proposed by those who identified capitalistic ideals with the decadence of the social and political institutions. CLC's relative success is particularly significant when we consider that, during the 1980s, while the media and most politicians sponsored the ruthless pursuit of immediate material gains, most people (including the industrial workers) clearly began to disbelieve the 'industrial miracle', with its promise of welfare for all.

As I have mentioned at the beginning of this chapter, the protest groups opposed precisely the 'technically rational control' over society brought about by industrial capitalism. They also singled out the party system as one that corrupts the essence of representation. And yet, as they institutionalized their protest, they became part of that system, in obvious contradiction of their essence as the (existential) representatives of a new political symbolism. Thus, it became obvious that their political discourse also remained embedded in the logic of 'technical control'. According to Suma, such institutionalization was the only possible way for CLC to put forward their political programme and vision of society. It is within the same logic that CLC negotiated their support of the ruling coalition led by D'Antonio, thus becoming involved in the very processes of decision-making they claimed to oppose. While their institutionalization alienated the cooperation of other protest groups, like the *Centro Sociale*, it was their involvement in decision-making that marked the beginning of their loss of representativeness and, then, inevitably, of support.

However, the crucial question seems to be less that of CLC's involvement in the process of decision-making as such than that of their failure to perform their new role in accordance with their principles. CLC were particularly weakened by the inability of a relevant part of their membership (i.e. the *Lega Ambiente*) to deal with the broader issues raised by the new power station. Indeed, while CLC as a unitary actor tried to provide answers to major problems, such as unemployment, housing and economic development, the *Lega* pursued 'short-sighted' and 'rigid' environmental policies. Thus, their elemental representativeness also became less credible, despite the observable role they had played in 'the system'; particularly regarding the substantial changes they had joined in imposing on the project originally accepted by an unquestioning town council.

Material Wealth vs Spiritual poverty (handwritten)

CONCLUSIONS   *Social political change from individual change* (handwritten)

It might be argued that instrumental interests carried a great weight in the construction of the power station. It seems clear, however, that the tendency of politicians to emphasize the pragmatic aspect cannot be seen simply as evidence of a strictly instrumental approach to politics. The case of D'Antonio is a significant example of genuine interest, among some of these politicians, in producing morally right policies that would solve the city's major problems. The degree of 'morality' of such policies, and the nature of the difficulty in promoting them, are, of course, equally significant.

A more complex explanation lies, perhaps, in CLC's inability, as a group, to escape the trap of what, borrowing from Weber, could be called the 'iron cage of technological thought'. A complex situation has, indeed, emerged from the study of the relationship between actors' material and non-material resources and motivations and their ability to manage these resources and the variation in their value over time (Pardo 1992, 1993). It seems reasonably clear that it is precisely in the management of this relationship that CLC basically failed, as did, in an opposite way, the materialist-minded 'politicians of capitalism'.

CLC, by showing that they were affecting local politics, may well have initially strengthened the popular support which they had attracted on ethical/moral grounds. But they were crucially restricted by the inability of the *Lega Ambiente* not only to expand its political discourse, as required by the complexity of the situation, but also to come to terms with the changing value of the issue in which it rigidly specialized. Nevertheless, although CLC failed to satisfy the hopes they had raised by proposing themselves as the bearers of a new form of representation, their experience has exposed the causal link between the environmental problem and the politics of *sottogoverno*. More generally, it has highlighted the limits of *sottogoverno* and the inadequacy of the Italian traditional parties as symbolizers of the wider society, a task that other forms of 'ecological politics', as different as the PDS[13] and *La Rete*,[14] are now trying to fulfil.

ACKNOWLEDGEMENTS

I am most grateful to Dr Rosemary Harris and Dr Italo Pardo, who helpfully commented on various drafts of this paper. Dr Nigel Rapport produced useful notes on the version presented at the Conference.

NOTES

1 I use fictitious names to guarantee a degree of confidentiality, on which some informants insisted.
2 One thinks of the position taken by George Bush at the 1992 Rio Summit, in particular his stated refusal to endanger American jobs for the sake of international agreements to protect the environment.

3 These people are now finding jobs in the redevelopment of the petrochemical plant.
4 The 'Social Centre' was formed by extraparliamentary leftist activists with the aim of addressing social problems independently of the political parties.
5 'League for the Environment'; this is a national organization which, though supported by different parties, claims 'political independence'.
6 CLC candidates included students, school teachers, clerks, professionals and industrial workers.
7 Galiano used green issues to defeat opponents in his own party. During his mayoralty, under pressure from CLC, opponent town councillors were prosecuted for pursuing private interest through public office.
8 The resignation of a ruling coalition does not imply the dissolution of the council. A bill passed in 1990 reduces the limit for forming a new coalition to sixty days, after which a new election must be held.
9 It was D'Antonio who, as mayor, allowed the popular consultation to be held in Brindisi.
10 For example, ENEL agreed to invest in public housing and to recycle the water from the cooling systems in greenhouse cultivation and fish farming.
11 Most members of *Presenza Democratica* have now joined the PDS (Democratic Party of the Left), i.e. the off-shoot of PCI. The PDS is now capitalizing on the experience of *Insieme per la Città* (cf. note 13).
12 Stasi, a founding member of the local *Lega* and a Green candidate, is described as a genuine believer in the green cause. In the 1987 events she advocated a policy of opposition.
13 In 1992 Brindisini elected only PDS candidates (a Parliamentary Deputy and a Senator). Many believe that by proposing D'Antonio's candidature for the Senate, the PDS gained the crucial support of a so-called 'cross-parties Party of honest people', who also voted for the MP candidate.
14 *La Rete* (The Network) is a new party formed by ex-Christian Democrats and leftist intellectuals, led by Orlando, the ex-mayor of Palermo.

REFERENCES

Abrams, P. (1982) *Historical Sociology*, Shepton Mallet: Open Books.
Apruzzi, R. (1979) 'Sviluppo capitalistico e organizzazione sindacale a Brindisi', unpublished Laurea thesis, University of Bari.
Bailey, F.G. (1970) *Stratagems and Spoils*, Oxford: Blackwell.
Bobbio, N. (1983) 'Italy's permanent crisis', *Telos*, 54: 123–33.
Cotgrove, S. and Duff, A. (1981) 'Environmentalism, values, and social change', *British Journal of Sociology*, 32 (1): 92–110.
De Pinto, V. (1982) *La Puglia e il Nucleare. Il Fallimento di una Scelta Energetica?*, Naples: Pironti.
Drudi, I. and Filippucci, C. (1988) *Il Sistema Industriale della Puglia*, Bologna: Il Mulino.
Gribaudi, G. (1980) *Mediatori. Antropologia del Potere Democristiano*, Turin: Rosenberg and Seller.
Harris, R. (1988) 'Theory and evidence: the "Irish Stem family" and field data', *Man*, 23: 417–34.
Heidegger, M. (1977) *The Question Concerning Technology and Other Essays*, New York: Harper and Row.
Kertzer, D. (1980) *Comrades and Christians: Religion and Political Struggles in Communist Italy*, Cambridge: Cambridge University Press.

Leach, E. (1964) *Political Systems of Highland Burma*, London: Bell and Sons.

Muller-Rommel, F. (1982) 'Ecology parties in Western Europe', *West European Politics*, 5: 68–74.

Pardo, I. (1992) '"Living" the house, "feeling" the house: Neapolitan issues in thought, organization and structure', *Archives Européennes de Sociologie*, 2: 251–79.

—— (1993) 'Socialist visions, Naples and the Neapolitans: value, control and representation in the agency/structure relationship', *Journal of Mediterranean Studies*, 3 (1): 77–98.

Parry, J. and Bloch, M. (eds) (1989) *Money and the Morality of Exchange*, Cambridge: Cambridge University Press.

Voegelin, E. (1952) *The New Science of Politics*, Chicago: University of Chicago Press.

Weber, M. (1949) *The Methodology of Social Sciences*, New York: Free Press.

—— (1970) 'Politics as a vocation', in H.H. Gerth and C. Wright Mills (eds) *From Max Weber: Essays in Sociology*, London: Routledge and Kegan Paul.

Chapter 13

Environmental protest, bureaucratic closure

The politics of discourse in rural Ireland

Adrian Peace

During the greater part of 1988, a group of independent property-owning families in east County Cork, in the Republic of Ireland, found their agricultural way of life and their rural environment to be under threat from an American multinational corporation. The corporate enterprise Merrell Dow – part of the Dow Chemical empire – proposed to locate a £30-million chemical factory in the midst of their prosperous dairy-farming region. Since the factory would without question produce prodigious quantities of effluent and waste, the local population felt that the threat of pollution to their environment was considerable. Despite there being no precedent for such a development in rural Cork, Merrell Dow's proposal was fully supported by national and regional institutions of the Irish state, including Cork County Council which, with undue haste, granted the corporation planning permission.

The goal of the ensuing local opposition movement, led and supported by moderate- and small-scale property owners, thus became to have rescinded the permission granted by the county council. This could only be done by an appeal to An Bord Pleanála, the Republic's national planning review body based in Dublin. Only a small percentage of appeals to the Board result in a formal hearing before its inspectors. But the Womanagh Valley Protection Association was a highly organized, politically skilful group heading a locality-wide movement against the proposed development. In December 1988 a fortnight-long public hearing was held in the chambers of the county council: this in itself bore testimony to the effectiveness of the movement. Yet in the event An Bord Pleanála rejected the appeal of the Protection Association and others allied to it, and by early 1989 Merrell Dow set their sights on constructing the factory and getting chemical production under way as soon as possible.

The concern of this chapter is to analyse these events and provide some explanation for the outcome of the bureaucratic review. The first consideration involves approaching the conflict between the locality's residents, and Merrell Dow and the Irish state, as a site of struggle (Kress 1985, Seidel 1985) between rival political discourses. I assume that a political anthropology of environmental movements in the modern global order starts from the premise that warring with words, managing meanings, and negotiating with knowledges is what much environmental politics is all about. Arenas of political opposition over environmental resources are to be approached as sites in which rival discourses are perennially in conflict with one another. To comprehend the processes on-going within these sites of struggle, it becomes imperative to explore how certain discourses come to exercise paramountcy over others. In brief, recent emphases in the political anthropology of language (Grillo 1989) and discourse (Fairclough 1989) have to be ushered into an anthropology of environmentalism.

The second consideration is to focus on the role of An Bord Pleanála in this conflict and so to render more broadly problematic the status of the independent review body in the political technology of contemporary governmentalism. The independent review figures widely in conflicts over the environment in both First World and Third World milieux. International institutions, national governments and regional state bodies frequently respond to conflictual environmental developments by setting up a commission of enquiry, a consultation panel of experts, a review tribunal, and so forth; and they undoubtedly do so secure in the knowledge that such bodies will in general provision the recommendations which favour the economic and political status quo. With none too many exceptions, they deliver the appropriate results. On the other hand, such review bodies consistently articulate their impartiality, they go to great lengths to broadcast their independence, they heavily invest in the rituals and the symbolism which underscore their political abstemiousness and moral integrity. Inasmuch as the review body is such a pivotal institution in the containment of local level movements, political anthropologists should pay due attention to their organizational mechanics and the construction of myths which envelop them. Borrowing a term from E.P. Thompson (1978), I shall dub these 'modern theatres of control'.

In order to unravel the politics of discourse which emerged in east Cork, the organization of this chapter is elementary. Following a brief overview of the locality, the first major section examines the emergence of the opposition movement and the populist discourse which dominated the political landscape for most of 1988. The second examines the course of the oral hearing at the end of that year under the auspices of An Bord Pleanála. The crucial process on which I focus is how the initial, encompassing and empowering discourse of total opposition to the chemical factory was rapidly and near-inexorably displaced by a scientific discourse which detailed the circumstances under which the factory might go ahead. This transformation effectively established the grounds for the Board finally and readily to endorse the earlier planning permission.

RURAL EAST CORK 1988: LANDSCAPE AND POPULATION

Fundamental economic and social change over the past thirty years is inscribed on every corner of the east Cork landscape, including close by the village of Killeagh (see Map 13.1) where the Merrell Dow factory was to be located. Modernization of intensive dairy farming and tillage has brought a moderate prosperity unimaginable three decades ago, so that across the gently rolling rural terrain, modern bungalows or refurbished dwellings stand alongside old cottages which have fallen into disrepair. Substantial cow sheds are filled with the best milking machinery on the market as well as evidence of yields being closely monitored. Concrete structures are filled with silage as winter approaches, while at other times beet, barley, wheat and other crops are harvested in by contracting firms. In farmyards are parked moderately expensive motor vehicles, while beyond in the fields graze the Friesian herds which are the source of farming families' affluence.

The one element of constancy has been the enduring pillar of the property-owning family which provisions its own labour and expertise to produce for the market-place. The characteristic unit of production is the farm family in ownership of inherited land to which it applies its own collective labour. Most properties are between fifty and two hundred acres; some have expanded through the incorporation of smaller units; but the indispensable input is always the labour of the farmer and his wife, variously supplemented by their children. These are the resources which have allowed them to take advantage of burgeoning regional markets (above all the EC – European Community), expanded capital investment availability (from national banks and regional cooperatives), and an elaborate system of subsidies and grants provisioned by the state (Breen *et al.* 1990).

East Cork families are enormously proud of their achievements. Fiercely independent, they exhibit unrestrained attachment to such communities as Killeagh, Mogeely, Castlemartyr and Ballycotton (see Map 13.1). All aspects of daily life are informed by an ethos of egalitarianism in which is distilled the essence of community membership. This creates endemic difficulties for any project requiring a modicum of hierarchy, but coming to terms with this consistent tension is itself a source of satisfaction. The embedded relation between individual achievement and collective identity is, in all these communities, the essence of *petit bourgeois* being, not only among property-owning farm families but also among those who possess fishing boats, community stores and public houses.

Conversely, this is a political culture at all turns critical of external hierarchies and the political and bureaucratic class which staffs them. Since the centralizing tendencies of the expanding state have been condensed within a brief and recent period, so this generalized suspicion – 'a pox on all your hierarchical houses' – is marked. A self-interested and secretive class of ruling elements is considered to have consolidated, over some sixty years of independent rule, their collective dominance; this in local parlance is 'the Establishment'. One major criticism of this body centres upon the thirty-year-long programme of recruiting foreign enterprises to establish industries on Irish soil with financial support from national and regional state bodies.

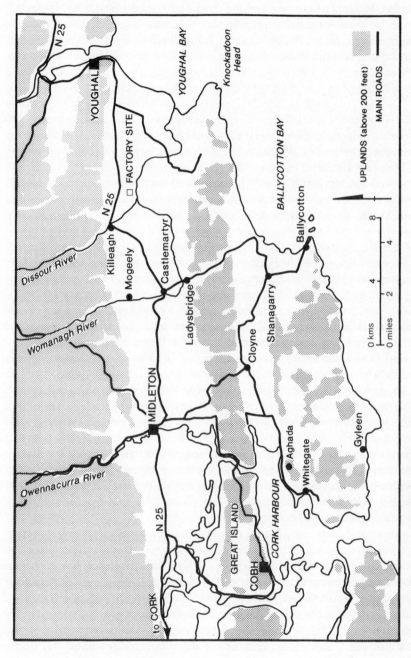

Map 13.1 The towns and villages of east Cork

While no one questions the need for industry, many seriously contest the enormous capital resources and other benefits allocated to multinational companies. Likewise damning is the view that the elected component (the politicians) within this Establishment is adjudicated to have restricted authority by comparison with the unbridled power of the non-elected (its bureaucrats).

CONSTRUCTING A POPULAR OPPOSITION: EXTERNAL RESOURCES AND COMMONSENSE UNDERSTANDINGS

Under these circumstances, once it became known that an American-owned chemical factory was to be constructed locally, Merrell Dow could be said to be entering hazardous terrain. The problem was compounded since Merrell Dow and the Industrial Development Authority (IDA), which was responsible for easing their entry into Ireland, determined to hold back details about the proposal for as long as possible. The bare information which did filter out spread as rumour, fuelling incipient alarm and reinforcing characteristically negative views as to how those with power exercise it.

The major pocket of disquiet developed among those families with properties closest to the ninety acres of agricultural land which were to be acquired by the American corporation. This was to become the core group which spearheaded the campaign, organized and funded the Womanagh Valley Protection Association, and finally presented the opposition's case in the oral hearing. Above all, this core brought together much of the information, knowledge and interpretive skills upon which a broadly-based discourse of popular opposition was to be constituted.

These were long-established Womanagh Valley families and so had little difficulty in establishing their credentials as spokespersons. They were also well connected locally with extensive familial and institutional networks through which they could disseminate information. A few were notably affluent and able to carry early expenses. Most important, they acknowledged at the outset that if Merrell Dow was to be halted, they would need to organize a broadly-based constituency of opposition not only from well beyond their own ranks but also from beyond Killeagh and its environs (a population of a mere 300 or so). Evidently it was necessary to become well informed about Merrell Dow and the chemical industry of which it was a part. This cosmopolitan-based knowledge was to be thoroughly integrated with the commonsense reasoning of local political culture.

The initiative was taken by an energetic and articulate housewife whose family residence overlooked the proposed site. Having accessed local library materials, newspapers, magazines and more specialist resources, Mrs Vaughan established a communicative network in Ireland and overseas, including the United States Environmental Protection Agency (EPA). From such sources it was learned that Merrell Dow had a dubious environmental record on a number of counts. Of especial concern was that the corporation had extensively polluted its own industrial location in Midland, Michigan, adjacent properties in the vicinity, and the Tittabawassee River into which it discharged effluent and waste. Moreover, when the EPA had attempted to examine closely Merrell Dow's manufacturing processes and its pollution, the corporation had placed all possible obstacles in the agency's path.

Word of mouth remains the predominant medium for the communication of information in rural Cork. As these items and much else were disseminated, concern soared among those who so far had been indifferent. The next stage compounded this, for in mid-June the core group had engaged the services of an environmental consultant. When the formal application for development was lodged in mid-July, Rory Finegan was in place to assess it critically; his report was to prove pivotal to later developments, and not only as a scientific assessment, for it was also a significant political text. While the scientist assuredly translated the technicalities of the application into lay language, Finegan described an entirely disastrous, almost apocalyptic, scenario were the chemical factory to proceed. Some of the likely consequences were a marked drop in local property values, degradation of water and air, chemical deposi- tions including acid rain, damage to farm animals' and residents' health, as well as 'a noisome, noisy and ugly manufacturing scene alien to the present way of life in this community' (the report's concluding remark). The political message was evident enough. The entire locality of east Cork, not just property-owners close to the proposed plant, had to mobilize quickly so as to protect their environment.

Finally, by way of extra-local resources which provisioned the discourse of opposition, Robert Allen was an investigative reporter with the monthly magazine *Magill*. Because of his sympathetic coverage of a notorious case in County Tipperary in which a doughty farm family had charged another American chemical conglomerate with destroying their livelihood through pollution, members of the Womanagh Valley group contacted Allen and brought him to County Cork. In an extended piece in *Magill* entitled 'Power and effluent' (see also Allen and Jones 1990: 124–59), he portrayed the core members as decent, hardworking, rural folk fighting their just cause against a ruthless, profit-seeking, American empire. The journalist especially focused on the unqualified complicity of the government in furthering the interests of Merrell Dow. On an interpersonal level, he shared with the objectors his experience of governmental bodies and his knowledge of the impact of expatriate industries on the environment elsewhere.

In short, the enterprise of the Protection Association leaders was well demonstrated in their ability to assemble the resources and expertise neces- sary to defend their environment. With this body of knowledge in hand, spokespersons began to draw together the groundswell of opposition through several public meetings and many more informal encounters.

PUBLIC MEETINGS, PRIVATE TALK

Well before these public meetings, 'the Merrell Dow business' (as it was locally termed) was already a recurrent topic of conversation even in contexts at some distance from Killeagh. Particularly marked was how ordinary folk established parallels between the growing conflict over the American development and other relatively current environmental issues. The inescapable backdrop was Chernobyl, just two years previously. But in 1988 other issues received mammoth media coverage, notably the loss of the Piper Alpha oil rig in the North Sea, followed by the pathetic plight of *Karin B* limping from one port to another.[1] The North Sea seal population was being decimated by disease reputedly due to toxic and other industrial discharges, while, more proximate to east Cork, pollution of the Irish Sea by Sellafield waste, and pollution of Cork Harbour by industrial facilities constructed around it (Baker 1990: 58), were also receiving media attention. It was by continued reference to these rough-and-ready, comparable circumstances that ordinary folk made sense of the development which seemingly threatened their own environment and livelihoods.

These comparisons also recurrently surfaced in the public meetings held under Protection Association auspices in the region's rural communities. As spokespersons began to tour the villages – itself a markedly symbolic development – they broadcast the detailed information now available, secure in the knowledge that whatever was said would be widely disseminated to those not in attendance. Linking the threat posed by Merrell Dow to environmental issues elsewhere proved particularly effective in countering claims being made by the management. For example, the latter stressed that half of the £30-million investment would be devoted to making the factory safe and minimizing its pollution potential. But, rejoined the spokespersons, no doubt this had also been claimed for the Piper Alpha oil rig, the chemical firms polluting Cork Harbour, and even Chernobyl?

Much of the political rhetoric of public meetings centred on the imagery of a ruthless company aiming for global expansion without due consideration for their own employees or neighbouring communities in the United States. How much more indifferent were they likely to be in an Irish milieu? It was emphasized that meetings with Merrell Dow and state representatives had quite failed to allay fears concerning effluent discharge into the ambient air and the Womanagh River. Much was made of the striking fact that the county council expected the corporation to monitor its own waste emissions rather than make some independent body responsible. Time and again, the IDA and the county council were subject to scathing attacks for their apparently supine posture in relation to the conglomerate; a couple of politicians who turned up to meetings were effectively humiliated. At times the atmosphere of these encounters was highly emotional. But in the midst of fiery rhetoric, a substantial body of information was being deployed in such a way as to extend ordinary residents' stock of knowledge about the development, as well as elaborating the threads of local political culture which condemned the Establishment. Here, it seemed, was a classic instance of how distant bureaucrats, senior politicians and a compliant media ignored the force of public opinion while capitulating to the power of a major corporation.

The spokespersons especially focused on the dangers of pollution to economic livelihoods and the environment at large; their emphasis was forthrightly materialistic. Yet more generally, an emergent theme in the meetings was that an American factory was essentially alien to the way of life which predominated in the Womanagh Valley, an area long farmed by the forefathers of current owners who knew the environment intimately and respected it. No industrial management could possibly comprehend that relationship. In addition to the obvious overtones of a latter-day colonialism, the characteristically conflictual relations between managers and wage-earners had no place in a locality where attachment to socially autonomous communities was the well-proven norm. In fine detail, what residents had in mind by 'our rural way of life' effectively meant different things to different people, but in public meetings these differences could be easily glossed under this highly emotive banner.

In similar fashion, when the phrase 'our rights' was deployed in open discussion, closer inspection revealed that this bore varied meanings, but encompassing most was the general notion that 'the right' of ordinary folk to maintain the way of life which they had themselves constructed over the years should be respected. Indeed the right should be defended by the institutions of the state; this was a reasonable expectation of its citizenry. Yet the entire course of 'the Merrell Dow business' indicated these expectations were not to be realized.

It is important to repeat that these same concerns were being visited in dialogue in the kitchens, on the streets, and above all in the bars so central in rural Ireland to the dissection of public issues. It is thus apt to talk of a crescendo of popular political discourse which, by October and November of 1988, commanded the social landscape. This discourse comprised a relatively comprehensive and systematic body of ideas and images, information and opinion. Its details were assembled from a diversity of sources, and they were integrated in a diversity of ways into the infinite exchanges of everyday conversation, out of which the essential traffic of rural social experience is always and everywhere constructed. By late 1988, there was no particular locus in which the Merrell Dow proposal was being discussed; rather it was everywhere a matter of public perusal. There was no particular group which monopolized informed opinion; rather it seemed everyone was formulating some set of judgements, and was more than ready to articulate them. Above all, the majority opinion was clear: under no circumstances should the factory proceed since it was so patently counter to common sense. While it was useful to have as much information as possible from external sources, and while it was proper to recruit specialists in order to have their informed opinions, in the last analysis it was the common sense of ordinary folk which was of real consequence. According to this distinctly superior, informed body of judgement, a chemical factory in a prime dairy-farming area was sheer folly.

BUREAUCRATIC PROCESS AND SCIENTIFIC REASONING: CENSORSHIP, CONTAINMENT AND DISCRETIONARY POWER

The circumstances which led An Bord Pleanála to conduct an oral hearing were not revealed to the residents of east Cork, the first of several discretionary – which is to say culturally arbitrary – exercises of bureaucratic power. The Dublin office had, however, received a substantial body of written objections to the chemical factory – again, a culturally arbitrary requirement – and a petition of objection bearing over one thousand signatures put together by the Protection Association. The granting of the hearing was met with elation by both leaders and followers; many felt they had the resources to persuade the Board that the planning permission ought to be rescinded. But as the hub of the site of struggle turned from the rural villages to the city-based council chambers for the fortnight-long public hearing, a major transformation was in motion. The discourse of popular political opposition was to be swiftly undermined and effectively marginalized by a bureaucratically orchestrated discourse of scientific reasoning. The pertinent question was no longer whether the factory should go ahead or not, but rather under what technical and scientific circumstances it might proceed. In this brief struggle between discourses was highlighted the uncontestable exercise of bureaucratic power.

From the outset the most signal property of An Bord Pleanála was its claim to be an independent, impartial and autonomous review body which conducted its investigations on judicial lines in the interests of fair practice and balanced judgement. These terms are taken from either the Board's literature or the two inspectors who conducted the Cork hearing. These were on the whole also the expectations of the opposition movement to Merrell Dow. It was felt that, provided their material was properly informed and effectively presented, the independent investigation would come round to their point of view. In brief, free from the stigma of political party practice and shielded from the prospect of government intervention – these being the taken-for-granted understandings of such terms as 'independent' and 'impartial' – An Bord Pleanála's claims and local residents' expectations were in agreement. Preliminary organizational arrangements as well as a myriad of rituals reinforced these understandings. In his opening remarks, the chief inspector pointed out that running the hearing on court-like lines was necessary for reasons of efficiency, impartiality and fairness. In the packed council chamber it would have been easy to miss his also mentioning that he and his fellow inspector had been trained in science.

Of similar significance was that the Protection Association leaders were henceforth wholly distanced from the population which had empowered them to speak. The bulk of concerned folk were not present at the hearing, but instead labouring on their farms, fishing out at sea, or minding their shops some twenty to twenty-five miles distant. But the geography was unimportant; rather, it was an extensive opinion that such an important institution as the Board would only pay attention to those with tangible and material interests to defend. So those who were downright alarmed were engaged in a form of self-censorship. This is under any circumstances a significant political act (Bourdieu 1991: 19), but in this particular instance it left the leadership who spoke at the hearing isolated and exposed. It could be argued they had specific interests to defend rather than a set of objections from the population at large which they were authorized to articulate.

Hardly had the hearing got under way, however, than another form of censorship became evident. For as farmers, fishermen, housewives and others – appearing in the role of appellants – entered the witness box, they made mention of Merrell Dow's questionable track record as well as Chernobyl, Three Mile Island, and Cork Harbour pollution, the reference points ordinary folk had used to make sense of their circumstances. Yet in each instance and repeatedly, the chief inspector interrupted and objected. All such comparisons, he insisted, were irrelevant to the Board's current brief. No one should try to use the witness box for political grandstanding, and anyway, he further emphasized, he, his colleague, and the full Board in Dublin were only concerned with 'the facts' and not 'subjective opinions'. Essentially this meant adhering to the scientific and technical details of Merrell Dow's application for planning permission and the county council planning department's response. Here was a clear ruling indeed: 'facts' were what scientists dealt with, 'opinions' were the currency of non-scientists.

Although the ramifications of these opening gambits were not entirely clear at the time, they were sufficient to disconcert those without experience of such a formal setting. A more decisive development in terms of the hearing's overall direction was the appearance of predominantly non-local institutions which were opposed to the chemical factory as currently pro-posed, yet could contemplate its being built provided that further measures to restrict the likelihood of pollution were incorporated into the plant's design, and that the factory was subject to independent monitoring once production was under way.

Before the November announcement of the hearing, the Protection Asso-ciation and others hostile in unqualified fashion to Merrell Dow had wel-comed the news that these external institutions were openly critical. It was felt – no doubt justifiably – that their collective weight added to the poss-ibility of a hearing. In the event, however, such bodies as the Southern Regional Fisheries Board, Bord Failte (the Irish Tourist Board) and several manufacturing firms proved to be allies only to a qualified degree. Not only could these non-local institutions contemplate the prospect of the factory going ahead, they had the technical expertise to provide the Board's inspectors with detailed specifications of improvements which could be incorporated into Merrell Dow's planning proposal. To give but one example, the Southern Regional Fisheries Board, an influential regional body, expressed strong concern about the discharging of enormous quantities of processed effluent into the Womanagh River. Three senior executives demolished the relevant section of the environmental impact statement. On the other hand, they put forward several detailed proposals as to how design improvements could be made, and monitoring procedures added, to Merrell Dow's development plan.

In other words, the opposition of such bodies was not intransigent. The result was that their presence contributed to the emergence of detailed, technical dialogues within the body of the hearing as to how the factory might go ahead. And this development was not only facilitated but encouraged by the inspectors, who drew on their own scientific expertise. There thus emerged the constituents of the scientific discourse which would eventually exercise hegemony within the hearing. The development which in paradoxical fashion compounded this process involved the professionally qualified specialists who appeared on behalf of the Protection Association and its closest supporters.

The most prominent was Rory Finegan, who authored the initial damning report; but his expertise as an environmental scientist was now supplemented by a highly qualified veterinary scientist, an academic expert in atmospheric pollution and air-modelling techniques, and a limnologist working as an independent consultant with reference to freshwater systems. The task of the first was to detail the likely adverse effects of the factory on dairy farming, that of the second to show how air-borne discharges would impact adversely on the surrounding locality, and that of the third to describe the effect of water-borne discharges on the quality of the Womanagh River, and the fish and shellfish populations of river and estuary.

In all three instances substantial and sophisticated confirmation was provided of the dire consequences anticipated by Finegan. Yet paradoxically, their combined influence also worked in the other direction. For a start, these (and other) professional consultants were providing projections; they were anticipating the effects of chemical production from a factory not yet built and about which many fundamental details were not available from Merrell Dow. In other words, while the projected scenarios were dire, they were also necessarily speculative – a point which had to be conceded time and again under hostile cross-questioning. Furthermore, with varying degrees of readiness, despite their appearing on behalf of the Protection Association, these scientific consultants also sketched out possible improvements to structural design and production-process monitoring, should it finally transpire that An Bord Pleanála upheld the planning permission.

At this stage it needs to be underlined that these developments surfaced in disjointed fashion during several days' extended and intensive presentations from the witness box. The emergent pattern was not clearly evident at the time. On the other hand, the combined effect was emphatically to reinforce and compound the technical dialogues which had earlier been set in motion. Indeed the experts in the hire of the Protection Association felt obliged to pick up on tentative suggestions introduced by their peers who had appeared on behalf of the Fisheries Board and like bodies. Since all consultants spoke to written submissions, and since they could be recalled by solicitors orchestrating the presentations, some of these technical exchanges became thoroughly involved. One particular refinement to this increasingly patterned dance of the scientists was that some gained authority as they deftly handled forays from legal counsels acting on behalf of Merrell Dow and the county council. Those who had impressed were called back to the witness box to answer specific queries from the Board's inspectors.

The final notable contribution to the growing hegemony of scientific discourse came from the corporation's own in-house technical managers, supplemented by officials from the county council bureaucracy. The former in particular – a ten-strong team bristling with tertiary qualifications and professional association memberships – presented detailed accounts of the plant's production technology, in particular its waste-treatment processes. In a systematic and coordinated series of presentations, a veritable barrage of scientific material covering all aspects of the chemical factory was put before the inspectors. From their questions it was evident that this was technical ground on which they felt at ease. Thus management representatives and the Board's inspectors in concert consolidated the paramountcy of scientific discourse in the body of the hearing.

There was one further decisive dimension to these technical presentations. At the outset of the hearing, a broad sequence for the proceedings had been ruled upon by the chief inspector. The one critical detail – the importance of which no one could have anticipated – was that the management of Merrell Dow corporation would present their case last. In other words, the critiques which came from Protection Association spokespersons and its specialists were all on the table before the multinational corporation's management took the stand. The latter were therefore able to incorporate measured rejoinders into their own presentations as well as comment on some of the issues raised in the dialogues which had gone before. More than this, the sequential order facilitated the most dramatic moment of the hearing, when the head of the management team put forward what he euphemistically termed 'a package of concessions . . . [for] our critics and future neighbours'. These ranged from technological modifications which would reduce air pollution levels caused by effluent discharge through to setting up a company–community consultation panel in which, so it appeared, community representatives would have access to Merrell Dow records.

The package seemingly incorporated some of the recommendations which had repeatedly surfaced during the hearing. Above all, it appeared responsive and conciliatory from certain vantage points, including the bench occupied by the inspectors. In the eyes of Protection Association leaders and supporters, the move was to be seen as a further exhibition of the company's unbridled opportunism and deviousness. While the concessions might impress in the immediate context of the hearing, what eventually transpired with the factory's construction might be quite different. Even the most strident of Merrell Dow's critics, however, had to concede this was a decisive move. It notably upstaged those who had presented the more vehement lines of opposition to the American corporation. It seemed to respond to the currents of scientific reasoning out of which the bulk of the hearing was by now emphatically composed. One prominent member of the Protection Association expressed it as follows: 'They've changed the position of the goal posts halfway through the game. And then kicked the winning goal straight through them.'

STRATEGY, STRUCTURE AND POLITICAL DISCOURSE: THE INDEPENDENT REVIEW AS A THEATRE OF CONTROL

The spokesman's game metaphor was undoubtedly apt. The dramatic announcement of modifications to the production process ensured that the company dominated the rest of the proceedings. To that extent, the corporate body's management had seized the decisive moment.

Having made this acknowledgement, the critical point is that this only proved possible because of the structure of the situation constituted by the due bureaucratic process as it had unfolded in the council chamber. For by this juncture, the discourse of science was substantially focused on the possible effects of the factory's construction on just the handful of farms within its immediate vicinity. The fact that the majority of residents in the area at large were hostile to the prospect no longer received any acknowledgement. Such terms as 'the rural way of life' and 'the rights of residents' had no currency whatsoever. Emotive considerations, dismissed earlier as 'subjective opinions', were no longer allowed voice at all. By this stage, the popular discourse had been wholly driven from a transformed and refocused site of struggle devoted to the analysis of 'hard facts'; that is, the scientific and technical details of the chemical factory's construction and operation. Indeed, a good deal of dialogue concerned the granting of an Air Pollution Licence and a Water Pollution Licence, which were precisely what their titles indicate.

Expressed slightly differently, the technical focus now was how to keep the factory's emissions to 'an acceptable level of pollution' and thus avoid posing 'a serious threat' to the environment. Both these phrases entered into the hearing's on-going dialogue as its persistent direction became to work out a reasonable compromise, a scientific *modus vivendi*, between the variously competing specialist opinions. Yet the most telling consideration was that within the structured context of An Bord Pleanála's hearing, the one party for which and with which no effective compromise was possible was that for whom the factory was unacceptable on any terms. Within the hearing, those speaking on behalf of the ordinary citizens of east Cork occupied the extreme end of a spectrum of positions variously exhibited towards the proposal. In distinctly ironic fashion, those men and women who, in the course of daily experience, were politically conservative and proud of it emerged as relatively radical elements! Elsewhere on this spectrum all parties seemed inclined to negotiate and compromise; the prevalent discourse of scientific reasoning not only testified to but also integrally facilitated this. Over the space of a fortnight's continuous submissions, a vast quantity of detailed material had accrued to the inspectors, who could now return to Dublin and draw up the recommendations which would give full, concrete and final form to this compromise solution.

In sum, the popular discourse of ordinary people as summarized in the slogan 'No factory under any circumstances' had been unceremoniously dispatched from view, while the discourse of science had become unambiguously privileged; and this effectively ensured that An Bord Pleanála's final ruling in early 1989 was in favour of Merrell Dow. Evidently, the determinant phase in this conflict between discourses turned on the advent of the independent review body, which proclaimed its impartiality and concern for a just outcome while imposing criteria of assessment, demanding modes of presentation, and encouraging types of dialogic exchange which all worked, in different ways yet also in concert, to the advantage of those with economic and political power and at the expense of those who enjoyed neither.

Within this comprehensive framework of bureaucratic rationality, it was especially significant that the review body was able to enforce its own criteria of assessment of the project as definitive and beyond challenge. This meant that the objectors had increasingly to phrase their own submissions in terms of those criteria, even though their case was thereby much weakened; and they had to look to the support of other bodies for whom opposition was not absolute but a matter of degree. Yet these specifics apart, the most telling consideration was that while in retrospect and from a distance, the social anthropologist might provision a persuasive account as to how one discourse came to exercise hegemony over another, at the time and from within, the sheer complexity of on-going influences and events served to obscure from view the decisive direction of the public hearing. The striking capacity of An Bord Pleanála to orchestrate in decisive fashion the theatre of control which was the public hearing, without the consequences being immediately evident, stands as testimony to the subtle political efficacy of this particular technology of modern governmentalism.

It has in no sense been the purpose of this chapter to provide a rounded account of the Merrell Dow conflict, only to analyse particular dimensions of it.[2] But it would be inappropriate not to mention in conclusion that the chemical factory was not built. The site which occasioned such dispute remains undeveloped. According to the American management the reasons are straightforward, if marked by notable irony. In the middle of 1989 the parent company determined that Merrell Dow should be merged with a second, recently purchased, corporate enterprise in order to realize the scale of production and distribution increasingly demanded by the intensely competitive global field of chemical manufacture. In the development programme of the newly formed multinational enterprise, there was no place for the factory at Killeagh. Plans for the location were shelved indefinitely. In their announcement, the management made a point of stressing that the opposition which they had encountered had played no part in this decision.

By contrast, and as one might anticipate, that same opposition saw their collective resistance as having proved enormously successful. The Protection Association and other groups which had emerged in 1989 considered that (as one newspaper citation had it), 'we have driven Merrell Dow into the sea'. Doubtless some detached account of this final phase would find some middle position between these two extremes. An attempt could be made to establish some interpretive space which offered a balanced and measured account of the newly rhetorical discourses emanating from the competing camps. But would not the effort to do so serve to resurrect and reinforce the same expectations of impartiality and objectivity so readily, yet falsely, claimed by tribunals, commissions, review panels, and the other theatres of control which proliferate in post-modern, late capitalist society? And would not such an exercise necessarily compromise on marking the significance of the myriad ways in which ordinary folk manage to exercise their capacity for opposition and resistance in structured circumstances which consistently work to deny them any effective voice at all?

ACKNOWLEDGEMENTS

I am obliged to Dr Kay Milton and other members of the 1992 ASA Conference for comments on an earlier draft of this chapter.

NOTES

1 In late July 1988, the Italian vessel *Karin B* set sail from Nigeria carrying some 21,000 tons of hazardous waste which had been illegally dumped in the country. The vessel's attempt to dock at Ravenna in August was prevented by protesting Italians. It was refused docking facilities in Wales, ordered out of UK territorial waters by the British government, and then banned by the Dutch. After a protracted period of uncertainty at sea, the *Karin B* was officially allowed to return to Italy from where the waste had been transported originally.

2 A full-length monograph is now in the final stages of revision. Its provisional title is *The Politics of Discourse: Political Protest and Bureaucratic Containment in Rural Ireland.*

REFERENCES

Allen, R. and Jones, T. (1990) *Guests of the Nation: People of Ireland versus the Multinationals,* London: Earthscan.

Baker, S. (1990) 'The evolution of the Irish ecology movement', in W. Rüdig (ed.) *Green Politics One,* Edinburgh: Edinburgh University Press.

Bourdieu, P. (1991) *Language and Symbolic Power,* Cambridge: Polity Press.

Breen, R., Hannan, D., Rottman, D. and Whelan, C. (1990) *Understanding Contemporary Ireland: State, Class and Development in the Republic of Ireland,* London: Macmillan.

Fairclough, N. (1989) *Language and Power,* London: Longman.

Grillo, R. (1989) 'Anthropology, language, politics', in R. Grillo (ed.) *Social Anthropology and the Politics of Language,* Sociological Review Monograph 36, London: Routledge.

Kress, G. (1985) *Linguistic Processes in Sociocultural Practice,* Deakin: Deakin University Press.

Seidel, G. (1985) 'Political discourse analysis', in T.A. van Dijk (ed.) *Handbook of Discourse Analysis. Vol. 4,* London: Academic Press.

Thompson, E.P. (1978) 'Folklore, anthropology and social history', *The Indian Historical Review,* 3 (2): 247–66.

Chapter 14

Eating green(s)
Discourses of organic food

Allison James

Although having its roots in traditional agricultural practices, contemporary environmentalist interests in relation to organic food production in Britain can be located in the teachings of Rudolf Steiner in the 1920s and, later, in the foundation of the Soil Association by Lady Eve Balfour in 1946. The Henry Doubleday Research Association (HDRA), which promotes organic gardening, was started by Lawrence Hills in 1955. However, the interests of these groups remained culturally marginal until the late 1980s when, seemingly, there was an almost overnight proliferation of concern over matters environmental in relation to food. Associations promoting organic growing registered steep rises in membership. The HDRA had increased its membership from 470 in 1961 to 18,000 by the end of 1990 and between 1988 and 1989 membership of the Soil Association increased by 22 per cent (Elkington and Hailes 1989). Special interest groups arose to monitor methods of food production, such as the Pesticide Trust (1988) and Parents for Safe Food (1989), adding their voices to those of more well-known organizations such as Friends of the Earth and Greenpeace, whose own memberships more than doubled towards the end of the 1980s. Reflecting this trend, there appeared a flurry of books about environmentalism and ecology and a developing populist literature about how to 'eat green' (Gear 1987, Elkington and Hailes 1989, Mabey *et al.* 1990, Taylor and Taylor 1990, Eyton 1991).

By the close of the 1980s, therefore, environmentalist concerns seemed to be very much on the agenda in Britain, but to what extent there is now a widespread commitment to environmentalist principles is less clear. Drawing on the images and themes in both populist and more specialized texts, this chapter considers this question through exploring some of the different ways in which organic food is currently represented and perceived.

Anthropological approaches to the study of food have shown that ideas about food consumption in any particular culture are intimately entwined with other conceptual domains, registering, for example, degrees of social intimacy and distance (Douglas 1975) or embodying more fundamental concepts of social order (Bulmer 1967, Lévi-Strauss 1970). The domain of food and eating thus speaks to and of the wider social and cultural context.

In this chapter it will be suggested that the concerns about food which emerged during the 1980s in Britain involved a questioning and reshaping of the relationship between the human and the natural world. However, although this has meant that organic food now occupies a more central position in contemporary thinking about food, the process of re-presenting 'nature' and the 'natural', which frames its marketing, cannot be taken as a sign of the integration of environmentalist principles into contemporary British culture. It reflects, instead, their absorption and incorporation into a continuum of existing discourses surrounding human beings and what they eat. In this way the political and ecological significance of organic food production and consumption is distanced through the diversity, rather than unity, of the social practices which may be called 'eating green'.

ORGANIC FOOD: THE UK BACKGROUND

Definitions of 'organic' in relation to food in Britain were, in 1989, finally agreed under the auspices of UKROFS (United Kingdom Register of Organic Food Standards). Based on a voluntary code of practice, these are little different from those established by the Soil Association in the mid-1970s (Mabey *et al.* 1990). Briefly, in relation to crops, 'organic' refers to foodstuffs grown without the use of artificial pesticides, herbicides or fertilizers; in relation to meat, it refers to animals raised in non-intensive farming conditions, free from unnecessary medication such as antibiotics and growth stimulants, and eating feed or grazing pasture which is itself organically grown. Other terms must be used for produce which is 'nearly' or 'not quite' organic. For example, 'conservation grade' is used for produce which, although it may not have been sprayed with pesticides, has been grown in soil containing certain non-organic fertilizers or chemical weedkillers. Both these are banned under the 'organic' rules. Similarly, 'free range' eggs are not equivalent to 'organic' eggs; to conform to the latter label, hens would have to eat feed which was made up of at least 80 per cent organically grown corn.

The urgency with which these standards were introduced during the 1980s is testimony to an increased interest being expressed in both the production and the consumption of organic food (Gear 1987: x–xi). It is now clear that organic food has established a firm foothold in the British market, despite the high price premiums that it commands (up to 35 per cent for organic beef),[1] and has moved out from peripheral health food shops into the large supermarket chains such as Safeway (co-sponsors of an organic research farm in Scotland) and Tesco.

The clear upturn in the organic food market is paralleled by the wider public airing which organic food is currently receiving. For example, it was pressure from growers and consumers for some consensus over both terminology and standards which forced the government to fund the setting up of UKROFS in 1987. In 1991 the Minister of Agriculture announced funding worth £3.5 million over three years for research into organic farming. While this amounts to only 0.4 per cent of the money which the Ministry pours into research into non-organic methods, it none the less suggests that organic food production is now on the political agenda.

There are signs, too, of a more common currency of ideas and a more general public awareness about organic food, illustrated by the diversity of contexts in which mention of it has appeared in recent years. *Good House-keeping* magazine, in addition to reporting on outlets for organic food, featured a lengthy article on the subject in April 1991 (Woodman 1991). The farming radio programme, *On Your Farm*, now allocates air time to the organic debate. Organic gardening has been promoted by TV programmes such as *All Muck and Magic* and *Gardeners' World*. Prince Charles has openly expressed his support for the organic movement, through the commitment of his own farm to organic agriculture, through his agreement (in 1989) to become the patron of the HDRA, and through his public statements both endorsing organic practices and criticizing intensive farming methods (see, for instance, *The Guardian*, 26 November 1991).

More prosaically, though of questionably greater significance, the mythical world of Ambridge continues to plot the rise in prosperity of Pat and Tony Archer's farm, which made the transition to organic agriculture some years ago. In its continuing role as a channel for public information, *The Archers* radio programme[2] recently drew attention to an ethical dilemma facing organic producers: in Pat Archer's refusal to sell their organic ice cream under a label other than that of 'Bridge Farm Ice Cream' we were led to understand that a commitment to organic food can also represent the commitment to a particular political ideology (see below). Should the organic grower retain a social identity as a small-scale and community-based enterprise or, effectively, 'sell out' to the demands of large-scale commercialism?[3]

DISCOURSES OF FOOD

The very diversity of cultural arenas in which organic food now appears suggests that there has been a significant 'greening' of attitudes towards food in Britain. However, in a culture where ideas and attitudes are packaged and sold alongside goods in the market place (Bourdieu 1986), it cannot be assumed that the purchase of an organic breakfast cereal, for instance, necessarily signals a simultaneous 'buying into' the environmentalist cause. On the contrary, as textual analysis will reveal, there are other discourses in which organic food is located. Thus, although the consumption of organic food may symbolize a commitment to environmentalism, quite different meanings may be invoked. Cohen has written of the polysemic nature of symbols that, 'the "*commonality*" which is found in community need not be a uniformity. It does not clone behaviour or ideas. It is a commonality of *forms* (ways of behaving) whose content (meanings) may vary considerably among its members' (Cohen 1989: 20).

Following Cohen, then, it will be argued that the different frameworks within which organic food is contemporarily represented constitute a conceptual continuum composed of multiple referents, which in some areas partially overlap, but in others are poles apart. Thus, the various texts considered – literature produced by organic growers, journalistic writings, promotional literature and advertisements – while seeming to share a focus on organic produce, are framed by quite different interpretations of its significance. As I shall suggest, their apparent commonality is fostered through the recurrence of two sets of binary oppositions which, in each text, are reflected and refracted in subtly different ways to register subtly different meanings.

The first, and more prominent, opposition is that between nature and culture. As Strathern has convincingly shown, although this binary pair is commonly evoked, it can never be fixed; there is 'no consistent dichotomy, only a matrix of contrasts' both cross-culturally and within cultures (Strathern 1980: 177). Thomas (1983), similarly, has demonstrated the changing face of the nature:culture divide over time. The second, and linked, opposition is temporal, differentiating and evaluating the past and the future. As a cultural construction this too eludes precision, slipping and sliding in its meanings as different moralities are pinned on it. Thus, although the writings produced by those strongly committed to the philosophy of the organic movement and the advertisements for supermarket organic or conservation grade produce share a set of recurring and interlinked themes – nature:culture:past:future – they are differently combined.

Williams (1985) has shown how these four themes recur constantly to mediate between the city and the countryside, a relationship which is central to the production and consumption of organic food. The appearance of these oppositional pairings in texts relating to organic food constitutes, therefore, a quadrant of dominating ideologies which shape the ways in which organic food is perceived in contemporary British society (Thompson 1984).

DISCOURSE 1: FOOD AND THE ENVIRONMENT

Within this discourse, a commitment to the philosophy of environmentalism is evident through organic farmers' adherence to its principles in their agricultural practices. Food production is geared to achieving a 'balance between crops and livestock . . . in ways that are in sympathy with, not hostile to the environment' (Mabey et al. 1990: 29–30). Organic farmers work towards future 'sustainability', i.e. 'the ability of the land to produce food indefinitely' (Mabey et al. 1990: 30). For the small-scale organic grower these principles are also central, as Lawrence Hills, the founder of the HDRA, shows in his reflections on its achievements and potential:

The scope of the HDRA has extended beyond gardening compost heaps and companion plants to population, pollution, diet and nutrition, because the concern of its members is for the Organic movement as a whole. We grow, we change, we learn. We correct our mistakes and above all we think ahead, drawing the line between 'organic' and 'inorganic' – between all that which we enjoy out of the income of the good earth, and that which will harm those who still need to use and love our land when we are gone.

(Hills 1983: 187)

These sentiments echo the general principles of environmentalism, popularly summarized by Porritt as follows:

a reverence for the earth and all its creatures; protection of the environment as a precondition of a prosperous, healthy society; sustainable alternatives to the rat race economics of growth; a recognition of the rights of future generations in our use of all resources; open, participatory democracy at every level of society.

(Porritt 1987: 25)

Within this discourse the binary opposition between humans and the natural world is represented as beginning to dissolve through a process of conceptual restructuring. It is represented instead as a partnership in which culture no longer has the dominant hand. Learning from their past mistakes, humans will, in the future, respect and revere nature's power. It is, therefore, as part of the natural world, rather than in control of it, that humans are depicted as aware of the restraints which must be placed upon culture by nature.

A commitment to such beliefs is apparent in the promotional letter which accompanies delivery of organically reared meat from a Northamptonshire farm. It begins with the statement that, 'Here at Church Farm we believe in keeping stock in humane conditions, allowing our animals to range free, feed and live naturally' (Church Farm, n.d.). The letter stresses the interdependence of the human and the animal world and, through its imagery, the world of humans is placed squarely alongside that of animals. Consumers are made to take on a moral responsibility for their own acts of consumption through encountering – face to face as it were – the pork or chicken destined for their tables. The reader is invited to 'enjoy looking at the ducks and geese on the pond', to watch the 'happy pigs as they chase each other round the fields'.[4] Similarly, the hens are depicted as being on a par with humans: they are described as 'friendly and accommodating', like welcoming landladies, and customers are invited to go and pick their own eggs. For Christmas 1990, the farm butcher offered an alarmingly personal introduction service between myself and the turkey I had ordered. As I left the shop to walk past the turkeys in the yard he called, 'Yours will be a Norfolk black.'

The farm letter firmly situates their produce within an environmentalist frame:

> In a world with increasing environmental pressures connected with both land and food, we decided five years ago to go organic. We now hold a Soil Association certificate to verify that our land is free from chemicals and our stock is reared to the highest conservation standards and fed, wherever possible, on our own organic grass, hay, cereals and beans.
>
> (Church Farm, n.d.)

A personal note ends the letter: 'We look forward to hearing from you, or better still meeting you on the farm.' This reflects the earlier invitation for a personal commitment to be made about food choice. In this way, the consumer is positioned as a responsible citizen who, through choosing to buy organic meat, personally confronts the environmentalist agenda.

This material somewhat contradicts Fiddes' recent claim that 'falling retail sales of the quintessential "red" meats speak volumes about our literal and metaphoric reluctance in these days of green consciousness to have the animal's red blood on our hands' (Fiddes 1991). While this argument is often used to account for the rise in vegetarianism, it cannot explain the increase in *organic meat* sales (see below). It would seem that a rising green consciousness has prompted meat eaters to change their butcher rather than their dietary practices, through an increased awareness of the interdependence of nature and culture.

This contemporary rephrasing of the nature/culture boundary is therefore in terms of a relationship of equality rather than domination and conceived largely in relation to the future. Within this discourse, therefore, the boundary between culture and nature has become ambiguous and must be more carefully located and positioned. This is achieved through temporal slippage between the representation of past and future agricultural practices.

For example, many of those committed to promoting commercially viable organic agriculture are keen to point out that although 'organic farming takes its cue from traditional agriculture', it takes only the 'best ideas from the past and grafts onto them a scientific approach coupled with modern techniques' (Mabey *et al.* 1990: 30). Thus it is *culture* (in the form of science and modern techniques) which is envisaged as the *future* salvation of both *nature* and of the *past*. And yet, this powerful control is represented as a metaphorically 'natural' activity. Coming, as it does, out of the past, it will not become a dominating social force in the future. Thus, in the above quotation, it is traditional 'agriculture' which is depicted as giving the go-ahead for humans to act, as they 'graft' (a horticultural term) the past to the 'scientific' present. Within this discourse, organic growing is not therefore envisaged as a return to the past with 'fields full of folk, rooting out weeds by hand, tending livestock and working horse-driven ploughs' (Mabey *et al.* 1990: 347). Commercial organic food producers are quick to distance themselves from the common caricatures of a romantic rural mythology which, as I shall show, frames other, more populist representations (Williams 1985).

This uneasy and fragile conceptual relationship between nature and culture, the past and the future, envisaged within this discourse, renders the concept of large-scale organic food production particularly vulnerable to criticism. For the majority of farmers, steeped in the world of agro-chemicals and factory farming, the agricultural practices of organic growers seem strangely bizarre, if not downright cranky (Taylor and Taylor 1990). From the perspective of agri-business, organic farming appears both 'alternative' and 'unrealistic', as the president of the Royal Agricultural Society recently argued:

> The image of an Arcadian style, 'green' agriculture, with a contrived non-intensive output, is incompatible with the aim of maintaining a competitive position in the market place. There is a need and duty to challenge more rigorously public statements on farmland and environmental care which are manifestly false.
>
> (Quoted in *The Guardian*, 26 November 1991)

As an agricultural strategy, organic farming is seen by its opponents as naive in its emphasis on future cooperation with, rather than domination of, the natural world. It is depicted as hopelessly Arcadian (locked in the past, tied to nature) through its hopeless vision of an agrarian Utopia (a radically different cultural future). However, this ambivalent representation of organic agriculture reflects a subtle historical irony. Compliance with organic standards means, effectively, a return to the kinds of mixed, non-intensive farming (animals and crops) which since the end of the Second World War have been in rapid retreat (Gear 1987). It was the post-war requirement for a cheap and plentiful food supply which stimulated agricultural research into more intensive techniques of food production. What are now seen as the 'conventional' methods of growing food are therefore a relatively recent phenomenon; those contemporarily depicted as 'alternative' or novel are conventional.

DISCOURSE 2: FOOD AND LIFESTYLE

A second discourse within which the concept of organic food can be contemporarily located is that which links food with lifestyle. While 'lifestylism' has been rightly criticized by health educationalists as an unsatisfactory explanation for people's resistance to change in food habits (Rodmell and Watt 1986), a more specific focus on the cultural meanings which particular foods have in people's lives offers a broader interpretive scope (James 1990). It can show how ideas about food permeate throughout society to structure many other aspects of cultural life and forms of consumption. Within this discourse of organic food the quadrant of nature:culture:past:future works in this manner to frame an 'organic lifestyle'. While in some respects it overlaps with aspects of the environmentalist discourse just noted, a primary focus on organic food as a symbol of 'alternative' lifestyles is revealed through the depiction of change occurring outside rather than within present social structures.

Recalling features of the 1960s counter-cultural movement, this discourse about organic food is associated with alternative ways of living, featuring centrally, for example, in the regimes of many New Religious movements (Baxter 1989). In a manner described by Atkinson (1980, 1983) for health and whole foods, the production and/or consumption of organic food symbolizes the rejection of modern industrial cultures through favouring a return to a more traditional and, by implication, more 'natural' lifestyle. Organic food, like whole foods and health foods, is seen to have less 'cultural' and therefore more 'natural' components and to belong to a different era: 'the imagery of the past in the present, and *rus in urbe*, is . . . central to the symbolic significance of health foods' (Atkinson 1980: 88). 'Eating green', when seen as part of an alternative lifestyle, similarly seeks to preserve the past for the future and works to erode the nature/culture divide through rejecting the technological 'advances' made in Western cultures.

In the small advertisements at the back of the HDRA newsletter, this anti-structural or counter-cultural vision is demonstrably present, alongside the previously described one committed to future environmental change. In the autumn newsletter for 1991, for example, which is printed on recycled paper, advertisements for organic gardening products are placed alongside those for recycled stationery and rare breed farms. With nature conservation, rather than preservation, as their focus, these advertisements situate an interest in organic food production firmly within the environmentalist discourse. However, other advertisements have a subtly different emphasis: offers for homes in an omnivorous community with a cooperatively run farm are found alongside those for smallholdings and for holidays in vegetarian/organic households. In these are envisaged not simply changed but alternative ways of living which, being predominantly rural, are divorced from the environmentalist concerns emanating from the large urban conurbations. Other small advertisements reinforce the conceptual links between organic food and lifestyle: advertisements for aromatherapy, house co-ownership, water purification systems and courses in yoga and spinning all foster a perception that the production and consumption of organic food must be part and parcel of alternative ways of living. One advertisement neatly summarizes the discourse within which this perspective is located. A group called 'Natural Friends' offers a personal service for putting people in contact with one another. It is for 'those with interests in organic gardening, vegetarianism, alternative medicine, yoga, meditation, "green" issues and all things natural' (HDRA Newsletter 1990: 36). Encapsulated in this is the 'alternative' way of life which 'eating green' can offer.

In these advertisements, therefore, semantic links are forged between nature and culture, the past and the future. Although sharing some of the environmental concerns embodied in large-scale organic agriculture, this discourse focuses on the rejection of, rather than making changes to, the commercialism and consumerism of contemporary Western life. Characterized as practised by 'sandal-wearing beardies', this view of organic food thus contrasts sharply with that found in the environmentalist discourse (Taylor and Taylor 1990: 41). Indeed, it is one which may be vigorously disclaimed by adherents to organic agriculture through appeals to the scientific culture and modernity of contemporary organic food production.

DISCOURSE 3: FOOD FOR HEALTH

The two discourses presented so far reveal some dissonance in contemporary representations of organic food. The conceptual boundaries between nature and culture, between the past and the future, are variously restructured and interpreted to sustain subtly different meanings of 'organic food'. Yet, at the same time, there are areas of overlap in, for example, both the New Ager's and the organic farmer's concern for the future well-being of the planet. Drawing on a continuum of ideas about food, both these discourses embrace aspects of yet a third perspective on organic food which, centred on health, stems largely from an urban environment. For the New Ager, for example, organic food consumption is seen as ensuring physical as well as spiritual health and well-being. For the environmentalist, organic food's freedom from pesticide residues is the body's bonus: 'organic food . . . is both healthier for you and healthier for the environment' (Elkington and Hailes 1989: 35).

Wider public opinion also situates 'organic food' within a discourse about food and health. A report published by the Consumers' Association, *Which? Health* (February 1990), indicates, for instance, that of those people who purposely bought organic food, only one in six did so for environmental reasons. A mere handful did so believing it to be kinder to animals. For the vast majority, health issues were the main motivation: one in two people said that they ate organic food because they believed it to be more healthy and one in three because it was free from pesticide residues and thus, presumably, was considered more healthy.

This suggests, therefore, that the rise in organic food consumption, achieved through retailing in large supermarkets, may have been contextualized by the discourse about food and health which has been gathering momentum in Britain from the 1970s onwards. From fats to fibre through to sugar consumption, 'healthy eating' emerged as a predominant issue of the late 1980s which, coincidentally, witnessed an unprecedented concern about food safety. Although this period also saw the acceleration of activity over 'green' issues, the timely appearance of organic produce on supermarket food shelves was, I suggest, more a reflection of anxieties about food safety than about the environment.

The 'salmonella-in-eggs-crisis' in 1988 was followed swiftly by lysteria in soft cheese, botulism in hazelnut yoghurt, BST in milk, and Alar in apples. As each scare hit the headlines, sales plummeted and parliamentary questions were tabled. The apogee of this alarm occurred in 1990 with BSE (bovine spongiform encephalopathy). Beef sales dropped dramatically and the Real Meat Company, which sells conservation grade meat, doubled its sales in the weeks following. The knackering industry all but collapsed. However, this was not a dramatic and sudden rush of environmentalist fervour, although its outcome may have been beneficial to those ends. It was instead motivated by a concern for health, as can be illustrated in the iconography of events surrounding the BSE scare.

The primary significance of BSE in relation to an increase in organic food consumption lay in the fact that it had ruptured the conceptual separation between the human and the natural world. BSE represented to humankind their own animality as part of the food chain and their vulnerability to the ravages of nature. The colloquial term for BSE – mad cow disease – reveals why, more than all other food scares, BSE appeared so alarming and prompted rapid government action. The threat of 'madness', a disease of the mind, rather than a disease of the body, struck at the core of Western understandings of humanity. Rationality, that which separated humanity from the animal kingdom, was under attack and the nature/culture boundary in a state of conceptual collapse. Furthermore, the virus bore an uncanny resemblance to a contemporaneous human virus – HIV. Sly, undetectable and lying dormant for years, BSE could suddenly and dramatically sicken an apparently healthy cow. Something had to be done, and quickly; culture had temporarily lost control over nature.

Although not framed by its concerns, the BSE scare thus had an environmental pay-off: the threatened pollution of the inner body through BSE came to be seen as symbolic of the environmental pollution in which human beings contemporarily dwelled. It starkly repositioned humans as part of the natural world in a chain of consumption – cows eat the brains of scrapie-infested dead sheep and humans eat the cows. Nature was threatening to pollute culture, as culture had earlier polluted nature by rupturing the boundaries between herbivore and carnivore, between life and death itself. While the fragility of this conceptual boundary was nothing new (Thomas 1983), BSE brought it sharply into focus as the nation was made to reassess its relationship to the natural world.

In the wake of this crisis, then, organically reared meat became a safe and healthy eating option, reflecting the previous year's demand for organically grown apples sparked off by the Alar pesticide scare. It became 'food you can trust' (Mabey et al. 1990), within a discourse centred on health.[5] This forging of conceptual links between organic food and individual health is commonplace and can be illustrated here by the marketing literature which accompanied the supermarket chain Tesco's introduction of its 'traditionally reared pork' in 1991. This meat, although not claiming to be 'conservation grade', is described as being produced under similar non-intensive conditions. However, although the promotional literature nominally addresses the concerns of environmentalism, through recourse to the same quadrant of concepts – nature:culture:past:future – environmentalist issues take second place to a stronger discourse centred on individualistic, personal health. Thus, the potential consumer is addressed not as a committed environmentalist, but as a person concerned with food safety and personal health. The natural and the cultural worlds are kept firmly apart.

First, cultural sensibilities are kept in check; it is 'pork', rather than pigs, which is being 'traditionally raised'.[6] This reluctance to acknowledge the relationship between the meat served at the table and the animal from which it came can be traced back to the eighteenth century (Thomas 1983). Beneath the cling-wrap on contemporary supermarket portions of ready minced, diced and spiced meat, there is little to recall the animal. Thus, unlike the organic farm, the supermarket does not choose to remind us of this connection. Second, this meat is described as both 'special' and 'traditional', both out of the ordinary and well established. Through recall of the 'past', with its associations of the virtues of nature, this meat is deemed safe despite its recent introduction. Further familiarity and assurance is provided through the inclusion of a map giving the location of Norfolk, where the pigs are raised. Significantly coloured green, the Norfolk landscape is sketched in pictorially by a watercolour of rural tranquillity, a source of comfort and reliability, 'a natural way of life: of peace, innocence and simple virtue' (Williams 1985: 1).

Assurance of food safety is reinforced through a personal introduction to those who take care of the pigs. These farmers and stockmen are described as having 'husbandry' skills, a word recalling traditional forms of non-intensive agriculture, when each animal would be known and loved, named as an individual, not numbered as stock. But lest this stress on 'husbandry' smacks of amateurishness or lower standards, these men are described as 'dedicated' in managing their modern (but also time-honoured) system, which is 'controlled by a strict and detailed . . . specification'. In this image, the modern agricultural world meets the natural and traditional: this system 'allows the pig to live in a natural environment' of 'spacious pastureland' and 'a warm comfortable straw-bedded house'. The pig is described as leading a 'happy and healthy stress free life'. The consumer therefore need fear no guilt about eating the pork – the pig after all has had a good innings. Indeed, by eating and demanding more meat produced in this way, the customer is depicted as making a positive contribution to porcine well-being: 'if enough people buy these products we will be able to switch more and more of our Pork production over to this method'. The pig depicted here, then, is not the 'horizontal human' of the nineteenth-century cottager's pig, whose death at pig-killing time is ambiguously perceived as a moment of both personal sorrow and happiness (James, forthcoming). These pigs are firmly part of a nature controlled by culture, producing pork fit for human consumption.

CONCLUSION

This chapter has identified a continuum of ideas about the place of organic food in contemporary Western society through consideration of a number of different texts. It has been suggested that the rise of an organic food market cannot necessarily be seen as an indication of the integration of environmentalist principles into British culture. Organic food has been incorporated into other food discourses centred on lifestyle and health. Thus, although the oppositional motifs of nature:culture:past:future pattern all these different representations, their semantic significance is subtly changed. In only one discourse is environmentalism a significant frame of reference.

However, this chapter has also shown how the organic food market may continue to prosper. In that each discourse refracts organic food through a communal repertoire of symbols, subject to different interpretations, these discourses are not mutually exclusive. For example, although it was the Alar scare which stimulated Pamela Stephenson to set up Parents for Safe Food, this group has now moved away from its narrow focus on personal health to embrace wider environmental principles. It is active in its promotion of organic food. What began as a self-help group promoting personal responsibility for health has become translated into a personal responsibility for the planet.

There are signs of change in other areas too. The Tesco campaign to promote their range of non-intensively reared pork was relaunched later in 1991 under the logo 'Nature's choice'. The leaflet for pork and bacon, printed this time on recycled paper, concentrates more explicitly on environmental issues. While much of the wording is the same, the pigs on this occasion are confronted in their animality. Less attention is given in this leaflet to the quality of the pork produced, which was a prominent feature in the earlier campaign. Instead, more emphasis is placed upon the pig's life and well-being:

> The welfare of the animals is of prime importance. If they become ill, medication will be given, but under strict veterinary supervision. Rearing pigs in this way means a contented life for the animals and also produces a premium quality product.
> ('Nature's choice, pork and bacon', Tesco Stores Ltd.)

These examples indicate, therefore, that although organic food remains marginal as a category within British food classifications and is largely absorbed by existing discourses, it may have a future role as a vehicle for the integration of environmentalist principles into British culture.

ACKNOWLEDGEMENTS

I am grateful to Nigel Rapport and David Woodman for their insightful comments on the first draft of this chapter. I am also indebted to Fast Facts for their information search on organic food.

NOTES

1 Several factors combine to make organic food significantly more expensive than non-organic food: the less intensive methods of organic farming produce lower yields while involving higher production and distribution costs, and with only just over 1,000 large-scale organic food producers in the UK, 60–70 per cent of organic produce has to be imported. The problem is compounded by the super-market requirement that produce should conform to EEC Grade 1 standard – which ensures that cucumbers are straight and that apples are of a particular circumference – which means that 60 per cent of the produce offered to them is rejected.
2 *The Archers*, a popular soap opera on BBC radio, has been running for over forty years.
3 These outlets for discussion may register a particular class bias in the framing, and therefore reception, of discourses about organic food. The higher prices of organic produce may compound this, in the way in which cost has been seen to play a significant part in the adoption of 'healthy' eating practices.
4 It was pointed out to me that inviting consumers to see the animals from which their meat will come does not only respond to an environmentalist discourse. It also draws on a discourse about food safety and health: the consumer will be reassured to see that the meat comes from animals which are healthy and well cared for.
5 An interesting report appeared in *The Guardian*, 17 October 1990, which con-firms the location of organic food within the discourse centred on food and health. A food minister, defending British practice over the use of pesticides in response to a BMA report, argued that his concern was about the 'natural chemicals in food, even organic food'. He argued that all foods are 'biological products which contain chemicals' but pesticides had the advantage of being 'checked out' by scientists. Natural chemicals, on the other hand, had not been tested for safety.
6 The following extracts are taken from a leaflet entitled 'Traditionally reared prime Norfolk pork', produced by Tesco Stores Ltd.

REFERENCES

Atkinson, P. (1980) 'The symbolic significance of health foods', in M. Tucker (ed.) *Nutrition and Lifestyles*, Barking: Applied Social Science Publishers.
—— (1983) 'Eating virtue', in A. Murcott (ed.) *The Sociology of Food and Eating*, Aldershot: Gower.
Baxter, E. (1989) *New Religious Movements: A Practical Introduction*, HMSO.
Bourdieu, P. (1986) *Distinction*, London: Routledge and Kegan Paul.
Bulmer, R. (1967) 'Why is the cassowary not a bird? a problem of zoological taxonomy among the Karam of the New Guinea Highlands', *Man*, N.S. 2 (1): 5–25.
Church Farm (n.d.) Promotional letter, Church Farm, Strixton, Northamptonshire.
Cohen, A. (1989) *The Symbolic Construction of Community*, London: Routledge.

Douglas, M. (1975) *Implicit Meanings*, London: Routledge and Kegan Paul.
Elkington, J. and Hailes, J. (1989) *The Green Consumer*, London: Victor Gollancz.
Eyton, A. (1991) *The Kind Food Guide*, London: Penguin.
Fiddes, N. (1991) 'Dying animal passions', *The Guardian*, 14–15 September.
Gear, A. (1987) *The New Organic Food Guide*, London: Dent/Henry Doubleday Association.
Hills, L.D. (1983) *Organic Gardening*, Wellingborough: Thorsons.
James, A. (1990) 'The good, the bad and the delicious: the role of confectionery in British society', *The Sociological Review*, 38 (4): 666–88.
—— (forthcoming) 'Piggy in the middle', in *Food, History and Culture, Proceedings of the London Food Seminar*.
Lévi-Strauss, C. (1970) *The Raw and the Cooked*, London: Jonathan Cape.
Mabey, D., Gear, A. and Gear, J. (eds) (1990) *Thorsons Organic Consumer Guide*, Wellingborough: Thorsons.
Porritt, J. (ed.) (1987) *Friends of the Earth Hand Book*, London: Macdonald.
Rodmell, S. and Watt, A. (1986) (eds) *The Politics of Health Education*, London: Routledge and Kegan Paul.
Strathern, M. (1980) 'No nature, no culture: the Hagen case', in C. MacCormack and M. Strathern (eds) *Nature, Culture and Gender*, Cambridge: Cambridge University Press.
Taylor, J. and Taylor, D. (1990) *Safe Food Handbook*, London: Ebury Press.
Thomas, K. (1983) *Man and the Natural World*, London: Allen Lane.
Thompson, J.B. (1984) *Studies in the Theory of Ideology*, Cambridge: Polity Press.
Williams, R. (1985) *The Country and the City*, London: Hogarth Press.
Woodman, A. (1991) 'Organic food: is it worth the money?', in *Good Housekeeping*, April.

Chapter 15

The resurgence of romanticism

Contemporary neopaganism, feminist spirituality and the divinity of nature

Tanya M. Luhrmann

In one of the earliest texts of British neopaganism, the naive protagonist, sick from asthma, awakes suddenly in the light of the moon.

> Now I cannot tell what I said to the moon, or what the moon said to me, but all the same, I got to know her very well. And this was the impression I got of her – that she ruled over a kingdom that was neither material nor spiritual, but a strange moon-kingdom of her own. In it moved tides – ebbing, flowing, slack water, high water, never ceasing, always on the move; up and down, backwards and forwards, rising and receding; coming past on the flood, flowing back on the ebb; and these tides affected our lives. They affected birth and death and all the processes of the body. They affected the mating of animals, and the growth of vegetation, and the insidious workings of disease. They also affected the reactions of drugs, and there was a lore of herbs belonging to them. All these things I got by communing with the moon, and I felt certain that if I could only learn the rhythm and periodicity of her tides I should know a very great deal.
>
> (Fortune 1978 [1938]: 15)

In a later novel of the genre, a retelling of the Arthurian legend, the protagonist, a priestess of the goddess, describes her struggle to regain the knowledge of her priestcraft after many years of dormancy.

> I learned again to count sun tides from equinox to solstice and back to equinox again . . . count them painfully on my fingers like a child or a novice priestess; it was years before I could feel them running in my blood again, or know to a hairline's difference where on the horizon moon or sun would rise or set for the salutations I learned again to make. Again, late at night while the household lay sleeping around me, I would study the stars, letting their influence move in my blood as they wheeled and swung around me until I became only a pivot point on the motionless earth, center of the whirling dance around and above me, the spiralling movement of the seasons.
>
> (Bradley 1982: 682)

Modern neopaganism – the 'new' paganism – acquired its shape as *The Golden Bough* was being written, and the first modern witches probably danced around their first bonfires in the years after Jessie Weston analysed the Arthurian grail legend as an ancient fertility rite. The magic was part of the mythic, folkloristic romanticism that flourished in the late nineteenth century. That romanticism arose out of the imaginative gap that widened as a mechanistic understanding of the universe took hold, as science and pragmatism increasingly dominated the foreground of the intellectual middle class. It still fills this gap. In its own way, neopaganism is a natural outgrowth of nineteenth-century romanticism, a child of the impulse to save traditional religious concepts by recloaking them in nature and thus in the scientifically 'real'. In neopaganism there is no god, masculine, separate and transcendentally aloof, but rather an ancient divinity immanent in the world, at once as metaphysical and as empirical as Wordsworth's daffodils. This is a world of stone circles and Celtic mythology, of British shamanism and a homespun web of Wyrd, of the 'Goddess' and her stag-horned consort, a world in which Frazer and Campbell are ransacked for details. And the natural world, from the mythicized perspective, is larger than itself, full of intensity and joy and pathos.

Those who now call themselves 'neopagan' tend to say that the world is divine and in some way alive. They are usually enmeshed in the mythology of what are called the 'old ways', the religions of pre-Christian Europe, and they see that mythology as part of their own spirituality. Some of them see themselves as involved with what they call 'magic', the 'art of change through will'. What they call magic the anthropologist would also call magic: an attempt to manipulate mysterious 'forces' by mind and ritual, and to invoke ancient gods to alter a present reality. Neopagans might invoke Hermes to make their secretary more efficient or Isis to make the world more loving to its poor. They might, however, be committed to a dreamy religious involvement with nature, but stop short of magic. This makes it difficult to estimate how many neopagans there are.

In 1983–4, while doing fieldwork in London on the magical sub-culture, I estimated that there were several thousand people actively engaged in magical groups. There were different groups of people – witches, Celtic ritualists, Egyptian ritualists and casual jumpers-over-fires – but their practitioners were more or less similar. Such people were middle-class and often middle-aged, book-oriented, interested in spirituality but not in a traditional form, and imaginative. One could estimate their numbers loosely, because they took courses, joined organizations and showed up at festivals. But neopaganism is a much broader category. Neopagans range from modern 'witches', who practise their nature religion in organized groups, to spiritually frustrated Green Party sympathizers. Most serious 'magicians' – members of witchcraft covens, Western Mysteries lodges and similar ritual organizations – consider themselves to be neopagans. There are probably at least three times as many people who think of themselves as neopagan, but who do not join groups, do not purchase home study courses in magic, and may, just, subscribe to one of the many magazines that fill this sub-culture. There may be many more. *The Mists of Avalon*, quoted at the beginning of this chapter, sold widely, and Jean Auel's novels – drugstore boy-meets-girl romances set against a neolithic tapestry – are remarkable best sellers which greatly appeal to the neopagan consciousness. If even a handful of those who read Bradley's book, and a thousandth of those who read Auel's, call themselves neopagan, this is a sizeable number.

Neopaganism (or paganism), loosely defined, is the term used in America and England to describe a romantic (in a nineteenth-century sense) attachment to nature in lieu of a more traditional religion. The term often implies a willingness to engage in a ritual practice using this pre-Christian imagery, and a conception of the divine as immanent in nature. An articulate neopagan describes neopagans thus:

> They share the goal of living in harmony with nature, and they tend to view humanity's 'advancement' and separation from nature as the prime source of alienation . . . They gravitate to ancient symbols and ancient myths, to the old polytheistic religions of the Greeks, the Egyptians, the Celts and the Sumerians. They are reclaiming these sources, transforming them into something new.
>
> (Adler 1986: 4)

To these old myths, she goes on to say, neopagans add the visions of Tolkien and Robert Graves, and the practices of the remaining aboriginal tribes.

The Pagan Federation and its publications give a good sense of the ethos of this world. The Federation was founded in Britain in 1970 as 'a focus for contact between the Craft of the Wise [also referred to as 'the Old Religion of Wisecraft'] and those who might find rapport with the Old Ways' (*The Wiccan* May 1990: 1). The group was then primarily aimed at witchcraft and its interested penumbra. Witchcraft, then as now, was a religion which took the great earth goddess and her consort as the central deities, and was practised in small groups called 'covens' which met on the full moon and on Frazerian fire festivals to do spells and perform seasonal rituals. Witchcraft is a modern phenomenon; it was started in the early twentieth century and has probably only an inspirational relationship with the sixteenth and seventeenth centuries (see Luhrmann 1989). By the 1990s, the Pagan Federation saw itself as reaching out to the broad, neopagan community, and considered changing the name of its newsletter, *The Wiccan* (thought to be the ancient term for 'wisecraft', white (healing) witchcraft), to *The Pagan*. The seasonal publications are dated by the traditional names for the fire festivals. The 1991 'Imbolc' (winter, 1 February) issue is representative. The cover is drawn to show herbs and candles, because the festival between winter solstice and spring equinox – in the Christian calendar, Candlemas –

celebrates the return of light to the earth; it also shows a new moon, for new beginnings. The newsletter describes the current activities. It announces an international Earth Healing ritual on 24 February, in which people will meditate to heal the earth from human hurt and pollution. A Hallowe'en Defence Campaign is being planned, to prevent the public from eliding neopaganism with Satanic ritual. There are announcements of an Earth Mysteries group in Bradford, a pagan evening in Luton, and other gatherings. There is a 'Cauldron Cookbook' column, an article on herbcraft and a discussion of pagan parenting. There is an essay on Nordic mythology, and a report of a Goddess Spirituality conference in London (*The Wiccan* February 1991).

NEOPAGANISM AND ENVIRONMENTALISM

Why now? What encourages this nature-drenched mythology to flourish in the contemporary world? I myself have argued before that people turn to modern magic – and, I suspect, neopaganism more generally – because they seek for powerful emotional and imaginative religious experience, but not for a religion *per se*. They have turned away from propositional belief in an external, separate god; they have chosen a playful spirituality with all the intensity of traditional religion but with few of its constraints. A neopagan remarks, 'I came to Neo-Paganism out of a search for a celebratory, eco-logical nature religion that could appease my hunger for the beauty of the ancient myths and visions without strangling my mind with dogmas or cutting off the continuing flow of many doubts' (Adler 1986: 374). Neo-pagans talk of ancient tradition, old ways, unknown powers buried in the earth, gnarled trunks and sun-scorched king-stones, strange forces access-ible to the gifted, and the powers of the forbidden, the mysterious and the beyond. They match the imaginative intensity with a deep spiritual involve-ment. The experience of this intensity without the demand to adopt some authority's belief is an important part of what makes neopaganism appealing to its modern enthusiasts.

Politics is another part. Neopaganism is also fuelled, I suspect, by the growing political power of environmentalism. Particularly in England, where the general cultural involvement with the environment is striking, the appeal of worshipping the divine in nature and that of protecting nature from human destruction are deeply intermixed. The May 1992 *Wiccan*, for instance, announces that the Pagan Federation will attend the Glastonbury Festival, hold an Earth Healing Ritual, sponsor a booth and donate all proceeds to Greenpeace. Pagans often see themselves as acting out political goals as part of their religious experience. One exemplar is Charlene Spretnak, a well-known writer whose books include an influential anthology (1982) entitled *The Politics of Women's Spirituality* (essentially, a feminist neopagan manifesto) and *Green Politics: The Global Promise*, co-authored with Fritjof Capra (1984). In *The Spiritual Dimension of Green Politics* (1986), she writes that environmentalism is in some fundamental sense about spirituality: 'a religion-based movement for social change is beginning to flourish that is completely in keeping with Green principles of private ownership and cooperative economics, decentralization, grassroots democracy, nonviolence, social responsibility, global awareness – and the spiritual truth of Oneness' (Spretnak 1986: 65). She refers to 'deep ecology' – a spiritual, philosophical elaboration of environmental principles – and depicts environmental politics without spirituality as an empty shell. Another American neopagan, Starhawk, explicitly equates political environmental action with spiritual engagement. She leads sit-ins at nuclear power plants, argues for environmentally sound disposal and encourages beach clean-up. Neopagans in general recycle, clean up beaches, and create rituals to 'heal the earth'.

But environmental politics in itself cannot account for the profound spiritual involvement in nature that many neopagans experience. I suspect that one of the motivations for a spiritual involvement in nature is the therapeutic power of that complex, rich imagery, and that this experience reinforces the commitment to environmental protection. Nowhere is that healing more evident than in neopagan feminist spirituality. While this strain of neopaganism does not represent the experience and orientation of all neopagans, it is salient to many, and it demonstrates more clearly than other realms of neopaganism the appeal that this imagery might have for an individual's life.

NEOPAGAN FEMINIST SPIRITUALITY

When I lived in London, in 1983–4, to do anthropological fieldwork among people who practised an occult and religious magic,[1] I encountered women who drew images of what they called 'the goddess', and who saw themselves as involved with a way of being religious which they sometimes called unique to women and to women's bodies. The goddess, they explained, is the divinity immanent in the world and represented through the earth, sea and moon; she was the pre-Christian feminine divine worshipped under many names and guises throughout the inhabited world.[2] In her myriad forms she represents the many different ways of being, and the women filled their rooms with pictures and statues of her in her different aspects. Many of these goddess images were tranquil: the beautiful young goddess, astride her horse in a shining robe; the goddess emerging from a flower's centre; the moon over standing stones. Many, however, were deeply disturbing: a woman crouched against a tree with her legs spread, blood streaming from her crotch; a thin, pink woman torn apart at the legs by demons; a black dancing goddess with a red tongue and a necklace of dead hearts.

The word 'goddess' means many things to those involved in the religion. They say that she is the earth goddess, the great goddess, venerated under many names in all early societies. A standard ritual opening reads thus:

'Listen to the words of the Great Mother: she who of old was called among men Artemis, Astarte, Athene, Dione, Melusine, Aphrodite, Cerridwen, Dana, Arianhod, Isis, Bride, and by many other names.'[3] To the extent that she is named she is conceptualized as a being or as many beings, but she is described in the literature as reality itself, as the vitality immanent in all earthly beings. In the words of Starhawk, perhaps the foremost voice of goddess spirituality,

> The primary symbol for 'That-Which-Cannot-Be-Told' is the Goddess. The Goddess has infinite aspects and thousands of names – She is the reality behind many metaphors. She *is* reality, the manifest deity, omnipresent in all of life, in each of us. The Goddess is not separate from the world – She *is* the world, and all things in it.
>
> (Quoted in Spretnak 1982: 50)

Such things are said of Christ, but the earth-centred ethos of this religion gives its followers perhaps a richer sense that the goddess is, literally, her rocks and streams, as well as 'that-which-cannot-be-told'. She is in nature, and she is nature. Authors repeatedly stress the in-the-world concreteness of the goddess, as well as her diversity of aspects and descriptive names. 'In the Craft, we do not *believe* in the Goddess – we connect with Her; through the moon, the stars, the ocean, the earth, through trees, animals, through other human beings, through ourselves. She is here' (Starhawk 1979: 78).

Through this diversity the goddess is understood as the life process – the process of birth, growth and death for individual, species and world.

> The revival of the Goddess has resonated with so many people because She symbolizes *the way things really are*. All forms of being are one, continually renewed in cyclic rhythms of birth, maturation and death . . . The Goddess honours *union and process*, the cosmic dance, the eternally vibrating flux of matter/energy.
>
> (Spretnak 1982: xvii)

The goddess thus represents interconnectedness, the sense of our incorporation into a web of natural objects. The symbols which represent her are often webs, nets, spirals, circles. Once when Greenham Common, an American military base in southern England, was surrounded by women protesting its existence, the women – many of whom read widely in neopagan feminist spirituality – encircled the military base with a yarn-woven spider's web, both a net to snare the men inside and a demonstration of the nature of their female power. The goddess is seen as that which surrounds, envelops, binds one to other humans and to the earth; she is both the concept of organic unity and social connection of the human animal, and the earth itself on which we live. The foremost American journal of feminist spirituality declares this in its 'statement of philosophy':

Our power as women arises from our understanding of interconnected-ness: with all people, all forms of life, the earth, and the cycles and seasons of nature and our lives. Through this understanding we commit ourselves to the transformation necessary for the revival of ourselves and our planet.

(Introductory statement of philosophy for *Women of Power*)

And again Starhawk: 'We encounter God/dess: the all, the interwoven fabric of being, the dance, the weaver – we say – and the web of connection, the pattern, the spiral' (Starhawk 1982: 72–3). We are not separate from the world, these women say. We are of the world, not autonomous individuals but connected wholes, and the important lessons come through letting go of that frightened separation from the world and other people. Our humanity lies in the recognition of these indissoluble bonds. The goddess, they say, becomes the representation of wholeness and union.

Yet many writings on feminist spirituality, and much of the conversation I had with practitioners, circle around the goddess as a demonic force. The goddess is often conceptualized through the three phases of the moon: the waxing moon as the virgin huntress, the full moon as the mother/lover, and the waning moon as the hag, who destroys. Starhawk gives these accounts of the different phases in an exercise meant to make possible the experience of 'connecting' with all three:

Visualize a silver crescent moon, curving to the right. She is the power of beginning, of growth and generation. She is wild and untamed, like ideas and plans before they are tempered by reality. She is the blank page, the unplowed field. Feel your own hidden possibilities and latent potentials; your power to begin and grow. See her as a silver-haired girl running freely through the forest under the slim moon. She is Virgin, eternally unpenetrated, belonging to no one but herself. Call her name 'Nimue!' and feel her power within you . . .

Visualize a round full moon. She is the mother, the power of fruition. She nourishes what the New Moon has begun. See her open arms, her full breasts, her womb burgeoning with life. Feel your own power to nurture, to give, to make manifest what is possible. She is the sexual woman: her pleasure in union is the moving force which sustains all life. Feel the power in your own pleasure, in orgasm. Her colour is the red of blood, which is life. Call her name 'Mari!' and feel your own ability to love . . .

Visualize a waning crescent, curving to the left, surrounded by a dark sky. She is the Old Woman, the Crone who has passed menopause, the power of ending, of death. All things must end to fulfil their beginnings. The grain that was planted must be cut down. The blank page must be destroyed, for the work to be written. Life feeds on death – death leads on to life, and in that knowledge lies wisdom. The Crone is the Wise Woman, infinitely old. Feel your own age, the wisdom of evolution stored in every cell of your body. Know your own power to end, to lose as well as gain, to destroy what is stagnant and decayed. See the crone cloaked in black under the waning moon: call her name 'Anu!' and feel her power in your own death.

(Starhawk 1979: 78–9)

The goddess is the cycle of the moon and the cycle of the seasons. She embodies all these aspects yet is each individually. She is the round of experience. Importantly, her appeal lies not only in her positive features, but also in her most destructive.

THE DARK GODDESS

It seemed to me that the women I met were most involved with the third aspect of the goddess, with the goddess as death, underworld, destruction – an aspect of the goddess which differs dramatically from Christian love, or from an angry, jealous Judaic god. The hag is the aspect of the goddess about which people spoke with the greatest awe. They spoke of being initiated through her, of reaching the 'deepest', 'truest' aspect of themselves through her; they spoke with scorn of people who thought of the goddess as 'sweetness and light'. Indeed the point of the goddess, for those deeply involved with her, seemed to be that this divine was as far from sweetness and light as it was possible to be.

The dark goddess, the Crone, eats and destroys. She is the madness of the raging tiger, the mother bear's fury, Kali child-eater and Clytemnestra man-slayer, Medea, the Furies and the witches on their blasted heath. The Old Woman, the hag, initiates the death which enables life to feed on death; to recognize the need for this moment is 'wisdom'. This aspect of the goddess the worshipper sees in old age, loss, pain and sorrow, as also in irrational rage, lust and all that is not 'nice'. She is the angry turmoil of the winter ocean and the overwhelming, drowning destruction of deep water. In the novel *The Sea Priestess*, the protagonist has a vision of such a woman:

I saw, sitting high on the stern poop, a woman in the carven chair . . . I knew that she was going to the high knoll that rose from the estuary some miles inland. On its crest was an open temple of stones and a perpetual fire, sacred to the sun; but underneath was a sea-cave where the water rose and took the sacrifices bound alive to the rocks . . . It was rumoured that the sea-priestess would require many sacrifices for her goddess, and when I remembered her cold strange eyes, I believed it.

(Fortune 1978 [1938]: 36)

and of the force she represented:

In the beginning was space and darkness and stillness, older than time and forgotten of the gods. The sea of infinite space was the source of all being; life arose therein like a tide in the soundless sea. All shall return thereto when the night of the gods draws in. This is the Great Sea, Marah, the Bitter One, the Great Mother.

(Fortune 1978 [1938]: 227)

When I was in London, a book on the goddess was passed from hand to hand among these women. Called *Descent to the Goddess*, it focused on the most ancient of Persephone tales, the Sumerian myth of Erishkigaal and Inanna, written on clay tablets in the third millennium BC.

In the Sumerian poem Inanna decides to go into the underworld: she 'set her heart from highest heaven on earth's deepest ground', 'Abandoned heaven, abandoned earth – to the Netherworld she descended'. As a precaution, she instructs Ninshubar, her trusted female executive, to appeal to the father gods for help in securing her release if she does not return within three days.

At the first gate to the Netherworld, Inanna is stopped and asked to declare herself. The gatekeeper informs Erishkigaal, queen of the Great Below, that Inanna, 'Queen of Heaven, of the place where the sun rises', asks for permission to the 'land of no return' to witness the funeral of Gugalanna, husband of Erishkigaal. Erishkigaal becomes furious, and insists that the upper-world goddess be treated according to the laws and rites of anyone entering her kingdom – that she be brought 'naked and bowed low'.

The gatekeeper follows orders. He removes one piece of Inanna's magnificent regalia at each of the seven gates. 'Crouched and stripped bare', as the Sumerians were laid in the grave, Inanna is judged by seven judges. Erishkigaal kills her. Her corpse is hung on a peg, where it turns into a side of green, rotting meat. After three days, when Inanna fails to return, her assistant Ninshubar sets in motion her instructions to rouse the people and gods with dirge drum and lamenting.

Ninshubar goes to Enlil, the highest god of sky and earth, and to Nanna, the moon god and Inanna's father. Both refuse to meddle in the exacting ways of the underworld. Finally Enki, the god of waters and wisdom, hears Ninshubar's pleas and rescues Inanna, using two little mourners he creates from the dirt under his fingernail. They slip unnoticed into the Netherworld, carrying the food and water of life with which Enki provides them, and they secure Inanna's release by commiserating with Erishkigaal, who is now groaning – over the dead, or with her own birth pangs. She is so grateful for the empathy that she finally hands over Inanna's corpse. Restored to life, Inanna is reminded that she will need a substitute to take her place. Demons to seize this scapegoat surround her as she returns through the seven gates and reclaims her vestments.

(Perera 1981: 9–10)

The last part of the myth involves Inanna's search for her substitute, whom she finally finds in her husband. I never heard any woman speak about that portion of the story. But many women spoke to me about the myth as the experience of being torn apart; they spoke of the experience of feeling the good girl within them – the Inanna-self – destroyed by their own Erishkigaal-like raging anger and lust. They explained the experience of the myth as the experience of menstrual cramps so bad they could not think, of suicidal despair, of abortions, of madness, of losing jobs and lovers, of discovering their hatred of their mothers, their culture, their selves. The tale had enormous power. Many spoke of the recognition they felt upon reading the tale, and some made extravagant claims. One woman, for instance, told me that the book had enabled her to become pregnant after she had failed to conceive. She told me that she had been raised by a father who despised her femininity. When she read this book – it is a short but scholarly text, and this woman lived behind net curtains in Clapham – she felt herself repeating the events of the tale in her own life, picking through grains in the kitchen (a tale from a later portion of the book), losing her jewellery, rotting like meat. Reading the book initiated her into womanhood, she said; it made her femininity vital and legitimate. When she finished the book, she conceived. This claim is only somewhat more extreme than many. To very many women, the experience of the dark goddess is the core of feminist spirituality, and the only real source of power.

And the literature of pagan feminist spirituality reiterates these concepts of a powerful dark goddess who is destructive, instinctual, chaotic, and yet the source of feminine creativity and wisdom. In this literature, daughters of the patriarchy are pretty. Experience of the dark goddess is anything but. And unlike the 'masculinized' women of the patriarchy, the dark goddess is said to be quintessentially feminine: 'If we have the courage to face into the dark, we may witness the slow epiphany or showing forth of the feminine' (Hall 1980: 19). Another woman writes:

> As I see her, the Dark Goddess is a manifestation of those aspects of female divinity and power that have become distorted because they have been split off, repressed and suppressed by patriarchal culture . . . if we are to become wholly empowered as women and stand up to the life-denying patriarchal forces, the Dark Goddess may and must be faced in each of us, her powers reclaimed and made accessible.
>
> (Reis in *Women of Power* 1988: 24)

These are in ways astonishing remarks: the truly feminine is a powerful, ugly, devouring hag.

SPIRITUALITY AND POLITICAL THERAPY

Why is this a woman's spirituality? Not all those who talk in this language think of it as uniquely feminine; some will tell you that the dark goddess represents the journeys of despair and hope all humans travel. Many, though, see the dark goddess as peculiarly female, fundamentally tied to what it is to be a woman. In part, this is because – they say – unlike men, women experience their bodies as a cycle of pain and pleasure. Only women, in menstruation and childbirth, face pain as a natural and healthy part of bodily process. Only women feel their bodies torn apart in the name of reproduction, and only women ride fluctuating hormones throughout their lives. And yet I think that this imagery works for them not because it is exclusively a woman's imagery, but because it enables these women to imagine their anger and transformation within a believable complexity. The concept that you must suffer in order to learn, brush with death to live truly, fail in order to succeed – there is nothing here that is not in some sense part of the bedrock of Western culture. The reason that it emerges now, to be labelled as a feminist spirituality, has to do with its use for these politically and spiritually minded activists, and that use depends upon the nature imagery.

Why is this a feminist spirituality? These images of anger and destruction are therapeutic for women who – by the very nature of their political orientation – have at least some anger towards their society and some desire to see it change. By 'therapeutic', I mean that the images encourage those who are drawn to them to identify their own anger, and that they legitimate those feelings while placing them within a constructive context. The most obvious answer to the question is that the image of the dark goddess permits women to be angry. In North American and UK culture, at least, women tend to repress their less 'proper' feelings in order to adapt to an approved cultural pattern. The symbol of the raging, devouring goddess allows them to lay claim to aggression and anger; they are of the goddess, they are allowed to feel rage. And one of the central concerns of a feminist politics is to liberate women's anger at the role accorded them in society, to encourage them to feel rage at their position. But the image of the dark goddess becomes relevant in more ways than this, for it is not only an image of rage but the representation of all the feelings which women (and humans in general) fear and deny. The image represents the unconscious, and the feminist politics which use the image are also arguing for the need for a kind of political therapy as a means to political power.

In feminism, famously, the personal is the political. The emphasis on the dark is a re-expression of this theme through the notion that constructive attention to the self will lead the collective to greater strength. The eighth issue of *Women of Power*, central voice of feminist spirituality, was entitled 'Revisioning the dark'. The heart of the editorial reads thus:

> The dark is the fear of loss of love, the fear of abandonment, the fear of failure, the fear of rejection, ridicule, and being shunned by our loved ones and by society . . .
> We have painful, hidden, secret memories and experiences of sexual abuse, child abuse and rape; and we are subjected to violent images of

women portrayed in pornographic magazines and the entertainment industry in general. We block these painful experiences and keep them buried in the recesses of our subconscious minds . . .

Revisioning the dark gives us a gift; the opportunity for soul-searching and reflection that leads to personal transformation. It allows us to reach deep within and bring our fears to the surface. We are then able to examine and confront them, and release their energies and move on. This work allows us to act on what we find unacceptable. It affords us the opportunity to move beyond our inactivity and open ourselves to life, to open our hearts and minds, and take responsibility for our lives and our actions because they affect all of us.

(Godavitarne in *Women of Power* 1988: 4)

We must transform ourselves in order to transform the world, the author argues, and to transform ourselves we must be prepared for an experience like therapy; we must confront feelings that frighten or anger us so that we can realize that our old patterns of behaviour – in place to protect us from these feelings – are no longer necessary to us. By confronting our personal lives we grow into more effective political beings. The dark represents the unconscious; the unconscious must be encountered in order to change current behaviour, and so feminists use the symbol of the dark to represent the change they seek to create in themselves and, through their own transformation, seek politically to transform society. When you come to know yourself and lose your fear of the unconscious – the dark – you are able to accept other people and the world as they are. 'People of integrity are those whose selves integrate both the positive and the negative, the dark and the light, the painful emotions as well as the pleasurable ones. They are people who are willing to look at their own shadows instead of flinching from them' (Starhawk 1982: 34–5).

Yet another aspect of this political therapy is the attempt to recast images of weakness as images of power. Starhawk named her coven 'Compost Coven', and her collective 'the Reclaiming Collective'. She calls herself a witch and talks about the crone and hag in every woman. 'Magic', she says, 'is the art of turning negatives into positives, of spinning straw into gold' (Starhawk 1982: 99). This idiom is quite common in this sub-culture. These women explicitly identify with the rejected and unpleasant – spiders, hags, organic refuse, menstrual blood, death. They do so, they tell you, to turn the symbol of the outcast into a source of strength.

And these images work because there *is* pain in the lives of those drawn to use them. We live in a world which is not often fair, or appropriate, or kind. These women are conscious of that messiness in a very particular way. They are bright, educated, determined. They see themselves as capable of doing effective work in the world. They also see themselves frustrated by traits they cannot control: their gender, their race, their body type and face. Unlike many frustrated people, they think that they can remake the world which has wounded them. But they are aware of the slow speed of culture's change. Political action can give them hope and constructive action can dull the hurt. Yet action does little to give the frustrations themselves much meaning. These women can and do use the process of explicitly identifying with the rejected and then redescribing, relabelling, that which is rejected as that which has the greatest power. In this way they give themselves a theodicy, and they use a very old, very powerful way of coping with suffering: to name despair by representing it. Why naming and redescribing an emotion should help one to feel mastery over it is the deep mystery at the heart of psychoanalysis, but to the extent that therapy works it does so through a process of this form. The dark goddess provides a kind of therapy for those coping with rejection.

Nature becomes important because it provides sufficient richness of imagery to engender these concepts, and at the same time a context to put these images of pain into perspective, in a world in which few complex religions are immediately knowable. It becomes both theodicy – explanation of pain – and therapeutic language. The religious power of the natural world is the range of the experience it can symbolize, and has always symbolized. We ascribe emotions to the natural world as readily as we use nature to describe our own. Storms rage, long sunny days are lazy and contented, fires hiss and crackle angrily. We thunder, bask, are cold with disdain or hot with sexuality. The turn of the seasons – a world in which vegetation sprouts, blooms, seeds and dies, the tension of the hunter and the hunted – provides the material for a dense narrative web. So too does the Bible, but few liberal intellectuals read that text these days. The natural world is immediately accessible. Its narratization proceeds on a foundation that all people know.

And the complexity, the richness, the depth and the breadth of the events of the natural world can match the variety and intensity of human experience, describe it, and give comfort. The solitude of nature gives us tranquillity and inner certainty, as Rousseau knew well, but it also helps us to pattern the complexity of our interaction with others. Inevitably, the emotions we need to understand are those which haunt and torment us: pain, horror, unutterable loneliness. As inevitably, we must set them in a world which gives us hope. In the implacable turn of the seasons but the annual renewal of spring, the absence of human justice from a world dominated by arbitrary predation but also the presence of birth and nurturance, we can find the narrative substance to transform uncomprehended pain into meaningful experience, and perhaps into transformative spirituality. Like Lévi-Strauss' Cuna shaman, the story gives the feelings imaginative reality, and allows us to confront and to contain them. Nature – red in tooth and claw – explains the existence of the pain, and gives it meaning, power, and the hope of winter's transformation into spring.

Spirituality, whatever we mean by the word, intensifies an emotional response towards a particular way of being. For feminist neopagans who see so clearly the frustrating irritation of their lives, the dark goddess of sea and storm becomes the means to transform frustration into tolerable vividness. For all neopagans, the natural landscape becomes a map for human feeling and aspiration, an environment for spiritual odyssey. And perhaps neopaganism suggests that imagination not only articulates life experience but ultimately is what is most real about that experience and also most human, that imagining the unimaginable, giving meaning to the meaningless, even transforming violence into creativity, are what being religious, and being human, are about.

NOTES

1 These were middle-class people who described themselves in various ways as practising 'magic'. By that term I mean a 'theory' of the world as interconnected by forces which scientists normally do not recognize but which can be affected by the mind, and a practice intended to use the imagination to alter the world through directing these forces in particular ways. A full description can be found in Luhrmann (1989).
2 It is standard practice in the literature of feminist spirituality to capitalize the word 'Goddess', and the personal pronouns which refer to the divine. I do not follow this convention here, although I maintain it in quoted remarks.
3 This is the introduction to the Charge, essentially the 'liturgy' of contemporary witchcraft. Not all people who call themselves witches describe themselves as feminists. However, many followers of the goddess describe themselves as witches, and use the witchcraft rituals as part of this woman's spirituality. The full text and description appears in Luhrmann (1989: 50) and in many other places.

REFERENCES

Adler, M. (1986) *Drawing Down the Moon*, Boston: Beacon Press.
Bradley, Marian Z. (1982) *The Mists of Avalon*, London: Sphere.
Fortune, D. (1978 [1938]) *The Sea Priestess*, York Beach, Maine: Weiser.
Hall, N. (1980) *The Moon and the Virgin*, New York: Harper and Row.
Luhrmann, T.M. (1989) *Persuasions of the Witch's Craft*, Cambridge, Massachusetts: Harvard University.
Perera, S.B. (1981) *Descent to the Goddess*, Toronto: Inner City Books.
Spretnak, C. (ed.) (1982) *The Politics of Women's Spirituality*, Garden City: Doubleday.
—— (1986) *The Spiritual Dimension of Green Politics*, Santa Fe: Bear.
Spretnak, C. and Capra, F. (1984) *Green Politics: The Global Promise*, London: Hutchinson.
Starhawk (1979) *The Spiral Dance*, San Francisco: Harper and Row.
—— (1982) *Dreaming the Dark*, Boston: Beacon Press.
The Wiccan, Beltane, May 1990; Imbolc, February 1991; Beltane, May 1992.
Women of Power (1988) Issue 8, 'Revisioning the Dark'.

Index